AVID

READER

PRESS

THE
PATHFINDER 3.0

HOW TO CHOOSE OR CHANGE

YOUR CAREER FOR A LIFETIME OF

SATISFACTION AND SUCCESS

NICHOLAS LORE

MONICA S. ROSE

AVID READER PRESS

NEW YORK   AMSTERDAM/ANTWERP   LONDON
TORONTO   SYDNEY/MELBOURNE   NEW DELHI

AVID READER PRESS
An Imprint of Simon & Schuster, LLC
1230 Avenue of the Americas
New York, NY 10020

This Avid Reader Press trade paperback edition April 2025

AVID READER PRESS and colophon are trademarks of Simon & Schuster, LLC

Simon & Schuster strongly believes in freedom of expression and stands against censorship in all its forms. For more information, visit BooksBelong.com.

For information about special discounts for bulk purchases, please contact Simon & Schuster Special Sales at 1-866-506-1949 or business@simonandschuster.com.

The Simon & Schuster Speakers Bureau can bring authors to your live event. For more information or to book an event contact the Simon & Schuster Speakers Bureau at 1-866-248-3049 or visit our website at www.simonspeakers.com.

Interior design by Dix Digital Prepress and Design

Manufactured in the United States of America

10 9 8 7 6 5 4 3 2 1

Library of Congress Cataloging-in-Publication Data has been applied for.

ISBN 978-1-6680-4823-8
ISBN 978-1-6680-4824-5 (ebook)

This book is dedicated to everyone who has ever cared deeply that their life and work make a difference— and not known exactly how to make that happen.

THIS IS THE PERFECT BOOK FOR YOU IF . . .

- You've walked a city street with other people on their way to work. Many of them look resigned, stressed, or a little blank. These people are obviously not looking forward to their workday. Suddenly you realize that you are not just an observer. You are one of them.

- Like a leaf in the wind, you have been blown into a career by the winds of circumstance and by decisions that seemed like the right thing to do at the time.

- You entered the job market with high hopes that you would be starting a terrific career. By now it is painfully apparent that you made some sort of misjudgment: somehow you have found yourself in the job from hell—or even worse, you are bored most of the time with the daily grind of tasks that don't even begin to make use of your intelligence and abilities.

- You used to really enjoy your work. It used to be full of challenge. When friends sang the career blues it never crossed your mind that anything like that could ever happen to you.

- You have visited career counselors and read numerous books on career and personal growth. You have done everything you could think of to find your true vocation. You know much more about yourself. And yet, dark clouds still obscure your future direction.

- You are a mindful young person. You and your friends are trying to figure out what to do with your lives. You want to have a career that really sings and soars. Your friends are deciding their fates the same way their parents did—and you know how that turned out.

- You had a job. You knew it wasn't the right one, but at least it paid the bills. Now it is gone or about to slip away. You could follow the crowd and repeat your last mistake or take this opportunity to carve out a new and better future.

- You are good at your job. You just don't seem to have a sense of purpose. You want to do something that means more to you personally. You definitely want to do something with your life that matters.

If this book is for you, let's begin.

CONTENTS

SECTION 3

DESIGNING YOUR CAREER

PART 1: WHO I AM

INQUIRIES

Preface to the 3rd Edition of *The Pathfinder*

Earlier editions of *The Pathfinder* were written primarily for people in mid-career, who were unhappy and dissatisfied with their jobs or the trajectory their career path had taken. When the first edition came out in 1998, the world of career decision-making was different. Earlier generations did not have the same expectations and resources that we have today. Counseling services and methods were more limited and were more focused on filling labor force requirements. Before the internet gave us access to an almost unlimited amount of information on any subject, most people had very little exposure to the idea of *designing or choosing a career path*. It was much harder to find quality guidance on how to make great decisions about your career. Nick's early work was pioneering. It helped shift the way society and career professionals approach working with others and their careers.

Since 1998, there have been many improvements to the knowledge and tools that school counselors, and other career professionals, use. Attitudes and approaches have advanced. There has been a broad culture shift. Darn it, a lot of people want work that they find rewarding. And . . . they believe it is possible to find it!

Today, there is a *massive* amount of guidance and information available on the web—much of it for free. This abundance of information, and change in expectation, has created a *new* problem. For those who want to make great decisions about their careers, there is *way too much* information. With all the contradictions and snippets of advice, it is hard to know where to turn. Not all of the advice you will find is good advice. Not all of it is clear. Very little is comprehensive. Very little is truly helpful.

Luckily, we've written *The Pathfinder 3.0* just for you. It provides you with a complete, step-by-step career design guide to work through at your own pace. Whether you are a student and just starting down your career path, or have already been down several avenues and alleys, if you want to make the best possible choices moving forward, you are in the right place. This is a comprehensive *manual of career design*. Enjoy the process.

—*Monica S. Rose*

SECTION 1

A LIFETIME OF CAREER SATISFACTION AND SUCCESS

This book is designed to take you through the process of *choosing* your future work. As you work through *The Pathfinder*, it will become your personal career coach and guide. Throughout this process, you will find that you have an opportunity to develop a personal connection with *The Pathfinder*—a relationship that will help you deal successfully with everything you need to consider and to learn practical, new ways to move forward from your present uncertainty. Here, you have the opportunity to design a career that will fit you as elegantly as custom-tailored clothes. Choose to be a participant—not just a reader.

If you have made the decision to make changes to your life, then you *have* found a book written just for you.

Whatever you can do, or dream you can, begin it.
Boldness has genius, power, and magic in it.

—JOHANN WOLFGANG VON GOETHE

CHAPTER 1

THIS CAN BE YOUR GUIDE

The Purpose of This Book

The purpose of this book is to guide you to your goal of designing a career that is both practical and perfect for you. Our methodology has already helped many thousands of individuals, from a wide diversity of backgrounds and experiences, reach certainty about what they will do with their lives. Do the work and it will work for you, too!

There are a multitude of things to consider in making life and career choices. It is complicated and interwoven. *The Pathfinder* will help you break everything down into small bite-size pieces and deal with them one by one. *The Pathfinder* will escort you through a series of inquiries into every aspect of your working life. Whether you are a student still preparing to enter the world of work, someone in mid-career wanting to make a next great move, or someone toward the end of their career seeking to design a fresh new project, this book is written for you.

The Method and Organization of This Book

The Pathfinder is a pragmatic set of tools and exercises designed to help you figure out what to do with your life and answer key questions like "How will I make the best use of my natural talents and personality?" "What workplace environment will support my best effort?" "How important is it to do something that personally matters to me, and what specifically will that be?"

Asking and answering key questions about your needs, skills, and preferences, is the most powerful way to design your career. Like an enormous jigsaw puzzle, as you become sure about one piece, it becomes easier to sort out the others. Some pieces will come easily. Others will take more consideration to sort out.

To help you move through this process, *The Pathfinder* is organized into sections and chapters.

The Sections

Each section has an overarching purpose, which is explained on the section page. Then each chapter in the section focuses in on a specific subject. Within each chapter, you will complete one or more exercises, called *Inquiries*, designed to help you uncover *Clues* and identify *Components and Career Ideas*.

This first section, "A Lifetime of Career Satisfaction and Success," introduces the intentions and methods of the book to you. We start you on the first part of a roller-coaster ride—the part where you slowly chug up the hill, heading with anticipation toward that first thrilling plunge down. Just your opening this book and reading these words means you have already begun the work you need to achieve your goals of understanding yourself and the features and factors that will lead to your career happiness.

Section 2, "Setting Yourself Up for Success," provides you with a structure to help you fulfill your goals. It will provide you with a handful of tools, tips, and perspectives that, if adopted, will help you move through any bumps or obstacles you encounter. Here we tell you to keep your hands inside the vehicle at all times—except when they are raised over your head in enthusiasm and wild abandon.

Section 3, "Designing Your Career," is full of Inquiries on different topics that will help you uncover, gather, and organize the factors that work best for you. Here you will work through four big questions: **Who am I?** which includes areas like your talents and personality; **What do I do?** which explores subject matter, work tasks, and activities; **Why work?** covers meaning, mission, purpose, values, and rewards; and **Work where?** is all about the workplace environment and culture.

In Section 4, "Putting It All Together," you will take the Career Components that you identified in the first three sections and use them to explore and identify potential career options. You will research, investigate, compare, and evaluate your options. You will narrow them down until, by the end of this section, you are able and equipped to make a choice about your future work.

Last but far from least is Section 5, "Communicating Yourself and Your Talents to Others and Staying in Action." This section will provide you with some tools and guidance on how to communicate yourself powerfully to others and translate your insights and decisions into actions. Our roller-coaster analogy breaks down a little here, since at this stage you are technically *off* the ride. How about . . . *you step forth into the wide world, ready to tackle any adventure with new self-knowledge and experience.* That will work.

Terms and Asides

We use special terminology throughout the book. You will find descriptions of important "Pathfinder" terms when they are first used.

For example,

The Pathfinder 3.0: *A particularly helpful "manual in a book" to help you design and identify real-world career options that will provide you with years of success and fulfillment.*

You will see a few special sections, called "Asides," which provide additional suggestions or comments slightly outside of the normal flow of the book.

ASIDE 1

A Few Fun Jobs You Could Have Had If You Lived in Victorian England

- Nurse
- Cook
- Academic
- Chimney sweep
- Leech collector
- Hokey Pokey Man (sold sweet treats in parks and on street corners)
- Ratcatcher
- Matchstick maker
- Tosher (who scavenged in sewers for valuables)
- Resurrectionist (who stole bodies from graveyards)
- Pure finder ("Pure" = poop; gathered and sold it to leather tanners)
- Accountant

You will also find a few tips that provide you with additional advice.

TIP 1

Read the Tips!

Your Guides

People who write how-to books are often missing the most important quality: first-hand experience. (You wouldn't be interested in a book about expert skiing written by somebody who had never stepped off a ski lift, after all.) So, here is a little bit more about us:

More than forty years ago, Nick realized that most of the career guidance available was quite limited or biased. He dedicated his life to inventing ways by which people, regardless of their situation or personality, could design a great future for themselves. He was one of the first people in the world to use the term *coaching* for anything other than sports. He founded an institute to study the subject and work with clients. He is the innovative author of the first two versions of this book (which have been read by several Super Bowl stadiums full of people).

Monica has worked with Nick for many years, both as a coach and developer of methodology. She has written interactive, online programs for public high school systems, trained school counselors and other career coaches, and created hundreds of helpful exercises. She is a subject matter expert on the aptitude and personality measures we use and has worked with thousands of individuals. She now works one-on-one with private clients.

Between the two of them, Nick and Monica have helped more than twenty thousand people design their future work.

Our Commitment

The intention of this book is to make it *as easy as possible* for you to step into a future filled with work you love! But, as you've probably already experienced, figuring out how to do this is a tricky venture. We (Monica and Nick, aka the authors) respect and appreciate you and your unique nature and situation. We won't mind if you jump up and down and curse us when you get frustrated. The whole process is designed to help build the clarity and certainty you need to make excellent choices about your future.

You Can Do It!

The world of work need not conjure up images of Bob Cratchit bent over his desk, freezing and working by the light of a single candle. Thankfully, you have better options. *Work* need not be a hard, dark, cold, dreary place. It can be a fabulous part of your life that fills you with satisfaction and joy. Even if you have made some mistakes or poor choices in the past, you can still find a career path that provides you with success. Even if you have faced difficulties, or feel confused and stuck right now, you can change things around. If you want to do something with your life that really lights you up, you are in the right place. No matter what your situation or past experiences, you can do it.

*I think that what we are seeking
is an experience of being alive,
so that our life experiences on the
purely physical plane will have resonances
within our own innermost being and reality,
so that we actually feel the rapture of being alive.*

—JOSEPH CAMPBELL

TIP 2

*For Those at Different Stages
of Their Working Life*

As mentioned in the preface to this third edition of *The Pathfinder*, the first two editions were written primarily to solve a particular problem—the lack of helpful information and guidance for people seeking success and fulfillment in their careers. The intended audience has been primarily two groups: 1. Those who had no idea how to go about choosing a career path that truly suited them; and 2. Those in mid-career who were already unhappy or confused and didn't know how to correct course. All editions of *The Pathfinder* are particularly helpful for these groups and also provide meaningful direction for all adults in the working world.

Throughout the book, you will see references to making a job or career change from an unhappy situation to a better one. This is because, historically, many of our readers and clients came to us because they felt confused or unhappy with their current job or career direction. They were looking for help out of a bad situation or in making a change. They were seeking a course correction. This may not be the case for you.

We assure you, *The Pathfinder* is appropriate for you, at whatever stage of your career you face, and even if you are happy with your current position and career path. Because the book would have quickly gotten very confusing if we tried to include options addressing every situation, we are relying on you, dear reader, to work it out to fit you and your situation.

That said, here are a few pointers for specific groups of readers:

Young Adults (Students and Those in Very Early Career)

- Later in your life and career, you will have more data from your own life to rely on. You may not have the same amount of life or work experience to draw on, but you still have plenty of insights to use.

- If there is a question about "work experience," look to your experience with education, classes, or hobbies for answers.

- Ask other people what they see and notice about you. (But please only ask people who you think "get you." And feel free to disregard or ignore their opinion if you don't find it helpful.)

- You can substitute the words *education, major, training program, vocational school*, etc., for the words *work, job,* or *career*. You can absolutely use this book to help you pick a college major or choose between a specialized training program, the military, or a four-year college. Swap out terms and make it work.

- If you are a young adult, still finishing school or training, or just beginning in the working world, it is okay (preferable?) to choose a more general direction than to pinpoint a specific position for the rest of your life.

- You will learn, grow, and have experiences that will inform your later decisions. Seek a general career trajectory (with a few clear-cut "must includes"), but leave some flexibility in your plan. Focus in on making specific choices about your next step—but you don't need to plan out the rest of your life. Save that for older folks.

Those Seeking Personal Exploration and Self-Awareness

• *The Pathfinder* is full of wisdom, self-exploration exercises (i.e., Inquiries), and, if you work through the book, you will gain a new and helpful self-awareness. It is perfect for you if you love personal growth and development. That said,

• New self-awareness and understanding is the opening to possibility. With it comes an opportunity to take new and different actions. If you don't love your life, your vocation, your work, or if you just believe that something more is possible, do all the work in this book. Make choices. Take actions.

Mid-Career Strategists

• You don't have to hate your job to get amazing results from the Inquiries. Also, perkiness is not required.

• If nothing is wrong and you have no complaints—fabulous. What are the best parts?

• If nothing is missing—where is the opportunity?

• If you aren't interested in how you feel about things—what makes sense to you? Run the numbers. Get the facts.

Self-Employed or Thinking about Self-Employment

• Throughout this book, we use the terms *employment*, *job*, *company*, and *organization* a lot. Most people prefer to work in an established business. Some do not. If you are self-employed or want to explore self-employment—fabulous.

• If you have a history of self-employment, you still have work experience, have held a position (even if you were the only person doing everything), and have had a work culture. You can draw on this experience as any employed person can.

- If you are considering becoming an employee (vs. self-employed), or are employed now but want to explore self-employment, we recommend that you consider both options. Explore employment opportunities and self-employment options.

- If you are considering self-employment (for the first time, as a structural/legal change, or a different business)—add "Create a Business Plan" to your list of mandatory activities. No kidding. We recommend starting out with a rough, simple plan first. If you are still interested, work through the details.

- There are a number of business plan templates and resources online. Do your research. Self-employment requires developing and taking specific actions on your vision.

Getting Ready to Retire/Don't Want a New Career

- We use the words *career*, *job*, and *work* a lot. If you don't want a new career, swap out the term *career* for one that suits you.

- This is a perfect manual to help you clarify how you want to spend your time and resources, and what legacy you would like to leave.

- Project, meaningful activities, lifestyle, part-time gig, small business, investment plan . . . you could swap any of these out for the term career.

The insights and guidance within these pages are not confined to those rewriting their midlife narratives. For the young adult just embarking on their career journey, or the proactive professional seeking to thoughtfully curate their next challenge, this book serves as a valuable compass. It's about making informed and you-prioritizing choices, regardless of where you stand on your career path—be it a trailhead, a plateau, or a peak.

CHAPTER 2

✦

CAREER SELECTION AND YOU

The trouble with the rat race is that even if you win, you are still a rat.

—LILY TOMLIN

Not Everyone Loves Their Job

A few statistics. Each year, Gallup, a global analytics and advisory firm, does a survey on employee engagement.* You can look up the current statistics, but, at the time of this writing, their most recent survey indicated that only 33 percent of Americans were engaged and enthusiastic about their work and their workplace. That means that 67 percent of all working Americans are *less than satisfied* in their careers. (And, for what it's worth, Americans are happier than many others—the global average of engagement is only 23 percent!)

Reported daily levels of anger, sadness, and loneliness have all increased since Gallup started its survey in 2009. And 49 percent of those surveyed are planning to, or are actively seeking, new employment. Half of us want to leave our current position. And . . . it's worse for managers. Ugh. This is not great news. Or is it?

One in three of us *do* have their important career elements worked out. Thirty-three percent of us are experiencing career satisfaction—either liking or loving their work. These statistics should give you hope.

---

* https://www.gallup.com/workplace/349484/state-of-the-global-workplace.aspx

LIFE IN HELL

© 1990 BY MATT GROENING

YOUR WORKING-DAY EMOTION CHECKLIST

9:00 AM ☐ PURE GRUMPINESS	9:05 AM ☐ CAFFEINE JOLT-O-RAMA	9:29 AM ☐ EARLY-MORNING STUPEFACTION	9:45 AM ☐ SPLITTING HEADACHE #1	10:04 AM ☐ MOMENTARY PANIC ATTACK	10:31 AM ☐ CAFFEINE OVERDOSE	10:37 AM ☐ PERVERTED DAYDREAMS	10:42 AM ☐ MID-MORNING NUMBNESS
10:52 AM ☐ SUDDEN FIT OF HOSTILITY	11:03 AM ☐ LINGERING SULKINESS	11:09 AM ☐ PRETENDING TO WORK	11:33 AM ☐ REBUFFED FLIRTATION WITH CO-WORKER	11:35 AM ☐ TEMPORARY DEMENTIA	11:57 AM ☐ "HEAD IN A VISE" FEELING	12:00 PM ☐ JOYLESS LUNCH-EATING	12:09 PM ☐ MIRTHLESS JOKE-TELLING
12:23 PM ☐ BELCHING DISCONTENT	12:35 PM ☐ SUDDEN AWARENESS OF ONE'S SHALLOWNESS	12:47 PM ☐ WAVES OF NAUSEA	1:00 PM ☐ RESENTMENT OF OTHERS	1:19 PM ☐ EARLY AFTERNOON CATATONIA	1:25 PM ☐ SPLITTING HEADACHE #2	1:42 PM ☐ GNAWING OF THE BOWELS	1:52 PM ☐ THAT "NO WAY OUT" FEELING
2:06 PM ☐ STRANGE TRANCE-LIKE STATE	2:30 PM ☐ URGE TO MURDER BOSS	2:44 PM ☐ FOOLING AROUND AT THE COPY MACHINE	2:55 PM ☐ WHINING TO THE PERSON NEXT TO YOU	2:59 PM ☐ UNREALISTIC PLANS TO QUIT THIS LOUSY JOB	3:09 PM ☐ MID-AFTERNOON TORPOR	3:14 PM ☐ EVEN MORE PERVERTED DAYDREAMS	3:36 PM ☐ EMOTIONAL DEADNESS
3:47 PM ☐ WATCHING THE CLOCK	3:59 PM ☐ WORRYING ABOUT SENILITY	4:01 PM ☐ SPLITTING HEADACHE #3	4:09 PM ☐ FEAR OF GETTING FIRED	4:25 PM ☐ LOTTERY FANTASIES	4:33 PM ☐ CONTEMPLATING TV TONIGHT	4:59 PM ☐ UNCONTROLLABLE JUMPINESS	5:00 PM ☐ TEMPORARY PERKINESS

From *The Huge Book of Hell* © 1997 by Matt Groening. All Rights Reserved. Reprinted by permission of Penguin Books USA, NY. Courtesy of Acme Features Syndicate.

A Little Experiment—Your First Inquiry

Inquiries: *The activities and exercises you will find in the chapters of this book. Each is designed for you to explore a topic that could hold rich and wonderful Clues and Components that will help you design your future work.*

With this first Inquiry, and all that follow, do the Inquiry. This usually entails some combination of reading, doing some research, thinking about things, picking out your preferences, and writing something down. In chapter 4, we will go over a great way to keep this whole Career Design Project organized, but for now, write or capture your responses and ideas in a place where you can collect them and refer back.

Inquiries are opportunities to use your experience, common sense, intellect, and imagination. Use them to identify components of work and work environments that would fit you fabulously.

This is your first Inquiry. It is a little experiment for you to conduct. See if the people around you fit with Gallup's statistics. Do one in three people really enjoy their work and feel like they regularly participate actively and happily?

INQUIRY 1

Ready or Dready

1. Tomorrow (or a day in the near future that makes sense), pay attention to others before, during, and after their workday. If you commute to work, pay attention to other commuters. If you work from home, find a way to observe others.

   a. How many look happy, excited, and eager for the day?
   b. How many look perky, open, and raring to go?
   c. How many look half asleep? Automated? Humdrum? Resigned?
   d. Any with sheer dread on their face?

2. Ask a few people how they feel about their job or career. Did they light up? Did they groan? Did they say something like "Well, it pays the bills"?

3. Now, if they were to ask *you* on a typical day, what would you say?

4. Did your personal research resemble the one out of three?

5. Jot down any thoughts or insights you had during this Inquiry. And, while you are at it, write "Clues" at the top of your notes.

A Very Brief History of Career Selection

Twenty thousand years ago, we all had the same career. We were hunter-gatherers. The men were hunters and made stone tools. Women hunted and did everything else: raising children, snaring small game, finding edible and medicinal plants, making the clothes, being the tribal social glue, and a thousand other tasks. We worked much less than people do now—spending roughly fifteen hours per week to acquire basic needs.

Ten thousand years ago, we became farmers. Suddenly, a work structure was born. There were better times of day, better times of year to harvest and to plant. There was preparation and cultivating and response to external weather and circumstances. We began to have specialized tasks and responsibilities. Skeletons of women from the early farming days show the wear and tear of endlessly grinding grain, day after day after day.

Communal living, semipermanent dwellings, agriculture, all these led humans to produce an abundance of life's daily necessities. Through specialization, people could produce more than they needed of certain things. But spending all their time on some things created lacks in other things. So, commerce was born.

A big jump in time later, in the early 1800s, approximately 75 percent of Americans (free and enslaved) worked on farms. By 1870 (thank you, Industrial Revolution and the Emancipation Proclamation!), less than half of us were. Quickly and steadily, work roles expanded to include more and more jobs in new industries including manufacturing, transportation, and professional services.

So, did industrialization and social change make life and work easier for the average American? Did it open up opportunities and options? Yes and no. Variety of roles and industries increased with technology and there were more options. Cities grew. The manufacturing, processing, and transportation industries grew. But with the good came some bad. More and more workers were being maimed, injured, or killed during the course of their repetitive labor jobs, and by the late nineteenth century, in the U.S., the typical workweek was about seventy hours long.

In reality, well into the twentieth century, most people simply did what their fathers or grandfathers did. Even with industrialization and the growth of cities, industry, and new technologies, one's ethnicity, gender, and social class determined most of your options. If you were not born a white American man of some privilege, you probably had *very* few options. Until shockingly recently, it was rare to find a person of color, or a woman, managing a shop or business or offered a professional opportunity. Up until the 1950s, main options for women included being a teacher, midwife, dressmaker, domestic servant, or sex worker. For men of color, it was no easier. Black leaders in politics, academia, and literature were exceptions. Realistic options mainly included fieldwork, semiskilled laborer, or tradesmen roles.

Jump forward to the 1970s, at the tail end of the social revolution of the 1960s. The world had experienced massive breakthroughs in technology and globalization and society. Still, most of us without wealth and family connections looked for available jobs in the local newspaper. Women were hired into clerical jobs and to make coffee, and men of color were still fighting to be seen and valued for more than their ability to lift heavy objects.

A lot has changed in the last fifty years! If you are twenty-five, or thirty-five years old, what we just described might seem completely foreign or like ancient history. It may not seem at all like the world we live in today.

But, across thousands of years of history—opportunities for education, self-direction, and career choice have been a luxury—certainly not the norm. Regardless of your personal experience in the beginning of the twenty-first century, *we have all inherited this legacy.*

ASIDE 2

A Few Stats from a Gallup Survey of 1.7 Million Workers

- Only about 20 percent said they used their best strengths every day at work.

- More than 70 percent of those surveyed thought they could have done a much better job of making decisions about their lives.

- The majority of successful professionals said that they had not known how to go about making choices in a competent way.

- Sixty-four percent of college seniors said they had serious doubts that they had picked the right major.

If you do not feel yourself growing in your work and your life broadening and deepening, if your task is not a perpetual tonic to you, you have not found your place.

—ORISON SWETT MARDEN

The Inherited Way of Career Selection

Even with all of our access to information and data, and the openness of our society and economy, few people choose their careers in an optimal way. Far too few people have access to the comprehensive, skilled guidance and coaching that companies like Career Matters provides.*

A Familiar Tale

For many of us in the U.S., the process of career selection usually starts around your sophomore or junior year of high school. Your elders, probably including your

---

* A shameless plug.

parents and guidance counselor, start bringing up your future. They start suggesting you prepare for the decisions you need to make. Of course, they love you and want you to be happy and successful, but it can sound a lot like "What are you going to do with the rest of your life? Decide now!" Yikes!

Because you are diligent (or lucky) enough to overcome some of your teenage angst and hormones, you start to think about it—a lot. *What should I do?* You ask your friends what they are doing. You ask them what they think you should do. You listen to the news. You consider your family's solid and practical suggestions. You even listen to your school counselor, who looks over your school records with you, *and* you talk to your uncle Bernardo, who seems to understand the job market pretty well. It's getting closer and closer to graduation; you need to decide.

Even if you are unsure about a lot, you are sure about one thing—you know you need to do *something*. There is something you need to do to be worthy of the jobs and employers of the world. So, clear, full of direction, and prepared, *or* unsure, unsteady, and bewildered . . . you forge ahead. The pressure mounts, time runs down, you consider your options, and you pick one.

You'll be an accountant. This is a trustworthy major that will make you hirable for a good job with advancement opportunities. Sure, you love science fiction, playing D&D, and have designed and crafted several stellar cosplay outfits, but those are only hobbies. Everyone knows that good incomes and stability lie in accounting and other financial roles.

To be an accountant, you need to get a degree in accounting. You need to pass all of the accounting classes, graduate, pass some additional accounting certifications, and get an accounting license. Then you can put all of that on a résumé and apply for accounting jobs. Then you will have accomplished the important things to make you acceptable and worthy of an entry-level accounting position. Then your life will be set. Hopefully, after you pass all of those classes and exams, you will have enough free time to study stagecraft, designing masks and costumes, and playing MTG on Fridays. Maybe you'll be able to retire early and then you can pursue your dream job—managing a traveling Renaissance Fair company.

Are you starting to pick up on our subtle hints yet?

Now, you got through your second-guessing and doubts and decided you want to graduate on time, and you've finished your degree in accounting. After you took six months off to recover from the stress of earning your degree, you studied and practiced and passed your CPA exams on the fifth try. You applied to only a few companies and got your first job. While not "exciting," it is a steady paycheck and has benefits.

It's a Monday morning four years later and you just woke up from a horrible dream. You'd been floating down a stream—being carried along. Then you notice that the stream has been building in strength and speed. You don't have a raft, you don't have an oar, you don't even know how to swim. You feel stuck—crashing through rapids, scrambling and scratching for air and for shore. You are just trying to keep your head above water. Hoping only to survive.

You look at the clock. It's 6 a.m. You realize that you are not happy. You are both bored and underperforming at work. Your partner mentioned that you seem tired all the time, have been grumpy, and are watching a lot of TV. You've called in sick three times this month, keep checking on your vacation days, and are wondering if you have COVID or clinical depression. You haven't even opened your sketchbook in two weeks.

BUT . . . you've invested all this time, energy, and money into your education and career. Your family would be disappointed if you didn't use your degree. You'll figure out a way to get through this. Maybe it's the company where you work. How could you even begin to make a change anyway? You feel stuck.

What? How? Why? While you've actually paid attention, followed the advice of others, and done some research, you have just started down a (potentially lifelong) career path that may have largely been decided by two things—how well you did in your school classes and which jobs your family, friends, and society think will be important and widely available in the future.

You are now following your inherited way of deciding your own future.

This method works really well for some people. Some are really clear what interests them, they did well in their classes, and they are pragmatic. They aren't second-guessing themselves or others, they are just doing the next thing in front of them. Their interests and grades line up well with the current jobs outlook, and they are off to a good start.

But . . . For those of us who weren't clear about our interests and priorities at age seventeen, who might have made a judgment error or two as a teenager, who don't perform well in conventional classrooms, or who just don't naturally follow mainstream society's suggestions—this inherited way of deciding is not so helpful.

> *I am not discouraged, because every wrong attempt*
> *discarded is another step forward.*
>
> —THOMAS EDISON

The Inherited Glitch

We could write several pages about the limitations we have seen in "the system," but we won't. The bottom line is: the biggest, inherited issue that most of us deal with in how we choose a career path is . . . drumroll, please . . . we overly limit our decision-making criteria to how we did in school and the current job market, we identify a job that fits what we have personal experience and knowledge of, then we check to see if our idea is acceptable to our friends and family. Then we figure out what we need to do to ourselves (education, training, and experience) to help us "become" hirable for that position.

The Glitch: We find a career box to fit in—then we figure out what we need to do to squish ourselves into that box.

While this method works perfectly well for some, it does not work for everybody—and generally, not for the people reading this book. For many of us, it is exactly how we start acquiring those tire tracks across our souls.

Fixing the Glitch

It is easy to drift along for years in a career that doesn't really fit you or your talents, interests, and values then wake up one morning and notice that you are miserable. It might be more subtle—like the slow suck of boredom and lack of purpose. Maybe you feel like you are compromising yourself or what's possible—like you are simply watching life pass you by.

If you worked hard trying to pick a satisfying career and it hasn't worked out, or you are concerned about that happening, please let the following statement seep into the very core of your being: it's not your fault. You do not have a psychological shortcoming or some fatal flaw in your character. It is simply that the tools you have been using aren't adequate. If you've worked really hard, have tried everything you can think of, and haven't been able to figure it out—it's okay. Trying to pound in nails with a sponge instead of a hammer is taxing!

The Solution. People who are engaged in satisfying, challenging careers that match their talents, personalities, and goals usually achieve a higher degree of success than people who do not care passionately for what they do. They are healthier, live longer, and tend to be more satisfied with other aspects of their lives. They feel their lives are meaningful and a source of joy.

To identify and choose a career path that provides you with satisfaction and meaning, you need to understand key aspects of yourself. You need to define your natural talents and abilities, your personality, your values and interests, and what you find rewarding.

The solution to achieving a lifetime of career satisfaction and happiness is first understanding who you are—what you are good at and what is most important to you—and then identifying jobs and careers that fit you.

Early Dreams of a Life Filled with Excitement

Let's shake off current stressors and considerations and look back to a time in which we had more freedom and life was full of possibilities.

Place yourself in the shoes of your eight-year-old self. Chances are, at that age, you were imagining an exciting future, without limits. You were passionately engaged in life, pursuing your interests. Perhaps you dreamed of being a movie star, an Olympic athlete, or the first empress of the galaxy. You might have envisioned yourself as a brilliant surgeon, as an artist, or an adventurer swinging from a vine over a bottomless chasm. Wiser now, you might smile at the naivety of childhood dreams. It may not seem reasonable or practical anymore, but those desires were valid—they put you in the middle of a life you were living fully.

INQUIRY 2

Early Career Dreams and Imaginings

Think back to your younger self as you consider and respond to the following questions. If helpful, after you do the exercise on your own, ask someone who knew you as a child if they remember anything about your career dreams.

1. Remember back to your childhood, back to the beginning of the journey. Look back on your childhood visions of the future. What were those dreams? What were those wild fantasies of yours? What seemingly perfect careers did you imagine as you were growing up?

2. How did you feel when you imagined yourself in the midst of one of those fantasies or plans? Can you feel like that again now?

3. What did you want to be when you were a child? Did it change? What about when you were eight? Twelve? Fifteen?

4. Write down any and all ideas that you remember. Do you remember what about them was so appealing? Write that down, too.

Everything you just noted down are Clues.

Clues: *Descriptions, opinions, experiences, and preferences of yours.*

An example of a Clue: *"When I was eight years old, I wanted to be an etymologist. I loved words and was fascinated by their derivations. I loved the history and culture of where they came from. I took Latin for fun in high school."*

As a child envisioning your future, *work* was full of wonderous activities and opportunities. *Work* was full of play. Consider what pops to mind when you think about *work* now. Is it still full of adventure and possibility? Have you separated the ideas of "work" and a "dream job"? Are they incompatible, forever destined to be separate things?

When people dream of being a lawyer, they aren't thinking about having to massage the egos of rich clients and being buried under endless piles of deadly, dull paperwork. They are picturing themselves as Atticus Finch, defending social justice and the rights of the falsely accused—taking a stand and being a hero.

INQUIRY 3

Current Career Dreams and Imaginings

Now we are going to magically jump forward in time. Consider and respond to the following questions. Try to remove doubts, considerations, and reality for your responses. And don't be afraid to dream big.

- If age, money, location, and practicalities were not an issue, what would you do with your time? In other words, what is your dream job today? Write down any and all jobs or career ideas that pop to mind. They don't have to be realistic, part of the plan, or things you are completely sure about. Just write them down.

- Now, for each of the Career Ideas you just listed, what about them is appealing to you? Write that down, too. (You are allowed to have as many reasons as you please.)

You just created more Clues *and* some Career Ideas.

Career Ideas: *Job titles or roles that popped to mind as a possibility or interest to you.*

Examples of Career Ideas: *etymologist, cultural anthropologist, forensic historian.*

When you get down to it, under all the sophisticated conversation and pretense, no one really wants to work if it means a life of suffering. One definition of the word *work* that is not in the dictionary, but nevertheless is a part of our internal dictionary, goes something like "Work—something I would rather do less of" or "something I have to do when I would rather do something else." Underneath all the serious reasons people give to explain why they want to change careers, lead a company, write a book, or drive an 18-wheeler, there is an essential, powerful motivation that's usually not discussed: we want to earn a living doing something we are passionate about. We want satisfaction, a sense of adventure or advancement. We want to have fun. We want to be brilliant at what we do, and to be appreciated. We want to contribute to something, help others, and make a difference. Our dreams are shaped by our own individual inner templates of what matters the most to each of us. Your inner template is uniquely yours, but may include one or more of the following human values: self-expression, adventure, accomplishment, belonging, creativity, personal growth, leadership, providing for a family.

The secret of success is making your vocation your vacation.

—MARK TWAIN

In chapter 3, *"The Pathfinder* Career Design Method," we will hunker down and discuss the nuts and bolts of how this thing is going to work. But first, let's do another fun Inquiry to get your imagination and your juices flowing (in a good way).

INQUIRY 4

Lifeline

One way to do this Inquiry is to use a large sheet of real paper, legal size or even bigger. If your world is paperless, use software that will let you draw curvy lines and add words so it looks like this illustration.

- Write "LIFELINE" in big letters at the top of the page.

- Next, draw your "lifeline." One end will represent your birth, the other, the end of your life.

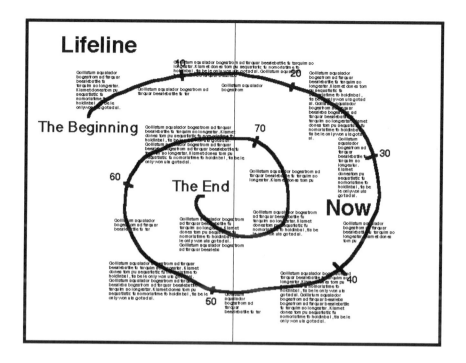

- With a heavy pen or marker, draw a long line across your document. The line can curve, curl, spiral, zigzag, or do anything else that pleases you. Leave room for writing on both sides of the line.

- At one end write "The Beginning." At the other write "The End."

- Draw short lines to mark each decade of your life—past, present, and future—as shown in the illustration. Write "NOW" in bigger letters at the place that represents your present age.

- Start at the beginning of your life. Write in significant events, from the time of your birth to the present time. Focus on events where you experienced significant growth, a personal transformation, a major life event, went after or accomplished an important goal, and times when your life was profoundly altered in other ways.

- Imagine your life continuing along this lifeline into the future. What significant milestones do you want to reach at various times in the future? Write them in, along your lifeline, at the appropriate place.

- What else can you add to your lifeline? Don't let yourself be bound by overly reasonable, practical thinking. This is about what you would really like to have. At the same time, though, don't write in entries that you know are just grandiose pipe dreams. Your favorite movie star will not fall for you and become your love slave. If you are fifty and out of shape, you will not become a world-famous ballerina (you might have a chance in opera, though).

- Keep asking questions that encourage you to visualize what you would like your life to be like. You need not confine yourself to career-related entries. Look in all the other areas of your life as well. Consider things like relationships, personal goals, financial issues, etc.

- Now look over your Lifeline. Many people notice that the past has many entries, but the future is almost completely empty. That alone can be a very powerful clue. People who get what they want know what they want. If you have not written much in your future, it may be time to do so now. On the other hand, it may be enough to simply notice that your future is kind of blank and work on this as you design your future career.

Look at what you have accomplished in this Inquiry. It may be that, by answering some of these questions, you have come up with some important clues about who you intend to be, and what you want to do and have in the future.

Your imagination is your preview of life's coming attractions.

—ALBERT EINSTEIN

CHAPTER 3

THE PATHFINDER CAREER DESIGN METHOD

Wouldn't it be amazing if you could snap your fingers and know what to do with the rest of your life? Wouldn't that be lovely?

Reality check. For 99.99 percent of us (we are leaving a tiny window of chance), no such instant solution is available. Choosing or changing your career for a lifetime of success and satisfaction takes a lot of thought and work. It is a process. And if you follow that process and do the work, to the best of your ability, you'll be amazed at the results you achieve.

The Career Design Process—in a Nutshell

6. Create an action plan

5. Choose your career path

4. Get facts to evaluate options

3. Use components to identify options

2. Develop clues, create components

1. Explore and gather clues

Become a Detective

To reach that answer, you need to be curious, investigative, and perseverant. In other words, you should become a detective—a **Career Detective**. As a Career Detective, your mission is to answer the question "Which career will provide me with a lifetime of satisfaction and success?"

What you now have is a big mystery. To solve your mystery, you must start at the beginning. So, put on your invisible detective hat (don't worry, no one will know you are wearing it) and get ready. You are about to investigate the world of *You and Your Career*. You will begin searching for and gathering Clues. You will follow up on and develop those clues until you identify key Components—the features and characteristics that your future work will include. You will work those Clues by observing, considering, and researching them from various viewpoints, identifying those of significance to you (your Components), and then identifying and investigating the potential suspects (i.e., Career Ideas) that meet the criteria (aka match your Components). You will move through an investigative process until you solve your case and answer the question "Which career do I choose?"

Your Detective Tools—Three Lists and a Bunch of Inquiries

To help you move successfully through the process, you will build three essential lists: Clues, Components, and Career Ideas. We've already introduced you to Clues and Career Ideas. You will refer to, and add to, these three lists as you investigate and build your case. Each list serves a unique purpose in the process and will help you organize your thoughts, develop your ideas, and consider specific career options. You will get to know them well.

- **Clues**—Insights, opinions, experiences, and preferences. A place to list everything you consider potentially useful or interesting about yourself. Individual ideas or noticings that *may* be important in your final career choice. Your Clues list is a gathering place for all kinds of information about you, what you are good at, and what is important to you.

- **Career Components**—Features or characteristics that you have determined are significant in your future work. A place to list the elements you have decided are specifications for your future work. Your Components are specific and as focused as a laser beam.

- **Career Ideas**—Job titles, roles, and positions. This is the place to list every job title or career that might fit you. An idea pops into your mind—add it to your Career Ideas list.

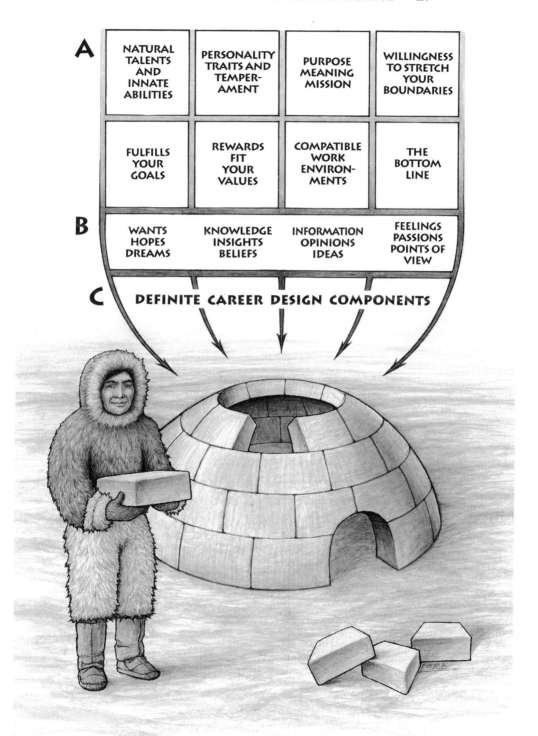

A

NATURAL TALENTS AND INNATE ABILITIES	PERSONALITY TRAITS AND TEMPER-AMENT	PURPOSE MEANING MISSION	WILLINGNESS TO STRETCH YOUR BOUNDARIES
FULFILLS YOUR GOALS	REWARDS FIT YOUR VALUES	COMPATIBLE WORK ENVIRON-MENTS	THE BOTTOM LINE

B

WANTS HOPES DREAMS	KNOWLEDGE INSIGHTS BELIEFS	INFORMATION OPINIONS IDEAS	FEELINGS PASSIONS POINTS OF VIEW

C   DEFINITE CAREER DESIGN COMPONENTS

We'll address these more in a bit.

You've already done several Inquiries. You will continue to work through them in each chapter of the book. Each is a subject matter–relevant exercise designed to help you explore ideas and generate insights about yourself and what is most important to you. Each chapter focuses on one or more topics that are career-relevant. Doing the Inquiries will help you build little islands of clarity in the midst of a vast ocean of career uncertainty. They will help you break the huge career design process down into bite-size pieces.

Working through the Inquiries, to the best of your ability, is a key to your success.

The Investigation Process

INVESTIGATE →		DESIGN →	EVALUATE
Gather Clues	Work the Clues	Career Design Components	Careers to Explore

Gather Clues. You, as the career detective, will take multiple steps to solve your career questions, just as a good detective does in solving a crime. You will **begin by collecting as many clues as you can.** A clue is any observation or information that might provide insight about the fit between you and the world of work.

At this stage you don't know what will ultimately be useful and what won't, so don't rule out too much too soon. You will notice that some clues might seem obvious. Others may be more subtle and harder to pin down. You may think to yourself, *There is something to this, but I don't know exactly what.* Try to capture those subtle ideas down on your Clues list to the best of your ability. It may take you a while to work them out. Still, especially as you begin, make note of them. Any of them might turn out to be important. Some clues will take a lot of work to uncover—you'll need to mull them over and possibly get input from others or do additional research. Be as open-minded and thorough as you can. The best detectives poke around everywhere for clues—leaving no stone unturned.

Work the Clues. As you come up with and work clues that will help you find the best fit between you and the working world, you don't want to jump to erroneous conclusions. Instead, keep searching and working the clues until you can point a finger with confidence at an answer.

You "work" the clues by investigating, researching, and considering them. Do they fit with your experience and common sense? Are they specific, or too generic or vague to be helpful? If you're comfortable, it might be a good idea to ask others to check your thinking or provide you with input and do some research and fact-checking on your behalf. The goal of working clues is to move them to the decision point and choose some of them as *definite career design components*.

Declare Career Components. Career Components are elements that you have chosen to be parts of your future work. Which Clues become Components, and what is deemed to be an important aspect of your future work, is completely up to you. (Though we will give you some additional guidance with this as you go along.) As you build your Career Components list, a clearer picture of your future work will begin to form.

As you move through *The Pathfinder* Career Design Process, you will keep yourself focused by repeatedly asking yourself an important question, "What am I sure will be a Component of my future career?" This question is different from questions like "What do I like?" or "What are some good careers out there?" Those questions relate to Clues. They are noticings: "I really love animals." Components are choices and declarations: "My work will involve working with animals."

As you declare Components and add them to your Career Components list, you are becoming the architect, author, and artist of your career.

As you work through the Career Design process, you may find it easier to come up with Clues than Components. But don't worry. Over time, you will build up that muscle. You can always go back and modify or improve them. You will also find that, as you add each new Component to your list, you get one step closer to having the clarity you need to step into future work.

Research and Evaluate Career Options. Once you have a well-rounded and meaningful list of Career Components, it is time to investigate how and where your list of criteria matches job and career options in the real world. Check out how well your career options fit your specifications. Research, investigate, and get the facts about specific fields, roles, and positions in the real world. Here, you start to match YOU to REAL-WORLD OPTIONS. Consider the preparation for, skills and aptitudes required, and other dynamics necessary to be happy and successful.

Choose. The goal is to reach the point where you can say with certainty, "I know exactly what work I will do. It is a great fit and within range of what I can accomplish." With this statement, you have solved the mystery.

ASIDE 3

How It Works—An Example

We just described an involved process with lots of pieces. To help show how it can feel like an organic, natural process, we thought we'd give you an example of how creating Clues and Components works in reality.

Gather Clues

A friend tells you that you never seem to get enough of talking with and doing things with people, face-to-face. This one hits you right between the ears as an accurate observation. Now you have a good clue. "I can't get enough of talking with, and doing things with, other people, face-to-face."

Work the Clues

You do some investigating, paying more attention to what you do naturally in your day-to-day life. You notice that what your friend said is completely accurate. You become more convinced that spending most of your time working with people may turn out to be an important career design component.

Declare a Component

You also look back at your past and realize that you are always happy dealing directly with people. This is so clear to you that you can now move to decision mode. You create a Career Component from your Clue and add it to your Career Component list: "My work will allow me to spend most of my time working directly with people, face-to-face."

Match Career Ideas to Your Component

You keep noticing things from your life, and have insights from doing the Inquiries, and you build a Career Components list. You have investigated and decided on enough pieces of the puzzle (definite career design components) to move forward. Two more Components you have identified are "My work will involve a lot of travel to different places" and "I will get to wear bright and fancy clothing at work." You have the pieces of a great career design and now move on to investigating your Career Ideas. On your Career Ideas list, you have three options: remote computer programmer, corner grocery store manager, and another.

Choose

Evaluating your Career Ideas by your Career Components, you excitedly choose your future career—a circus clown! You love the idea, but had never thought it could be a reality. But you have thoughtfully created a meaningful list of Components that you have decided are essential to you. You have identified and investigated a variety of careers that might fit that combination of Components. You have done the research and gotten the facts about job requirements and availability. As you researched specific careers on your Career Ideas list and learned more about them, you tossed out careers that didn't fit. You talked with three successful circus clowns and feel you have a basic understanding of what it's like to be one. You are ready to get started.

Next Action Steps

Your research has shown you that, although not all circus clowns go to clown school, many do. You find a clown school that you like and determine that a next step for you to build your knowledge, experience, and skill is to attend that school. They even have a placement program when you get your certificate of completion. You have a plan to pursue your Career Choice—circus clown!

Reality Check

Aside 3 provided a simplified example to illustrate the process. Your process will probably not be this simple and straightforward.

Your process will probably involve you identifying some Clues and Career Ideas, then a single Component, then more Clues, then another Component, etc., in a "complete one step before you start another step" way. This is normal and helpful.

You will also likely become confused and uncertain about some of your Components, crossing them out and reworking them repeatedly. You may also run into difficulty finding ways to express yourself and not know who to turn to for the best answers. All of these are normal experiences.

When you run into roadblocks, overwhelm, or confusion—go *back to basics*. Read over your Clues, Components, and Career Ideas lists. Reread a section or chapter of this book that you found informative or inspiring. That may be enough to get you grounded and reoriented. You can also talk to a trusted friend or adviser or hire an experienced career coach, like Monica, to help you progress and push through the roadblocks.

Every great journey starts with a single step.

—MAYA ANGELOU

SECTION 2

SET YOURSELF UP FOR SUCCESS

The three chapters making up Section 2 are here to provide you with a structure to help you fulfill on your goal of designing your career.

Chapter 4: Your Career Design Project—gives you some project management tips to help you organize yourself and your work and achieve your goals.

Chapter 5: Important Questions—discusses how to ask and answer questions that are important and relevant to designing your career.

Chapter 6: The Voices in Your Head—provides you with some thinking tools to keep you engaged, empowered, and in action.

This section contains several activities and Inquiries to help you plan, organize, and complete this important project. It provides support and wisdom that will help you overcome challenges here and in other areas of your life.

A good plan is like a road map: it shows the final destination and usually the best way to get there.

—H. STANLEY JUDD

CHAPTER 4

+

YOUR CAREER DESIGN PROJECT

The best way to reach your goal, and choose that fabulous career path, is to treat this career design and decision-making process as an important project.

One of the most important gifts you can give yourself is to take the time and effort to thoughtfully design your own career. Congratulations for being willing to step up and take it on!

But how do you do it? How do you find your path in the complex and dynamic world of work? How do you avoid the pitfalls of settling for less, following the crowd, or drifting aimlessly?

The answer is simple: Treat this as a project.

Project Management 101

Most results and achievements in life don't just spontaneously occur or appear out of thin air. Someone set a goal, put a plan together, then managed their time and activities until they were done. A project is a well-defined and structured process for achieving a specific outcome. A project has a clear plan, a timeline, and an intended outcome or result. A project is organized, focused, and purposeful. Similarly, a career is not something that happens to you by chance, or luck, but something that you create with intention and purpose.

In this chapter, we will lay out the principles and tools of project management. With them, you can enjoy the same benefits and outcomes successful project managers experience. You can watch as your progress builds and you achieve your goals.

An effective project has four main phases:

1. Defining the goal.

2. Creating a plan and structure for how the goal will be achieved.

3. Executing that plan by taking relevant actions.

4. Concluding the project by producing a result that meets your goals.

Here in chapter 4, you will formally define your goal and set up a basic structure for working toward your goal (parts 1 and 2). You've probably already been taking relevant actions by reading the first chapters and doing the Inquiries. It's official now: you will continue taking relevant actions (part 3) until you declare your project complete (part 4).

Goals are an active intention, not a prediction.

Career Project Step 1: Define Your Goal

The first step in setting yourself up for success and achieving your career goal is to create and define the specific goal you want to reach. Being clear and specific will help you achieve the outcome you want. It will focus your energy and direct your attention toward things you desire to accomplish. Being specific will help you plan, execute, and adjust as necessary.

Besides being clear and specific, your career goal should be measurable. Something that you can "check the box of" and something about which you can say, "Yes, that exists" or "No, that has not occurred." If your career goal is not measurable, how will you know when you get there?

(David Allen's brilliant work, *Getting Things Done*, has a great tip: the best way to word a goal is as an event or result that has occurred.) Let's play with some examples.

Goal	Rating
"I'm going to work on my website."	☹
"I will have a website."	☹
"I will have a published website."	☺
"I have a published website with at least three pages of content and my contact info listed."	😃

The top example is vague and without time or scope constraints—too open-ended. Things improve as the examples continue, but can you see how much easier it becomes to plan and fulfill on the goal in the fourth example? In the two "I will have . . ." goals, there is a someday quality to it. The third example adds an element of specificity that is helpful, but the fourth example is most productive and clear. There is something specific to aim toward—you either have three pages of a published website or you don't. *Kapow!*

Now let's define your Career Design Project Goal.

Define Your Goal

Since you are now in chapter 4 of a book on how to have a career that you love, our guess is that you have a goal in mind that involves figuring out which career path you should follow, or what specific jobs or positions you should pursue, or which college major to choose. You may even have more than one goal you'd like to address.

Here are a few examples of specific and measurable career goals:

- "I have identified one to three specific jobs or careers that fit my talents, interests, and values."

- "I have decided which college major or training program I will apply to in the fall."

- "I have identified three organizations whose values and missions align with mine, and that I would feel proud to work with."

- "I have rewritten my résumé in a way that highlights my experience attractively and effectively in a career change."

You are more than welcome to adopt one of these example goals. Just make sure that your goal sounds like something that you would say and that is meaningful to you. Create your own or modify the examples in a way that suits you.

My (specific, measurable) Career Project Goal:

_____

_____

_____

_____

_____

_____

_____

_____

_____

_____

*Feel free to create more than one goal.

Inquiry 5 Bonus Activity: Write, draw, or print out your GOAL(s) in an attractive way. Place it near your desk, bed, door, mirror, refrigerator, or any place that will help you keep it in mind!

Career Project Step 2: Plan and Structure

A plan is a detailed description of how you will achieve your goal. A plan is a road map that guides you from where you are to where you want to be.

By having a plan, you can clarify your vision, focus your efforts, and measure your results. It will also help you avoid procrastination, confusion, and overwhelm by knowing exactly what to do next, and when to do it.

Your plan, and the actions you take, should not be fixed and set in stone, but should be adaptable.

Time Frame

By when do you want to complete this career design process? Is there an externally provided deadline ("I am being laid off with three months of severance, pay, and want to know what's next for me before that income runs out," or "School application deadlines are December 1"), or is it more flexible? If nothing else is guiding you, or forcing your hand, what is a time frame that makes sense for you?

Some people work more quickly and intensely than others. Some value, and do better with, more time to reflect and process information. Take a moment to think about which of these people you might be. How do you prefer to work, and to lay out these kinds of projects and assignments? Remember to set yourself up for success by thinking realistically—if you are someone who never works well without a specific deadline, for example, a time-sensitive approach might be more suitable.

INQUIRY 6

Setting Up My Time Frame, Calendar, Organizational System

Inquiry 6A: Time Frame

You have full say in the time frame in which you work through this book and complete your career design project. And . . . setting a deadline or a completion date for yourself will help you manage the rest of the project and achieve your goal.

Note: It might take months, not weeks.

By when would you like to complete this project? _____[add a date]

Another key part of project management is actually scheduling time to work on the project. How and when is completely up to you. You may like to work on it half an hour or an hour each day, or for four hours every Sunday or two chunks of three hours a week. Whatever it is, marking the time in your calendar will help hold your accountability.

Let's do that now.

NEW CAREER
Target Date: 3/1
Choose a new career that is practical, that I will enjoy and fits me perfectly

Vision/metagoal: Play like a kid in a sandbox, having the time of my life

		Fully understand my natural talents	10/15
✓	1	Go through chapter 17 of *The Pathfinder* again	9/25
✓	2	Do the career testing program to learn about my natural abilities	10/1
	3	Ask friends and mentors (listed below) their opinions of my best talents	10/1
		Decide what subject matter will be central to my work	10/30
	1	Do chapter 21 in *The Pathfinder*	10/15
	2	Read appropriate books, articles, find themes	10/20
	3	Make a list of what matters to me and narrow down	10/20
		Learn about careers that fit my natural talents	12/15

Milestone ⟶

Completed ⟶
action "✓"

Action ↗

Action ⟵
target date

Milestone ⟵
date

Inquiry 6B: Put It on Your Calendar

With your time frame/deadline in mind, get out your calendar and block out specific times that you will spend working on this project.

❑ *Check this box off when you have blocked off time on your calendar to work on this project. Any notes about it:* _____

Now, we all know that the best made plans and intentions can get waylaid or shifted around. This is to be expected and not a problem at all. We're just going to plan for it. If you need to change or shift a time you have scheduled to work on your project, do so. Just replace the existing time to another that works well for you.

Another thing that you can plan on is that the time that it will take to get through this project will probably be at least twice as much as you just scheduled for. Plan on this. Go back and double the amount of time you have allotted to work on this project.

❑ *Check this box off when you have blocked off more time on your calendar to work on this project. Any notes about it:* _____

Tip: If you have a tendency to limit planning to what seems reasonably within your comfort range, rather than planning what will be most effective, stretch yourself. Even if you don't quite make an ambitious milestone by the desired date, you will have gone further than if you had planned on playing it safe. If you are committed to a plan that seems more challenging than what you think you can handle alone, hire a coach. (See the back of the book.)

Organizational System

You're going to be doing a lot of work for this project, including a lot of writing, typing, and research. As part of your project plan, decide how and where you're going to organize your work. We've provided some space in the book for you to write in, but you are **also going to need an additional notebook or digital system.**

TIP 3

Should I Use an Analog or a Digital Notebook?

There are both benefits and downsides to using either a pen and paper or digital notebook to work on and organize your career design project. There's good evidence that writing by hand aids memory and creativity; everything from how you arrange things on the page to the motions your hands move through can have very positive impacts on your thought process and your creativity. But, at the same time, writing it all out by hand can get messy to revise, and you're probably a slower writer than you are a typer. It's also not search or copy-paste friendly and is harder to share with others. Using a physical notebook also means remembering to have it with you whenever possible.

Digital notebooks or folders, such as Google Drive and Docs or Microsoft OneNote, are convenient, accessible, and efficient for when you want to re-order, modify, copy and paste, search for, add to or delete, or share content. Later on in the career design process, you are going to be doing a lot of research, much of it online, identifying and gathering URLs and descriptions off the web. It will be much easier to copy and paste, gather, and organize your work if you use a digital system.

This is your plan. Whatever you want is going to work best for you. If you want to use a handwritten system, great! We just recommend supplementing it with something digital.

Inquiry 6C: Organizational System— Create a Notebook

If you have not already done so, set up the basic organizational system or systems you will use for this project. Designate a folder or notebook in which to keep all of your work.

❑ *Check this box when you have completed this planning and organizing step.*

If you have created a digital notebook, where is it? Which account is it attached to? Do you easily remember the log-in info?

If helpful . . . make a few notes about where it is and how you access it:

_____

Career Project Step 3: Execute Your Plan

The skill you bring to bear on managing the action phase of your project makes all the difference in the results.

Okay, now you have a goal or goals, and a plan with a time frame, a rough schedule, and an organizational system. **Now it's time to take action.**

This means *reading* the next chapter, writing down your responses, *sending* that email, *doing* that online research, *having that conversation*, *narrowing down* your options, and *making that decision*.

To help keep yourself in action, and help stave off overwhelm, keep your end goal or goals in mind, and write out the next one to three specific steps you will take to get there. This work can become emotional and complicated. There are a lot of options. There are a lot of unknowns. Most of the answers you provide, and values you attribute to different things, are subjective. There are many pieces to this puzzle.

Your access to successfully completing this project and reaching your goal is always in taking concrete actions.

TIP 4

In the Event of Confusion or Overwhelm

If at any point in this project, you start to feel lost or overwhelmed—pause. Take a breath. Find and read the goal(s) you wrote down. Do you remember why you are doing this work? The possible bright and rewarding future you saw for yourself? This is tricky stuff. We know it. It's okay. You're okay.

Then, with your goal in mind, write down the next one to three specific actions that you need to take. If that is rereading chapters 1 and 2—do it. If it is reviewing all of your notes so far—do it. If it is looking something up online—do it. If it is having a conversation or sending an email—do it. If it is taking a walk and talking to your dog—do it. Don't worry about planning out every detailed element, just focus on specific next steps to take.

"Performance is a direct result of action."

TIP 5

The Importance of Writing It Down

In career design, writing it down is not just a note-taking exercise. Writing it down is a critical-thinking and learning exercise that enhances your understanding and awareness of yourself and your work. Writing it down is also a form of creative expression and is preparatory work for how you will communicate yourself to others. Capturing your ideas in writing is essential for several reasons:

It helps you clarify your thoughts and intentions. Writing forces you to articulate your ideas and goals in a clear and coherent way, and to complete the thought—first for yourself, and then in a way that you can communicate to others. It will help you refine and improve your insights and choices.

It helps you commit to your actions and decisions. Writing helps you stay focused and motivated on your tasks and objectives. When you think a thing, or even speak a thing, it doesn't last. It just disappears into the ether. Writing down or typing things out provides you with a concrete and usable record you can return to.

It helps you track and measure your progress and results. By writing, and recording, your work, you will be able to see the progress you are making. This is highly motivating. Be as detailed and consistent as you can and your efforts will be rewarded tenfold.

Be as realistic and flexible as possible.

A great (and fun!) way to keep your project in mind and keep yourself in action is to create displays.

In small-town America, a common display used to be a giant vertical thermometer set up in front of the fire station when volunteers raised money for a new fire engine. As money came in, the mercury was painted ever higher until the goal was reached. Devise your own cheerful, visual way of tracking your project. This just might be your chance to award yourself those gold stars you've always deserved. Make it big, if possible: bigger than a file folder, smaller than the firehouse thermometer. A display can also remind you of your goal. If you want a career that allows you free time to garden, for example, you might create a collage of magnificent gardens with some sort of project-tracking chart in the middle. A display helps you track progress visually and keeps your vision for your project in front of you.

**Your brain is a bad place to keep your plans,
and time is a great pickpocket.**

Career Project Step 4: When You Have Decided— Declare Your Project Complete

We will have more to say about completing your specific Career Design Project toward the end of the book (when it is time to do so). But, the final step in your Career Design Project is declaring it done.

TIP 6

The Power of Completing Things

That said, here is some wisdom that would be helpful for you to consider now.

- **Without declaring the project complete, people can get stuck in the past,** which hampers their being alive in the present.

A common way to get stuck is to leave a project in a state that does not meet your level of satisfaction or to leave it "not finished." For example, let's say you spend many evenings designing and making a beautiful coffee table. You planned to put a multi-coat finish on the whole thing, top and bottom, but after six months, you're tired of it and skip the underside. Forever after, whenever you see your gorgeous table, you don't see the intricate inlay work. All you're thinking about is the unfinished underside.

A more obvious way to get stuck is by abandoning a project midstream: the half-knit sweater, the abandoned tuba in the attic, the PhD program you put on hold, and so forth.

- **You can free yourself from being stuck in unfinished business by declaring it "complete."**

"The underside of that table is unfinished and I say I'm done—it's a fabulous table as it is."

"I never liked the color of that sweater; I'm rolling the yarn back into a ball that the cat can play with."

"I'm never going to play the tuba again; I'm giving it to the high school."

"I stopped the PhD program for a good reason, and that's the past. I will pay off my student loans as promised, but I'm going to stop beating myself up about it and am creating a new project with a new goal."

- **Natural cycles tend to move naturally toward completion.** We pay a psychological price for resisting the flow of creation, action, and completion.

While there is nothing wrong if you abandon working through this book when you are halfway through it and don't pick it up again for five years, you will find yourself enlivened and free in completing this project.

CHAPTER 5

+

IMPORTANT QUESTIONS

Questions are the creative acts of intelligence.

—FRANK KINGDOMY

In chapter 3, you learned about *The Pathfinder* **Career Design Method** and how it works. **Your access** to being able to choose future work that engages you and brings you satisfaction **is in asking and answering questions.**

You will never find, or think up, every question worth answering, but you can ask some key questions that will provide you with the guidance you need to make excellent choices about your future.

Ask Resourceful Questions

As you know, answering life's important questions means wrestling with the unknown. You can, however, make the process as painless as possible by enhancing your skill in the art of questioning; if you are experiencing difficulties in resolving uncertainties, the problem may lie in the questions you are asking. The people around you who are making significant contributions are masters at answering difficult questions. They are not necessarily more brilliant than the rest of us—they just **know how to ask the questions**. Most of us give little thought to crafting our questions; we go with whatever pops into our minds. The quality of any answer, however, depends heavily on the quality of the question.

Take the question "Do I need more education?" You could print this question in huge letters on your bedroom ceiling and think about it every morning and evening, day after day, month after month, and never move an inch toward resolution. That's because it's not quite addressing a real concern. Instead, you might want to reframe the question as "Am I willing to go back to school?" or "Is there any realistic way I could go back to school, given my finances and crazy schedule?" Sometimes the real question is just an attack of insecurity: "Wouldn't I feel completely out of place in a classroom with a roomful of twenty-year-old undergraduates?"

Sometimes there may be several distinct questions collapsed into one overly general, fuzzy question. "Do I need more education?" may mean "Am I certain enough that X is my ideal career that I should risk pouring more time and money into school? How much suffering am I willing to endure? Is there any way possible to go back to school full-time? How long would it take if I went at night? Am I willing to work all day and study every other waking moment? Could I get into the local school that has the courses I need? Would I be willing to move away from Frog Hollow to get more education?" By brainstorming, you will discover whether or not the general question leads to more specific questions. If you find more than one specific question lurking beneath the surface, see if one of them is the primary question, the dealmaker, or the deal-breaker.

As you work through this chapter and, for that matter, the rest of this book, see if you can discover what essential questions are hiding under the ones on the surface. You probably don't need therapy to uncover your real life-planning questions. You just need to poke around a little.

How to Answer Important Questions

We will either find a way or make one.

—Hannibal

If half of finding the right answer is asking the right question, the other half is answering it skillfully. You would be amazed how often people get stuck working on an Inquiry because they don't know where to look—or because they keep looking for something that doesn't exist.

Even for the big questions, there are only three places you can possibly look to find the answers:

Looking inside yourself is the best way to find answers to questions about your preferences, personality, wants, needs, hopes, dreams, ideals, requirements, experiences, and so forth. These answers are subjective and personal to you. They come from your head, your heart, and your unique mix of experiences. "What matters to me most?" "What would I like to do this weekend?" "How do I feel about squid?" are all questions that are answered by looking inside yourself. You may discover that you already have some specific, definite requirements for your future career that you can access by simply asking yourself the right questions.

You can also **look out to the external world.** The answers to "Is there a growing job market for acrobats?" "What training is needed to become a master electrician?" and "What is the difference between a data scientist and a data analyst?" do not exist within your own mind. Research (looking outside) and fact finding is the key.

You can also **invent the answer.** One of the great myths is that you can find all the answers within yourself if you only know how and where to look. Sometimes there is not a correct answer or fact we can find on the internet, and no single solution or conclusion presents itself in our mind or experience. When this is the case, it is time to create the answer. This offers a way out of being permanently stuck in neutral. To invent an answer is to make a choice, a declaration, to get out in front of the train and lay your own tracks instead of remaining merely a passenger in your life. You make an existential leap, point to what you most want, and claim it as your own.

A common struggle for clients who have come to us for help is that they have spent *years* in a futile search to discover their calling in life, or to know what purpose-driven work is right for them. Some believe that they are here on earth for some preordained purpose, yet the answer eludes them. They all feel that resolving this conundrum would bring peace and direction to their lives. What might happen if you stopped looking for the answer to appear—and created a purpose instead?

So, which direction do you take?

How do you know which of the three doors has the answer hidden behind it? First, decide if the answer can be found inside or outside. If the question is "How do I feel about moving to a colder climate?" the answer is obviously found internally. If the question is "How much do charter boat captains make in the Virgin Islands?" you will need to ask people with experience.

Where people run into difficulty is in determining if the answer is to be found internally or if they must invent the answer themselves. This is unbelievably easy to determine. Here's how you do it. First, look inside. Poke around and see if the answer is in there. If it is, it will appear. You may have to give it some serious thought, meditate on the subject, give it a few days to bubble up, or wait for circumstances to develop. If you cannot come up with the answer within a few days, most likely you never will—most of what is inside you is readily accessible. If you cannot find the answer inside yourself, it is probably hopeless to continue to look there. You will have to make up the answer and decide for yourself.

Making up the answers is quite simple. Here's our favorite method: first, figure out what you would most like the answer to be. For example, if the question you have been unable to resolve by looking in or out is "Am I willing to start my own company?" look to see what answer you would prefer, if you had a choice. Which answer would move your life forward the most? Which answer do you have more passion for? The next step is simply to decide that the answer you lean toward is the one and only answer for you. Then commit to doing whatever it takes to make it happen. That's all there is to it, folks. Inventing an answer can be nothing more than selecting the most desired possibility, hanging your star on it, and being responsible for making it happen.

Sometimes the answer may involve looking in more than one place. For example, if you are trying to decide what sort of organization you want to be associated with, you may want to look for answers both inside and outside. Unless you are intimately familiar with a wide range of organizations, you need to do some research. Then you check out how you feel and what you think about what you uncover in your external research.

Each of us is more comfortable in one of the three places that answers can be found. "Innies" introspect. "Outies" extrospect. Hardly anyone is adept at making up the answers her- or himself. Identify your preferred source for answers, then practice leaving home base to visit the two less familiar areas. You will find the answers to your thorniest questions in the places you visit least often.

Career Design Questions

As we've stated several times, the process of powerfully choosing a career consists of asking and answering questions. Section 3 of this book is full of subjects and questions on specific topics, and you'll be able to explore and work through them in depth. But first we're going to give you some practice in looking for answers to questions that will help you decide what to do with your life.

The questions in Inquiry 7 (below) will be the jump-start to your Career Design! It is not only practice in asking relevant questions and considering whether the answer lies in your own preferences and experiences, from some outside source, or is one that you need to invent yourself. Here you will dive into the world of Clue creation. Many (or all) of your responses will be Clues that you can add to your Clues list. You may also come up with a Component or Career Idea or two! You may already have some key insights and direction toward your great-fit future, but this will make clear the progress you have already made. And, bonus opportunity: if you do whatever you need to do to answer all of your important questions, you will reach your goal (or discover more questions you hadn't thought of that you need to answer, and then will reach your goal).

INQUIRY 7

Answering Important Career Questions

Below is a format you can use to organize your responses to this Inquiry. Copy it or find a way that works for you to capture down your questions and responses.

Important Career Questions

The Question	Where to Find the Answer (inside, outside, invent)	Answer

Keep in mind that some of the questions you recognize as being important to you may not have immediate answers—you may need to do some real investigation. This is normal and expected. Use this Inquiry, and the document you create for it, as a resource that you can refer to again and again. From it, you will generate many Clues and Components, but it will be a good place to record questions that arise as you work through the process.

Don't be surprised if it takes more than one approach to work through this Inquiry. It is a long one.

Pace yourself and keep perspective—there are no "right answers" to any of these questions. You can always come back to them later. You can always update your answers when you have new information and insight.

Step 1: What questions do you already have? Consider what you already know might need to be resolved to choose your future career.

- What have you been wondering about?
- What decisions do you know you have to make?
- What ideas have you already been batting around?
- Are there questions you've already asked and answered?

Step 1 (cont.): Note down all your questions and responses. Where did you find, or where do you need to look to find, the answers?

Focus on the big, weighty, important questions—the ones you absolutely must resolve to make your career decisions. Don't get bogged down in every little question, or you will drown in your own thinking.

Make sure that you have really thought about your important questions before you continue with this Inquiry.

Have you done that? Really? Okay. If you feel you have, keep reading.

Below is a list of questions that are important to many people designing their career. Some may be important to you, others may not. Read over each and think about your career and how it might fit you and your life. Focus in on those questions that seem important to you. And don't be wimpy! If you think a question is important, even if you have no idea how to answer it now, put it on your list. Working through *the important but confounding questions* makes all the difference!

Several of the questions below will be referred to again in the chapters of Section 3, and some of them are only addressed here.

Step 2: Read over the questions below. Write down the questions that stand out to you as important for you to answer. Answer all of them that you can now. Begin to wrestle with the ones you cannot answer fully. And, certainly, if you think of an alternative important question—write it down!

Geographical Environment

- Would you prefer to work or live in a specific geographic area, locality, or a certain type of physical environment? (Beach, mountains, prairies, etc.)

- Do you prefer an urban, suburban, or rural environment?

- Do you want to live near family (or far from them), or in proximity to specific recreational opportunities?

- Are there particular cities, states, or countries for you?

Transportation and Commute

- How about transportation—drive a car, walk to work, public transportation?

- Remote work, in a busy place of business?

- How long of a commute works for you?

Physical Environment, Movement, and Portability

- Inside or outside work—or a combination of both?

- Do you work from a single place or do you move from location to location?

- How much travel is okay? Local, regional, global?

- Do you have any physical, emotional, or mental characteristics that need to be accommodated for?

- Would you be happy sitting at a desk in an office all day? Would you rather have lots of physical activity during work? A mix?

- Would you like to be able to work from anywhere? Would you rather have a stable home base, where you have everything at your fingertips?

Money, Status, and Lifestyle

- How much of a priority is having a high income to you? What is a high income to you?

- Is it important to you to have a large home, a fancy car, or belong to a country club?

- Is it important that others view your position and your work in high regard? Is the social status important to you? (Dealing straightforwardly with this question is very helpful and can help you quickly narrow down your career options.)

- Are you willing to work fifty, sixty, seventy hours a week for a higher income or status?

- Are there other hobbies, activities, or priorities that your work needs to allow for?

- Is there a certain schedule (time of day, days of the week) that work, or don't work, for you?

- Do you have religious or spiritual practices or mandates that impact your availability?

Organizational Culture and Stability

- How formal or casual would you like your work environment and dress?

- How much structure and order is comfortable for you? Would you prefer the rigor of the military or the casualness of a beach vacation?

- For-profit, not-for-profit, academic, artistic, government, or entrepreneurial priorities?

- Huge corporation, small company, boutique shop, self-employed, contractor, home office, partnership, firm, government work?

- Would you be willing to work for a new, high-tech start-up with no history? Would you prefer a tried-and-true, stable, long-standing corporation?

Human Environment

- How much will you be in direct contact with others?

- Is your workplace social or is it all business?

- Are your colleagues your friends? Do you share personal information with each other?

- How rigorous is the hierarchy? Is there a clear and specific chain of command?

- Do you regularly interact with a wide variety of people or interact with a smaller, known group?

- Do you work in a highly interactive way, with lots of collaboration and teamwork, or do you work largely independently?

- Are the people you interact with coworkers, clients, customers, patients, adults, children? Do they share any characteristics (intellectuals, kind and caring people, innovators, or artists)?

Work Priorities and Characteristics

- Who does your work benefit? The organization, the less fortunate? Specific groups? The environment?

- How defined are your responsibilities and goals?

- Is the pace of your workday relaxed, moderate, or fast?

- What kind of problems do you work on?

- How much variety does your work provide? Do you do many things in many areas, or specialize and perform one or a few specific tasks?

- Do you have a set schedule and routine or is there a high degree of variability?

Creativity and Self-Expression

- Do you want to be able to be freely and fully expressed, in a personal or social way, at work, letting your freak flag fly? Or would you prefer to remain private about your personal life?

- Is your work a personal expression, a work of art, uniquely yours, and in need of limited constraints? Or do you like to have clear and firm parameters to work within to produce an excellent product?

- How important is it to you to make full use of your gifts—talents, personality, and so forth?

- Is there a particular way, or ways, that you like to express your creativity? Creating beauty, producing excellence, innovating, or improvising?

- How does your creativity express itself? Scientifically, in human relations and understanding, with logic, with music, the visual arts, or generating novel solutions?

- Do you want your work to involve a lot of imagination or storytelling?

- Is it important to you to get direct credit for the authorship or results of your work?

- What careers would you be proud to pursue? What would you do for free (if only that were realistic and possible)?

Leadership and Decision-Making

- Do you report to a boss?

- Do you have a managerial or leadership role? If so, what sort?

- What do you want to have responsibility and authority for? Do you want to set all of your own goals or have them provided for you?

- Do you want to direct, delegate, and supervise others?

- What kind of decisions do you make?

- Are you willing to be responsible for the health and safety of others? Their lives? Their money?

- Is your work detail-oriented? If so, in what ways? Big picture? If so, in what ways?

- Does your work provide you with new and regular challenges? Are you learning and applying new ideas or tools regularly? Or are you working with familiar tools and knowledge with a high degree of mastery?

More Lifestyle Factors and Plans

- What plans or commitments do you (or other people in your life) have that may affect your career choices?

- Personal plans or nonwork goals?

- Are you planning a marriage? A divorce?

- Whose career comes first—yours or your partners? What factors do you need to consider?

- Are there children involved? Will there be? What accommodations and considerations need to be made for them?

- Aging parents or grandparents?

- What about retirement?

Future Demand, Barriers to Entry, and Risk

- Do you need to be in a field that is in high demand? Where you feel confident that you will always have plenty of options to choose from?

- Is it more important for you to find your unique and specific role that speaks to your unique interests and abilities—even if it is harder to find a position?

- Would you be okay with creating a position that doesn't exist now?

- How much preparation are you willing to put in to secure a position? Is spending eight years in university to become a doctor something that you would be willing to do?

- Are you willing to constantly add to your training and education to stay competitive in your field?

- How much competition are you willing to face? Would you strive to fill one of eight Mission to Mars seats—and go head-to-head with an elite group of astronauts?

- How much uncertainty for success are you willing to face? Would you be willing to risk instability and irregular income for a chance at fame or to create your art?

- What types of risk are you willing to take on? Physical risk (like a fire-fighter, merchant, fisherperson, or mountain climber)? Artistic or political risk (facing the public criticism or rejection)? Financial risk (having little certainty of financial reward or stability)? Intellectual risk (are you willing to be wrong)?

Pheww! That was a lot of questions.

Step 3: Now go back and look at your list of Important Questions. If you haven't already done so, consider where you are likely to find the answers to them. Is there an external source of information in which you need to turn to get some facts? Is there a personal preference or priority to identify? Or is it something that you can simple choose?

Let's take a pause and acknowledge the hard work and effort you just put in. Whether you have five unanswered questions on the page or two full pages of questions and answers, you have made progress in your Career Design. You have increased your clarity and certainty about what work would be a great fit for you and you are that much closer to making a Career Choice. Well done.

What is something you can do to appreciate yourself and your work? Go for a walk? Get an ice cream cone? A massage? Give yourself a little treat. Even if you think your work is imperfect, or incomplete, we can celebrate the progress.

Have you done something good for yourself? Great! Let's keep up the momentum. We have one more step to take to complete our work here with these Important Questions.

Step 4: Review your Important Questions document and look for Clues to add to your Clues list. Remember, Clues are insights and observations about your preferences, opinions, experiences, needs, and wants. See what you can add to your list.

Here's an example: Let's say that you have the following item on your Questions List:

The Question	Where to Find the Answer (inside, outside, invent)	Answer
Would I be happy sitting at a desk in an office all day? (#12)	Inside	"While I love using a computer, I can't stand sitting on my butt all day. I don't want to sit behind a computer all day and want to be able to move around."

From this question and answer, you could quickly and easily add the following Clue to your Clues list: "While I love using a computer, I can't stand sitting on my butt all day. I don't want to sit behind a computer all day and want to be able to move around."

Step 5: Review your Important Questions document and look for Components to add to your Definite Components list. Again, Components are elements or aspects of your work or work environment that you have identified as being significant and important to you. It is a Component only because you say it is one.

Sticking with this example: "My work and workplace will not require me to spend eight hours a day sitting or in front of a computer" is a Component. An alternative could be "I will be able to freely move about my workspace, go for walks, and engage in noncomputer activities at least half of my workday. I will spend more time talking and working directly with others than I will sitting at a computer."

Step 6: Did any Career Ideas pop to mind? If a job or Career Idea popped to mind—they don't have to be directly related to any of the questions—add it to your list! Easy breezy!

Example: Career Ideas: museum exhibit specialist and docent, field quality-control specialist, marriage and family mediator.

CHAPTER 6

+

THE VOICES IN YOUR HEAD—
EXPECTATIONS, GOALS,
AND COMMITMENT

A Cure for Upsets, Delays, and Confusion

People who run marathons don't expect running 26.2 miles to be comfortable. They expect the preparation for, and the event itself, to be exhausting, frustrating, and sometimes painful. They expect that they may have to make certain sacrifices and that they might fall down. People who run marathons have as many doubts and problems as you and me—they just don't let those things stop them.

Like a person training for a marathon, you've taken on an important project—identifying a career that you find meaningful and rewarding. You've already begun the process and are at work on it. You just (chapter 5) created a goal, put things on your calendar, and set up a notebook to keep yourself organized. Perfect. Now everything will be smooth sailing, and you'll reach your goal ahead of schedule with perfect clarity and intention, right?!?

We hope that is the case.

But . . . if *your* experience of working on important projects is anything like ours have been, you may hit one or two snags or bumps along the way.

Snags and bumps happen. What would be helpful is to avoid having those snags and bumps turn into potholes and unravelings.

This chapter will provide you with some guidance for troubleshooting and persevering through the difficulties and breakdowns you might experience while working on this, or any other, project.

When humans make plans, God laughs.

Expect Snags and Second Thoughts

You have chosen to undertake a project in order to look at who you are, what you're good at, and what's most important to you. You have a big goal—identifying a career path that truly suits you. This is not a simple task. You are playing for high stakes—a truly exceptional and highly satisfying future!

As you work through this process, you may feel stuck or like you are wasting your time. At some point, one or more of the following statements will probably come to mind: "This is stupid," "I am stupid," "What was I thinking?!" "I don't really need this," "I don't understand," "I don't really want this," "I'm okay where I am," or "This isn't working." You may feel frustrated or confused or irritated or sleepy. You may want to quit.

All of these thoughts and feelings are completely normal. It is simply good ol' crazy human nature hard at work. Your biology is trying to reduce your risks, keep you safe, and make you comfortable. When you are facing change, or something that seems difficult or confronting, it is very human to want to reach out for the couch, a bag of chips, and another Netflix series.

**The secret to not being stopped by snags
and second thoughts is to expect them. It is that simple.**

Why Not Stretch Yourself?

Consider the following scenario:

Sam just got back from visiting friends at the shore and was inspired—picturing a wonderful future full of fresh, salty air, sunrises over the ocean, and the squawks of happy seagulls. In no time at all, Sam went through the following internal dialogue:

"I am going to buy a lovely house at the seaside—one with ocean views! That would be amazing and I could wake up every morning to the sounds of surf and seagulls! But . . . I bet seaside homes are incredibly expensive! Maybe I should find a smaller house near the sea. Yikes, there aren't many of them, and I probably won't find one I like. I can look for a house within driving distance of the sea (or another large body of water). Well, that would still require going through all my finances and finding the right real estate agent. That seems like a lot of work. I think I'm better off staying where I am. I'll reorganize my sock drawer."

It only took Sam moments to start compromising on dreams and goals of living by the sea. Possibly without realizing it, you compromise on what you really want, and what you see as possible for yourself, all the time.

When you start having thoughts of reducing, ignoring, or compromising your goals or dreams, of letting go of that vision of your wonderful future, we want you to take an opposite action. Instead of making your goal smaller, we want you to stretch yourself. This will require you to expand what you believe is possible and what you are capable of achieving.

In the long run, you only hit what you aim at.
Therefore, though you should fail immediately,
you had better aim at something high.

—HENRY DAVID THOREAU

We believe in you. You can have anything you want for yourself—including the job of your dreams! We're not talking about wishful thinking—it might take something for you to get it.

We don't care if you have quit everything you have ever started in your life, if you don't have the right background or experience, or if you have ADHD and are neurotic (who isn't?). You don't need an IQ of 150 or a life of privilege to fulfill any goal you set for yourself. You are capable of having a life that you love and a career that suits you brilliantly.

Are you willing to stretch yourself and your expectations of yourself to have what you want?

Because it would be very human for you to start compromising on yourself when things get challenging, let's plan on that happening. Here's a little exercise to help you recognize the compromising when it shows up . . . and to help you refocus on the goals and future you really want.

INQUIRY 8

Stretch Yourself

Draw a line across a piece of paper.

At the right end of the line, write down what you really want and would go after if you had no barriers to achieving it. This may even be a goal that seems completely over the top and into the realm of impossibility. The whole "If age, education, and time were not an issue" thing.

At the left end of the line, write down what would be a reasonable goal to go after. Pretty easy to do. Something that would be nice, a simple improvement.

Then fill in the space between the two extremes with intermediate goals that represent a progression from your more reasonable, safer goal to your outrageous one.

Now consider and respond to the following questions:

- Which of these goals are you likely to meet?

- Where along the line lies your expectation of yourself?

- If you were going to allow yourself to stretch beyond your past and expectations of yourself—where could you reach?

- What would it feel like to set a big goal (the one on the far right) and persevere until you accomplished that goal?

- What would that perseverance and accomplishment make possible for you?

Remember that each part of your life is interwoven with other parts. You don't need to limit this exercise to looking at career goals. You can explore and create big goals for other aspects of your life, such as marriage, hobbies, community involvement, or health and fitness.

Having Bigger Goals Does Not Make You a Better Person. But Why Not?

Nothing is ever accomplished by a reasonable man.

—GEORGE BERNARD SHAW

Yeahbuts

As you work through *The Pathfinder*, you will have to deal with a litany of reoccurring doubts. We call them *Yeahbuts*.

Yeahbuts are the thoughts, opinions, and doubts that pop into your head whenever you are contemplating change. They are the intruders that show up as a little voice that says something like "Hmm . . . are you sure about that?!"

A Variety of Yeahbuts

Some Yeahbuts are really useful and fit almost any purpose:

> *"I'm too tired."*
> *"I'll feel better tomorrow."*
> *"I have other priorities now."*
> *"I forgot."*

While some Yeahbuts address your perceived inadequacies:

> *"I'm too young."*
> *"I'm too old."*
> *"I'm not smart enough."*
> *"I never finish anything."*
> *"I don't have enough money/talent."*
> *"I have this fatal flaw/it's my karma."*
> *"What makes me think I can decide now when I have failed for all these years?"*

Others address your past, your experiences, or your identity:

> *"I didn't have the right opportunities or upbringing."*
> *"I'm too sensitive."*

"I'm an artist."
"My skills are antiquated/outdated/underrated."
"My head and my heart don't match."

Or address general anxiety or fear of the unknown:

"It's too complicated."
"I don't know what will happen."
"The world is not fair."

You surely have some little gems of your own. If you strung them together, you would probably have the lyrics for a musical number called "It's Not Fair." You could sing it in the shower.

If you noticed that Yeahbuts sound a lot like reasons and excuses, you are right! But . . . they can get even more colorful than that. These voices in your head are often accompanied by feelings, emotions, and other really good reasons and excuses.

Let's do an Inquiry and take a look at your personal orchestra of Yeahbuts.

My Yeahbuts

Make a list of the Yeahbuts that are familiar to you. Get some hints from those we shared.

Look back through your memories to times when you had a big decision to make or were considering doing something that was a stretch. What were the objections your mind came up with? What did you worry about? Which Yeahbuts hooked you?

Do you have a few common themes to your Yeahbuts? One or two that are strong enough to kill off any plan or dream? Do you remember the first time you thought that? What were the circumstances?

If you haven't already done so, add a page to your notebook/workbook titled "Yeahbuts." Like the Clues, Components, and Career Ideas lists, add Yeahbuts to this list whenever one or more of them arises. This is an ongoing assignment.

Something to remember: While your Yeahbuts might be a pest, they are not a problem. In fact, they are part of your internal survival mechanism. For example, if you were about to spray-paint "My boss is a total idiot" on the side of your office building in the middle of the day, the Yeahbut that tells you, "Maybe this is a bad idea. Wait until dark" might be worth paying attention to. As would a Yeahbut that asks, "Well, will you be able to pay the rent if you quit your job today?"

For better or worse, Yeahbuts pop up to keep you out of harm's way. Like well-meaning relatives, they butt in and give their opinions. This said, these well-intentioned Yeahbuts can be a bit shortsighted.

A Few More Characteristics of Our Lovable Yeahbuts

And in the night imagining some fear,
how easy is a bush supposed a bear.

—WILLIAM SHAKESPEARE

As you create new goals for yourself, and intentionally work toward them, you are stepping into new territory, into the unknown. **Yeahbuts love the status quo.** They don't want things to change. They love your familiar and safe home, to take the familiar and safe route to the grocery store, to hang out with your familiar and safe friends, and to go to your familiar and safe job. Even if you complain about them the entire time, you know what to expect from the familiar. For better or worse, you know you can survive it. If you are just beginning your career life, you are leaving the safety and familiarity of school, friends, and family. Any time in your career, when you consider a job or career change, you are increasing risk. Even setting the goal to improve your circumstances is a threat to your survival system and will **launch a Yeahbut campaign!**

Your Yeahbuts have been with you a long time. They increase in number and intensity whenever you intend to create something new in your life—anything that involves change or what your biology perceives as risk. The bigger the perceived change or risk, the more adamant the Yeahbuts become!

Yeahbut Management, Part 1

Security is mostly a superstition. It does not exist in nature, nor do the children of men as a whole experience it. Avoiding danger is no safer in the long run than outright exposure. Life is a daring adventure, or nothing.

—HELEN KELLER

News flash: Your Yeahbuts are not going away. They were there yesterday (and long before that), they are here today, and they will be there tomorrow. They are automatic, biological responses to stimuli. But they do not define you and they do not need to stop you.

To combat them, notice when a Yeahbut shows up, then simply take a pause and recognize it for what it is—a Yeahbut. A caution, an automated response to stimuli, a biological reaction to keep you and your life from expanding or changing. Choose to see it for what it is, instead of getting swept away again and again. Add it to your list. Say hello to the old familiars. Thank it for looking out for you. By focusing your attention on your thoughts and recognizing when they are automatic survival reactions, your Yeahbuts will have less power over you. You can then use them as an asset, to help you see when and where there is something that needs a strategy or some information. Noticing and staying present to your Yeahbuts is like working out—the more you do it, the more strength you build.

You are more powerful than your Yeahbuts. You do not need to heed them or obey them. You do not need to be stopped by them. You can have a brilliant future and create amazing things in the world despite them. You have a powerful ally in your drive to have the life and career you want. When you set your goals high, and expect to hit bumps along the way, you are off to a strong start. Then when the nagging doubts, fears, and Yeahbuts start swarming, you have a secret weapon—commitment.

"And in the night imagining some fear,
How easy is a bush supposed a bear"
- Shakespeare

Commitment

Whatever you can do, or dream you can, begin it.
Boldness has genius, power, and magic in it.

—W. H. MURRAY

If you really thought about the human dilemma, your human dilemma, as you read the last sections, it should not now be a mystery why so many good intentions go no-where. Most New Year's resolutions vanish like dew in the desert. All human beings walking the earth suffer from a serious case of Yeahbuts when they seek to expand their personal horizons into unknown territory.

Yeahbuts do not need to stop you! They can help you think about potential trouble spots that need some extra attention. You can think about them as problems to solve rather than deal killers.

The best way to work through most Yeahbuts is to change the questions that arise from "Is it safe?" or "Can I do it?" to "Am I willing to do what it takes?" and "Am I willing to put actions behind my intentions?" What you need in order to pursue your goals and dreams is the commitment to move it forward.

Commitment begins with a possibility and an intention. You create a possible future for yourself when you imagine your life with a rewarding career, doing work you love, and being acknowledged and rewarded for it—and then declare it to be the truth. *I'm going to have a rewarding career, doing work I love, and be acknowledged and rewarded for it!*

That goal can only be achieved if and when you commit to doing whatever is required to fulfill on your intention and achieve your goal. It is your access to achieving anything you want for yourself and your life.

> *There are really only two ways to approach life—as a victim or as a gallant fighter—and you must decide if you want to act or react, deal your own cards or play with a stacked deck. If you don't decide which way to play with life, it will always play with you.*
>
> —MERLE SHAIN

The Power of Commitment

The word *commitment* comes from Latin, meaning "to bring together or join." Its effect is binding: bringing together a promise from the present with a reality for the future. The shapeless goal of wanting to be a rock star, going to medical school, or tripling the income of your company is only half of the equation. A commitment is *a pledge to do something.* It puts you on a journey from your speaking it in the present to the fulfillment of what you spoke in the future. If you master the art of creating and living from commitments, they can be the most powerful tools in your toolbox.

Let's say you want a large lily pond in your backyard. You know how big you want it to be and where you want it. It is hot and humid outside, and you must dig it today because this is your only free week for the next six months. You also know yourself all too well. You know that if the soil is rocky or filled with roots, you are likely to get discouraged. You know that as you get tired and sweaty, your mind tends to come up with increasingly compelling reasons (Yeahbuts) why the pond should be smaller, shallower, maybe even abandoned altogether. But you truly want a big, glorious pond. To make it happen, you pull out the right tool for the job— commitment. Remember, a commitment is a pledge to produce a specific result. So, knowing that the pond is likely to shrink the hotter the day gets, you make a commitment in the form of a specific promise: "I will dig the pond and finish it within a week, no matter what difficulties arise. It will be *x* long by *y* wide and *z* deep. Having my home be a sanctuary is important to me, and a lily pond will definitely enhance my experience of that." When you start having thoughts of quitting, you are more likely to be able to contextualize those thoughts as an attack of Yeahbuts rather than the voice of a reasonable, universal truth coming down from on high. (It's also not a

bad idea to tell everyone in the neighborhood about your plans so you're threatened with looking like a jerk if you come up with a pond the size of a pothole.)

With a clear commitment, and action consistent with that commitment, something amazing happens. Your commitment transforms your mindset and guides your actions. It means honoring your word more than your fears and feelings. It means getting support if you need it, and it means getting back on the proverbial horse, and recommitting, if and when you fall off.

You are an intelligent, creative, and capable human being. You have full say in where and how your life goes. Yet, sometimes, you seem to forget this. You disempower your ideas, your intentions, and your dreams by listening to the Yeahbuts more than to your commitments.

You are fully capable of being the person you want to be. And, it might take something.

**To have the life you want—honor your commitments
more than your Yeahbuts.**

Simple. Not easy.

Distinguishing Yeahbuts as Yeahbuts, and identifying and accepting that feelings, reasons, and excuses will swarm you whenever you step out on life's skinny branches is your first and most helpful step in keeping your commitments and achieving your goals.

Committed Action

What saves a man is to take a step.

—ANTOINE DE SAINT-EXUPÉRY

Keeping promises and honoring your commitments requires an essential element—taking committed action.

Thinking won't make it so. You can *wish* you were thinner, you can *hope* to have a career you love, you can *want* to get married. Wishing, hoping, and wanting will make no difference. Going to the gym, applying for the job, and asking for someone's hand will be far more fruitful.

Performance is a direct result of committed action.

With a clear commitment, and actions consistent with that commitment, something amazing happens. Your commitment transforms your Yeahbuts into a to-do list. No longer are they fears, reasons and excuses; they are items to handle and actions to take to have what you want.

Now you can start realizing your goals and stepping into the future you choose.

INQUIRY 10

Commitment—Practice

For the sake of building a muscle in making and keeping commitments, you might want to start with something relatively small. Gain the success. Then you can repeat this exercise as many times as you like.

What is something that you've been saying you want? Something to do or complete? An action you keep meaning to take . . . ?

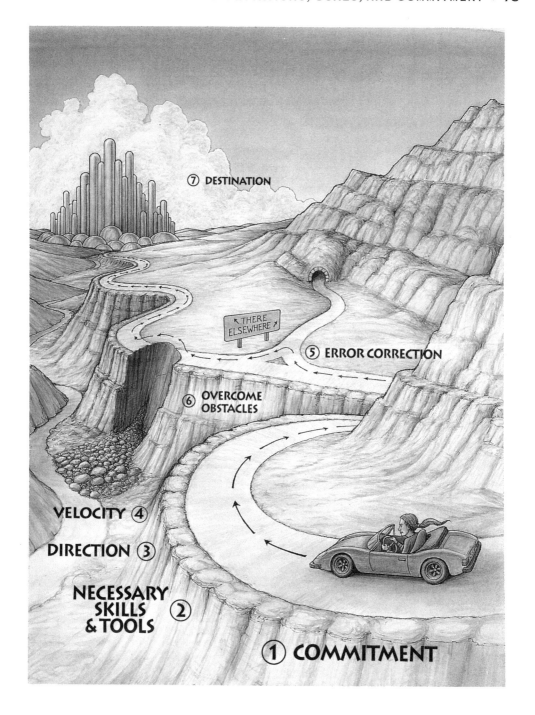

What Yeahbuts or concerns pop up when you think about it?

_____

Transform your Yeahbuts into questions you can answer or problems you can troubleshoot:

_____

Declare your commitment and write it down as a specific goal:

_____

What is the next action you need to take to achieve your goal and honor your commitment?

_____

By when are you going to take that action?

_____

What will help you keep your commitment and keep in action?

_____

Example:

My want: *I want to take an aikido class. I've found a place that teaches it.*

My Yeahbuts include: *"I got hurt last time I started aikido," "What if I don't like it?" "I'm thinking of moving," "What if it is only for children?" "What if they don't offer classes at times that work for me?" "It might be really expensive."*

A to-do list generated out of my Yeahbuts: *"Tell them I got hurt before," "Try it!" "Ask them their fees and policies about moving," "Find out what ages attend their classes and what their class schedule is."*

My commitment and goal: *I will investigate the aikido club near me and register if it fits my schedule, budget, and age group.*

Next actions: *1. Look at their website and confirm their hours of operation. 2. Go there, check it out, and speak with someone and get my questions answered.*

By when: *Look at website—today at lunchtime. Visit—on Monday during their business hours. Decide to register or not—by Wednesday, close of business.*

To keep me in action: *I will look at the website now, write myself a sticky note and put it on the refrigerator, and put the visit to the club on my calendar as an appointment for Monday.*

The secret of creating anything new in your life consists of creating new commitments, getting support, and then holding the tiller to your new course until it becomes established as a behavior. This works equally well whether you want to create a new career that truly fits and expresses you or be more effective in some other area of life.

When in doubt, gallop.

—FRENCH FOREIGN LEGION PROVERB

ASIDE 4

If You Need a Motivation Boost

Tell me, what is it you plan to do with your one wild and precious life?

—MARY OLIVER

Anytime you work on a long project, especially one that requires a lot of thought, insight, and creativity, it is normal and expected that your energy and motivation will ebb and flow.

This Aside contains a short but powerful exercise you can do if or when you could use a little boost.

Quick Question: *In regard to working on your Career Design Project, where are you on the energy and motivation spectrum?*

_____

1–I'm dragging myself and cleaning my room to avoid this.
2–I'll get to it soon.
3–I'm reading the book and doing what it says. Maybe it will turn out.
4–I'm working through the process. My enthusiasm ebbs and flows, but I am committed to completing it.
5–I'm actively engaged in the process and am excited about what is next.

If you rated yourself as a 4 or a 5 on the current energy and motivation spectrum, feel free to skip ahead to the next chapter. Come back any time your engagement is waning.

As discussed in Section 2, creating specific goals and making a commitment to complete the work will help you stay on course. Go back and review (or read!) those ideas if they might be helpful.

Another way to boost your motivation in a project is to remind yourself of the reason(s) why you started it in the first place.

Grab your notebook and answer the following questions.

• What is your goal, the outcome you want, for working through this book?

_____

• Why did you initially start this project?

_____

• What is an insight that you have already had about yourself, what is important to you, or what is possible?

_____

• How would having a job or career that you were really good at, and that you really enjoyed, make you feel?

_____

- How would having a job or career that you were really good at, and that you really enjoyed, impact your life and relationships?

  _____

- What outcome could you produce that would make the time and effort you are spending on this Career Design Project worth it?

  _____

Look back at the energy and motivation scale.

If you rated yourself less than a 4 before, did your self-rating go up at all? Even a smidge?

If you still rated yourself less than a 4, regardless of how you feel, the next best thing you can do is immediately dive into the next section and chapter. The entire next section is filled with specific activities that are all about you and what is natural and important to you. You will find it interesting and informative.

Remember: The number one way to succeed in this (or any) project is to stay in action!

SECTION 3

DESIGNING YOUR CAREER

In the first two sections of this book, we discussed the importance and benefits of having a career that fits you, and introduced you to some ideas and tips to help you move successfully through the process of designing your career.

The next three sections will guide you through the process of:

- Designing Your Career (Section 3)
- Exploring the world of career options and Making a Choice (Section 4), and
- Communicating and Pursuing Your Future (Section 5)

By the end of Section 5, you should have the clarity you need to make great choices for yourself and to take further action!

If you just had a mini surge of panic—worry not! We are still early in the process of figuring out what work fits you! You have laid the groundwork for success in the reading and Inquiries you completed in the first two sections. If you have anything written on your Clues, Components, or Career Ideas lists, you have already made progress. We hope that you have already had some fabulous aha moments and insights.

This section is designed to help you piece together, to design, a great-fitting career that suits your talents, personality, values, and goals. Each chapter addresses an individual topic that is important to consider in your career design. Along the way, you will identify and collect new Clues, Components, and Career Ideas. Then, like pieces of a great mysterious puzzle, you'll put them together and see what they create.

Section 3 is divided into four subsections:

3.1 Who I Am—Personality, Talents, Social Orientation, and Natural Roles
3.2 What I Do—Job Functions and Subject Matter
3.3 Why I Do It—Meaning, Purpose, and Values
3.4 Where to Do It—Workplace Types, Environment, and Culture

When you have answered some key questions, and created Components, from each of these sections, you will have a remarkable new clarity about who you are, what you have to offer, and what is most important to you.

Let's get started!

WHO I AM

Throughout the next four chapters, we will **explore different aspects of you—traits, aptitudes, and qualities**—and identify fundamental ways that you approach and process information about yourself and the world around you.

We already know that you are an intelligent, interesting, and competent individual. We also know that you have a unique set of talents and gifts. This section will help illuminate key aspects of what makes you *you*.

You'll address WHO I AM through several different lenses:

Chapter 7: *Personality and Temperament*
Chapter 8: *Natural Roles*
Chapter 9: *Social Orientation*
Chapter 10: *Aptitudes and Talents*

As you work through these chapters you may notice that ideas and distinctions overlap. They certainly do. Researchers and psychologists are always debating how to categorize things. For our purposes, whether something is a personality trait or a social orientation doesn't really matter; what matters is that you identify *how it is for you*. So, don't sweat the categories. If an idea or response shows up several times across a variety of Inquiries, that is great news! That means that there is a lot of evidence for something being important to you. This is a bright red flag that a Component is calling you.

As you work through the next chapters, look for key points or characteristics that you identify with. Later, we'll show you how to use these insights to look for opportunities, roles, and work environments that are naturally suited to you.

Note: It is normal and expected that you may relate better to some of the topics and chapters covered in this book. While these chapters are written to be completed in the order provided, they are whole and complete subjects in themselves. Mix it up if you prefer. Lean in and deeply explore the topics that resonate with you. And . . . we strongly recommend that you do work through all the chapters. Like in yoga, the position or posture that you find the most uncomfortable may be exactly the one you need the most.

✦

CHAPTER 7

PERSONALITY AND TEMPERAMENT

Knowing yourself is the beginning of all wisdom.

—ARISTOTLE

In our relationships with other people, sometimes we seem to easily get along, and sometimes, well . . . we don't. Haven't you ever met someone that you just liked immediately? Is there someone in your life that just doesn't seem to get you or who you just don't like? As with our relationships with people, we can match or clash in our relationships with our work and workplace. This is why we should never underestimate the importance of having our personality fit our work.

About 60 percent of the clients who have come to us seeking help in making a career change, with a personality clash within their workplace, or with their work, is a key factor in their unhappiness. And it is often an undiagnosed problem. **Great-fit work provides you with an environment that suits you, tasks and responsibilities that engage you, and aligns with your natural preferences.** A clash of your personality with your work can be devastating.

Having a basic understanding of your personality, and how it relates to your success and happiness in the working world, will help you:

- Diagnose existing issues (aka problems) with other people and work environments.

- Seek out opportunities and situations that fit your personality.

- Make better, self-empowered choices and decisions.

What Do We Mean by "Personality"?

- A set of enduring characteristics or traits that influence an individual's behavior across different situations. For example, someone may be described as extroverted if they consistently display outgoing and sociable behavior in various social contexts. (*Traits*)

- Observable patterns of behavior exhibited by an individual. For instance, if a person consistently displays punctuality, organization, and neatness in their daily routines, they may be said to have a conscientious personality. (*Behaviors*)

- The cognitive aspects of personality, such as an individual's thoughts, beliefs, and attitudes. For example, someone with an optimistic personality might consistently interpret events in a positive light, expect favorable outcomes, and maintain a hopeful outlook. (*Cognitive Processes*)

- Underlying motivational forces that drive an individual's behavior. For instance, a person with a high need for achievement may constantly strive to set challenging goals, pursue success, and demonstrate a strong desire for personal accomplishment. (*Motivation*)

- One's core sense of self and identity that differentiates one person from another. For example, someone with an independent and individualistic personality might prioritize personal autonomy, express unique preferences, and resist conformity to societal norms.

- We view all these aspects as intertwined and related. (*Self-Identity*)

Taking all of that into account, here is our simplified definition: **A set of enduring characteristics that influence an individual's thoughts, attitudes, motivations, and behaviors across different situations.**

Whether or not you are born that way, or it developed out of your environment and experiences (reality: it's probably a combo—nature and nurture), **identifying your personality type is extremely helpful and useful when determining your best-fit career.** Millions of people have gained **self-knowledge and awareness, and made better choices and decisions,** from doing the same.

What follows are a few Inquiries that will allow you to explore your personality in a few ways. You'll start with a self-assessment of positive character traits, then will look for Clues with one of most popular ways of understanding individual differences in personality—the 16-Types Model of Personality. We'll finish this chapter with a short Inquiry on temperament.

Character Traits

Your exploration of personality starts with an Inquiry into your character traits. By *character* traits, we mean *individual qualities that combine to form your personality.*

In this first Inquiry, you'll begin to identify and collect ways to describe yourself. You'll do this by considering, and choosing, terms that capture aspects of your personality.

It's okay if you are unsure about how objectively or accurately you see yourself. We are interested in how you view yourself. Subjectivity is expected. And we are looking out for you—for some additional perspective, you'll be asking other people to describe you as well!

INQUIRY 11

Character Traits

Here is an Inquiry to get you started thinking about your personality traits.

Directions:

Below is a series of paired personality traits.

Read each pair of traits and consider where you fall on the spectrum between the two contrasted characteristics.

Mark • at the appropriate place on each scale for each pair.

Example: Cautious ← |—|—|—|—|—| → Impulsive

If you are really cautious, mark,
Cautious ← ♦—|—|—|—|—| → Impulsive.

If you are balanced in cautiousness and impulsiveness, mark
Cautious ← |—|—|•|—|—| → Impulsive.

Recommended: Use a pencil if writing in this book. We've provided you with an extra set of Inquiries (in the back of the book). In several Inquiries (including this one) we will ask you to get input from others. Seeing your responses could influence theirs—we want to avoid this.

90 Character Traits in 45 Pairs

Self-indulgent ← |—|—|—|—|—| → Disciplined
Cautious ← |—|—|—|—|—| → Impulsive
Low need to influence others ← |—|—|—|—|—| → Persuasive
Suspicious ← |—|—|—|—|—| → Trusting
Warm ← |—|—|—|—|—| → Cool
Content ← |—|—|—|—|—| → Ambitious
Joiner ← |—|—|—|—|—| → Socially independent
Shy ← |—|—|—|—|—| → Bold
Follow urges ← |—|—|—|—|—| → Controlled
Leader ← |—|—|—|—|—| → Follower
Conventional, conforming ← |—|—|—|—|—| → Unconventional, rebellious
Comfortable ← |—|—|—|—|—| → Adventurous
Optimistic ← |—|—|—|—|—| → Pessimistic
Tortoise ← |—|—|—|—|—| → Hare
Proactive ← |—|—|—|—|—| → Responsive
Self-expressed ← |—|—|—|—|—| → Reserved
Subdued ← |—|—|—|—|—| → Enthusiastic
Quiet ← |—|—|—|—|—| → Talkative
Gather information ← |—|—|—|—|—| → Process information
Loner ← |—|—|—|—|—| → Super social
Private ← |—|—|—|—|—| → Open book, sharing
Curious ← |—|—|—|—|—| → Observant
Realistic ← |—|—|—|—|—| → Imaginative
Practical ← |—|—|—|—|—| → Conceptual
Like the tried-and-true ← |—|—|—|—|—| → Like to innovate
Concrete ← |—|—|—|—|—| → Abstract
Traditional ← |—|—|—|—|—| → Original
Organized ← |—|—|—|—|—| → Free-flowing
Trust experience ← |—|—|—|—|—| → Trust intention
Correct ← |—|—|—|—|—| → Creative
Logical ← |—|—|—|—|—| → Insightful
Reasonable ← |—|—|—|—|—| → Compassionate
Self-indulgent ← |—|—|—|—|—| → Disciplined
Accommodating ← |—|—|—|—|—| → Questioning
Interdependent ← |—|—|—|—|—| → Self-sufficient
Provide information ← |—|—|—|—|—| → Provide wisdom
Facts matter more ← |—|—|—|—|—| → My perspective matters more
Scheduled ← |—|—|—|—|—| → Spontaneous

Strict ← |—|—|—|—|—| → Tolerant, permissive
Consistent ← |—|—|—|—|—| → Variable
Expedient ← |—|—|—|—|—| → Sophisticated
Decisive ← |—|—|—|—|—| → Open-minded
Self-confident ← |—|—|—|—|—| → Complicated
Assertive ← |—|—|—|—|—| → Easygoing
Early starter ← |—|—|—|—|—| → Pressure-prompted
Results-focused ← |—|—|—|—|—| → Process-focused

Look over your responses. Does that sound like you?

It is often helpful to get some input from people in our lives. If they see you the way you see yourself, that is helpful. If they see you differently than you see yourself, that is also helpful. The perspective of others can be validating and/or enlightening.

Ask someone who knows you well to do this Inquiry about you. Do they see you the way you see you? If there are any differences, why do you think that is? Make a note about it:

Write a description of yourself that contains the traits that stand out most to you. Be honest—not you on your best day, or your worst.

For example, you might write:

"I am imaginative, enthusiastic, flexible, optimistic, independent, and empathetic."
Or *"I am a restrained, conventional, pessimistic loner."*

Look back at the description of yourself you just created. Is this a Clue you can add to your Clues list? How about creating a Clue about how others see you.

Example: *"Others see me as witty, independent-minded, and creative."*

Did any Components come to mind? If you think to yourself, "I want to be allowed to be my enthusiastic and curious self at work—not be stifled." Make it a Component!

Example: *"My workplace and colleagues allow me to fully express my natural enthusiasm and curiosity."*

See how this works?!?

16 Types of Personalities

At some point, you may have heard someone say, "I am an ENFP" or "That is a characteristic of an ISTJ." They are referring to individual personality "types"; "ENFP" and "ISTJ" each refer to personality types, or groups, that tend to share certain traits, characteristics, and tendencies. These traits and tendencies strongly influence how a person naturally and comfortably interacts with others and with the world around them.

All models are wrong,
some are useful.

—GEORGE E. P. BOX

The most well-known personality typing system, or model, categorizes individuals into one of sixteen types. You can find many variations of the sixteen-types model, but most of them are based, at least partly, on the work of Dr. Carl Jung. Later, a mother and daughter team, Katharine Cook Briggs and Isabel Briggs Myers, expanded upon Jung's ideas and created the Myers-Briggs Type Indicator (MBTI)—a widely recognized personality assessment tool.

Many alternatives to the MBTI exist. **We have created a simplified sixteen-types tool for you to explore your personality and its relevance to your career.** This is a straightforward exercise to help steer you toward your "best fit" type. Then you'll see descriptions and some career ideas for each.

Let's investigate!

A happy life is one which is in accord
with its own nature.

—SENECA

INQUIRY 12

What's My Type?

On the four pages following these instructions, you will find (four) paired lists of traits or tendencies. Each pair of traits corresponds to one of four dimensions:

E	Extroversion	Introversion	**I**
N	Intuition	Sensing	**S**
F	Feeling	Thinking	**T**
P	Perceiving	Judging	**J**

Consider each pair of traits, on each page, and mark the one that more closely describes you.

Example:

E I

___ Outgoing, chatty   ✔ Reserved, shy
✔ Many social relationships   ___ A few deep, personal relationships
___ Expressive, quick to engage ✔ Reflective, a quiet observer

This can be tricky. Try not to overthink it. In this Inquiry, it can be best to go with your first thought (i.e., gut, instinct, intuition). If not an easy choice, try to consider how you have responded or reacted over time and across a variety of situations.

You probably can think of examples of how both responses would fit in certain ways. Do your best to pick one from each pair. What is your natural inclination (before you learned, struggled, or worked hard to be better at the other)?

If you absolutely can't choose a "better" option, between a particular trait pair, leave them both blank.

When you are done marking your choices on all four pages, go back and total the number of marks for each (vertical) list.

Note: If you know you are not a math-y or detail-oriented person, add them up more than once. Then, add that to your Clues list! (E.g., "I am not a math-y person"; "I am not good at detail-oriented written tasks.")

Ready to begin?

WHAT IS MY TYPE?

INQUIRY 12

E

- ◯ Outgoing, chatty
- ◯ Many social relationships
- ◯ Expressive, quick to engage
- ◯ Saying it out loud is helpful
- ◯ Studying in a loud café is great
- ◯ Proactive
- ◯ The more the merrier
- ◯ Just do it!
- ◯ Talk
- ◯ Lonely when alone often
- ◯ Easily begin new relationships
- ◯ Discuss everything with everyone
- ◯ Speak first
- ◯ Love to be in the middle of the action
- ◯ Seek out the input of others
- ◯ In the world
- ◯ Like being the center of attention
- ◯ An easy day is lots of conversations

I

- ◯ Reserved, shy
- ◯ A few, close friends
- ◯ Hard to read, observant
- ◯ Need time to consider my response
- ◯ Studying in a loud café is difficult
- ◯ Reactive
- ◯ Prefer one-to-one
- ◯ Look before you leap
- ◯ Listen
- ◯ Savor and seek alone time
- ◯ Slower to enter new relationships
- ◯ Desire time to think through things
- ◯ Respond
- ◯ Prefer quiet environments
- ◯ Seek to work out things on your own
- ◯ In your head
- ◯ Avoid being the center of attention
- ◯ An easy day is lots of time without distraction

Number of E responses_____   Number of I responses_____

WHAT IS MY TYPE?

INQUIRY 12

S

- ◯ Focus on what IS
- ◯ Reality
- ◯ Now
- ◯ Concrete
- ◯ Action
- ◯ Tradition
- ◯ Organize
- ◯ Interact with the world
- ◯ Observe the details
- ◯ Pragmatic
- ◯ Practice makes perfect
- ◯ Trust experience
- ◯ Down-to-earth
- ◯ Tangible results
- ◯ Trust tried-and-true
- ◯ Develop and refine skills
- ◯ Appreciation
- ◯ Reproduce or build accurately

N

- ◯ Focus on what COULD BE
- ◯ Possibility
- ◯ Future
- ◯ Abstract
- ◯ Ideas
- ◯ Novelty
- ◯ Plan
- ◯ Understand the world
- ◯ See the connections
- ◯ Imaginative
- ◯ Find a new way
- ◯ Trust insight
- ◯ Free-spirited
- ◯ Prefer quiet environments
- ◯ There's always a better way
- ◯ Be creative
- ◯ Inspiration
- ◯ Modify or re-imagine

Number of S responses_____   Number of N responses_____

WHAT IS MY TYPE?

INQUIRY 12

F

T

○ What is important
○ Personal values
○ Important to be understanding
○ Protect other's feelings
○ Appreciate
○ Inclusion
○ Influence
○ Share
○ Personal
○ What feels right
○ Interested in the impact on people
○ Tactful
○ Harmony
○ Authenticity
○ Socializing at work is important
○ Understanding
○ Mentor
○ Empathize

○ What is true
○ Principles
○ Important to be competent
○ Be direct
○ Analyze
○ Efficiency
○ Inform
○ Explain
○ Impersonal
○ What is logical
○ Interested in ideas and things
○ Straightforward
○ Results
○ Competence
○ Getting to the work is important
○ Knowledge
○ Train
○ Sympathize

Number of F responses_____

Number of T responses_____

WHAT IS MY TYPE?

INQUIRY 12

P

- ◯ Flexible
- ◯ Seek more information
- ◯ Often finish projects at deadline
- ◯ Resist deadlines, but need them
- ◯ Adaptable
- ◯ Make a plan
- ◯ Prefer to keep my options open
- ◯ Spontaneous
- ◯ Process-oriented
- ◯ Effort and focus ebbs and flows
- ◯ Remain open to new inputs
- ◯ Like a flexible or varied schedule
- ◯ Autonomy
- ◯ Prone to indecisiveness
- ◯ Tolerant
- ◯ Find the best way to do it
- ◯ More information is better
- ◯ Tentative, contingent

J

- ◯ Consistent
- ◯ Meet the parameters
- ◯ Often finish projects before deadline
- ◯ Of course I meet the deadlines
- ◯ Dependable
- ◯ Follow the plan
- ◯ Comfortable after decision is made
- ◯ Structured
- ◯ Goal-oriented
- ◯ Deliberate
- ◯ Decide once
- ◯ Like a regular schedule
- ◯ Security
- ◯ Prone to inflexibility
- ◯ Exacting
- ◯ Find a sufficient way—get it done
- ◯ This will work
- ◯ Definite, final

Number of P responses_____   Number of J responses_____

SCORING YOUR RESPONSES:

1. Transfer your totals, from Inquiry 12, for each of the eight "functions" here.

    ___ Number of **E** responses   ___ Number of **I** responses

    ___ Number of **N** responses   ___ Number of **S** responses

    ___ Number of **T** responses   ___ Number of **F** responses

    ___ Number of **J** responses   ___ Number of **P** responses

The letter with the higher score for each pair (E-I, N-S, T-F, J-P) becomes part of your four-letter type. For example:

10   Number of **E** responses   5   Number of **I** responses

6   Number of **N** responses   2   Number of **S** responses

5   Number of **T** responses   12   Number of **F** responses

3   Number of **J** responses   9   Number of **P** responses

In this example, the scores were higher for E, N, F, and P. The test taker's type would be ENFP.

2a. If you have clearly higher scores for each of your trait pairs, write your four-letter code here: _____. You can go on to "Exploring Your Type."

2b. If one of your trait pairs is equal or within a point or two, you will need to do some additional investigation. Write a "?" in place of each ambiguous trait pair in your four-letter code. For example:

10   Number of **E** responses   5   Number of **I** responses

6   Number of **N** responses   2   Number of **S** responses

5 Number of **T** responses   5 Number of **F** responses

3 Number of **J** responses   9 Number of **P** responses

Since the number of responses for (trait pair) T-F were even, this test taker should write their type as: EN?P. And should read and consider both ENFP and ENTP profiles.

If this is the case for you, write both of the types you should review: _____ and _____

2c. If more than one of your trait pairs is equal or within a point or two, the number of personality profiles for you to review can become confusing. To see if you can narrow down your options, we recommend the following activity:

For each trait pair with a "?," go back and review the lists of common characteristics for each letter in the pair. Look at them as two "groups," or "sets," of characteristics. If you consider them holistically, does one stand out as "overall, more like you" than the other? Swap that letter out for the relevant "?."

Do that for each trait pair with a "?."

Write your "revised" personality type four-letter code here: _____.

In the pages that follow, there are encapsulated descriptions of all sixteen personality types. Remember, the point of doing this is not to pigeonhole yourself with a four-letter type, but to get clear on important aspects of your personal blueprint. Use it as a mirror to see yourself more clearly, and to find Clues. That's the main value of all career tests. If you are in the middle in more than one pair of opposites, don't worry; it's perfectly natural. Many other people have scores in the middle. It doesn't mean you are wishy-washy or undecided. It means your personality might be a combination of more than one type. If you highlight the traits that best describe you in each of the temperament types that seem to partially fit you, you will wind up with a list of your temperament traits, even if you do not exactly match one type or another.

Also remember that the careers suggested for each type are only examples, not a list from which to choose your future career. These careers are suggested as possible matches for your *personality*, not your talents, your interests, or what matters to you; often, an in-depth look at these other areas suggests careers that are very different. Some people feel the need to have a career that is a direct expression of their temperament, or will be most attracted to careers similar to ones listed for their type. Others are perfectly satisfied if they can do whatever they do in a style that allows them to freely be themselves at work, without having to manufacture a business persona. For example: someone whose personality includes a built-in tendency toward helping people to be their best could choose a career where that quality would be of profound importance, such as teaching, coaching, or counseling. That trait could also be expressed less directly in many other careers. But in some careers, this trait might be less important or valued. As you read through the key words that describe your type, ask yourself which ones are most important for you to express. If most of the key words for your type describe you accurately, and you are committed to finding work you love, wouldn't you think it necessary to choose a career that would fit elegantly with those descriptive words?*

Before we begin, remember . . . none of this is "the truth." We are looking for insights and Clues about what is so for *you*. This whole book on career design and decision-making is intended to empower you to identify what is natural, important, and motivating to you. **Read through as many descriptions as is helpful or interesting to you.** You will probably recognize yourself in several of the descriptions. Look for the one or two that seem, holistically, the most like you.

It also may be helpful to have another person or two read through your "top contenders"—and get their input. But, remember, they will view you through their own filters and biases . . . and others will notice your outward-facing characteristics more than your internal ones. Though, you are the one who has the final say in which type is your best fit.

INQUIRY 13

Personality Type Clues,
Components, and Career Ideas

What type did your responses indicate was your best fit? _____
[four letters]

Any alternative types you should read? _____

---

* If you want to delve deeper into your personality, we recommend that you pick up a copy of *Do What You Are* by Paul D. Tieger, Barbara Barron, and Kelly Tieger. It is an absolutely terrific, in-depth guide to the subject of temperament and work.

- As you read the descriptions and are considering your "best-fit type," look for Clues. If it doesn't fit, don't include it. Add any terms or phrases that ring true to your Clues list.

- Ask yourself, "Is there anything I am willing to choose as a Component?" Anything that strikes you as being significant or important to you? Something that you are clear that great-fit work for you would include? Or avoid? Add these ideas to your Key Components list.

- See any careers listed that are interesting to you? Do any other careers/ jobs come to mind? Add them to your Career Ideas list.

The 16 Types—Descriptions

ENFP

Enthusiastic, expressive, emotional, warm, evocative, imaginative, original, artistic, improvisers, perceptive, affirming, supportive, cooperative, positive, open, responsive, sensitive, playful, fun-loving, multifaceted, gregarious, zestful, spontaneous, idealistic, initiators of new projects and possibilities, agents of change. Their focus is on self-expression and possibilities, "what could be" rather than "what is." Life is a celebration and a creative adventure. Enthusiastic initiators of new projects, relationships, and paradigms. Masters of the start-up phase. Lose interest when the project or relationship gets routine or when the primary goal is well on the way to accomplishment. Often eloquent in expressing their vision of a world where ideals are actualized. They might say the glass is full rather than half-full or half-empty. They are quick to see the potential in people and situations. Frequently have a positive attitude in situations others would consider to be negative. May enjoy a rainy day as much as a sunny one. Management style is focused on the people rather than task-oriented. They encourage and serve as mentors rather than command. Work in bursts of enthusiasm mixed with times when little gets done. Need careers that are personally meaningful, creative, and allow for full self-expression and that contribute to other people in some way. Extremely versatile. They may have friends from many walks of life, a wide range of interests and hobbies, and they gain a professional level of mastery without formal training.

Activist: social causes	Agent for actors, artists, writers
Actor	Buyer

Clergy in low-dogma faiths
Coach: personal growth and
    effectiveness
Counselor: relationship, spiritual,
    career
Consultant: communications,
    education, human resources,
    presentation personal
    effectiveness
Director/producer: films
Entrepreneur
Fundraiser
Healer: alternative disciplines
Human resources specialist

Journalist
Midwife
Ombudsman
Passenger service representative
Physician: family, holistic
Psychologist
Public relations
Recreation leader
Religious activities director
Social scientist
Teacher
Therapist in active, participatory,
    growth-oriented discipline
Trainer

INFP

Idealistic, warm, caring, creative, imaginative, original, artistic, perceptive, supportive, empathetic, cooperative, facultative, compassionate, responsive, sensitive, gentle, tenderhearted, devoted, loyal, virtuous, self-critical, perfectionist, self-sacrificing, deep, multifaceted, daydreamers, persistent, determined, hardworking, improviser, initiator of new projects and possibilities, agent of change. Drawn to possibilities, "what could be" rather than "what is." Values-oriented with a high level of personal integrity. Their focus is on understanding themselves, personal growth, and contributing to society in a meaningful way. Under surface appearances they are complex and driven to seek perfection and improvement: in themselves, their relationships, and their self-expression. If their career does not express their idealism and drive for improvement, they usually become bored and restless. Dislike conflict, dealing with trivialities, and engaging in meaningless social chatter. Thrive on acknowledgment and recognition so long as they are not the center of attention. Needs a private workspace, autonomy, and a minimum of bureaucratic rules.

Activist
Administrator: education or
    social service nonprofit
Architect
Artist
Attorney devoted to righting
    wrongs

Clergy in low-dogma faiths
Coach: personal growth and
    effectiveness
Consultant: education, human
    resources
Counselor: relationship, spiritual,
    career

Developer of training programs
Director of social service agency
Editor .
Entrepreneur
Healer: alternative disciplines
Health-care worker
Human resources specialist
Librarian
Medicine: family
Midwife
Nurse
Physician: psychiatrist, family,
  holistic
Psychologist
Researcher
Social scientist
Social worker
Songwriter/musician
Speech pathologist
Teacher
Therapist
Writer, poet, or journalist

ENFJ

Enthusiastic, caring, concerned, cooperative, congenial, diplomatic, inter-active, facilitators, diligent, emotional, sincere, interpersonally sensitive, warm, supportive, tolerant, creative, imaginative, articulate, extraordinary social skills, smooth, persuasive motivators, teachers/preachers, verbal, nat-ural leaders, active, lively, humorous, entertaining, witty. Values-oriented. Uncannily perceptive about other's needs and what motivates them. Often rise to leadership positions. Concerned with the betterment of humanity and work to effect positive change. They have such a gift for persuasively using language that others may consider them to be glib and insincere when actually they are forthright and openhearted. Don't deal well with resis-tance and conflict. Easily hurt and offended if their well-meaning crusades are met with criticism and rejection. Take everything personally. Put people before rules. Strong desire to give and receive affirmation. Manage by en-couragement.

Actor
Advertising account executive
Camp director
Clergy
Consultant
Counselor: career, relationship,
  personal growth
Dean
Director of communications
Director of social service
  nonprofit
Entrepreneur
Fundraiser
Health practitioner: holistic
Mediator
Newscaster
Outplacement counselor
Politician
Producer: films, television
Promotions
Public relations
Public speaker

Recruiter
Sales
Sales manager

Supervisor
Teacher
Trainer

INFJ

Gentle, introspective, insightful, idealistic, intellectual, inquisitive, sincere, quiet strength, steady, dependable, conscientious, orderly, deliberate, diligent, compassionate, caring, concerned, peace-loving, accepting, intense, sometimes stubborn, dreamers, catalysts, many interests, seek and promote harmony. Many feel at home in academia, studying complex concepts, enjoying theory-oriented courses. They are quietly aware of the dynamics between people. Because they are gentle and quiet, their gifts and rich inner life may go untapped. Their caring, nurturing nature can remain unnoticed, since they may not find it comfortable to express these feelings openly. Consequently, they may feel isolated. Need a great deal of solitude and private personal space. Dislike tension and conflict. Give a great deal of focused energy and commitment to their projects, at work and at home. Although usually compliant, they can become extremely stubborn in pursuit of important goals. Seek careers that further their humanistic ideals and engage their values.

Accountant
Administrator: health care, social
  work
Analyst
Architect
Artist
Clergy
Composer
Consultant: organizational
  development
Coordinator
Editor
Entrepreneur
Human resources planner
Judge

Librarian
Management analyst
Novelist
Photographer: portrait
Physician
Physical therapist
Poet
Psychologist
Researcher
Scientist
Social scientist
Social worker
Technician: health care
Writer

ENTP

Enthusiastic, puzzle masters, objective, inventive, independent, conceptual thinkers, creative problem solvers, entrepreneurial risk-takers, improvisers, competitive, questioning, rebellious, rule breakers, gregarious, witty, involved, strategic, versatile, clever, adaptable, energetic, action-oriented agents of change. Improve systems, processes, and organizations. Relentlessly test and challenge the status quo with new, well-thought-out ideas, and argue vehemently in favor of possibilities and opportunities others have not noticed. Can wear out their colleagues with their drive and challenging nature. See the big picture and how the details fit together. The most naturally entrepreneurial of all types. Usually not motivated by security. Their lives are often punctuated with extreme ups and downs as they energetically pursue new ideas. They have only one direction: ahead at full speed, leaving a trail of incomplete projects, tools, and plans in their wake. Their idea of fun and best creative self-expression involves devising new conceptual modeling and dreaming up imaginative and exciting ventures. Need lots of room to maneuver. When forced to dwell on details and routine operating procedures, they become bored and restless. Respect competence, not authority. Seek work that allows them to solve complex problems and develop real-world solutions. Often surrounded by the latest technology.

Advertising, creative director	Manager: leading-edge company
Agent: literary	Marketer
CEO: high-tech companies	Political analyst
Computer repair	Politician
Consultant: management	Public relations
Designer	Publicity
Engineer: high-tech	Sales
Entrepreneur	Software designer
Industrial designer	Special projects developer
Inventor	Strategic planner
Investment broker	Systems analyst
Journalist	Technician: high-tech
Lawyer	Venture capitalist

INTP

Logical, original, speculative quick thinkers, ingenious, inventive, cerebral, deep, ruminative, critical, skeptical, questioning, reflective problem solvers, flaw finders, architects and builders of systems, lifelong learners, precise, reserved, detached, absent-minded professors. Seekers of logical purity. They love to analyze, critique, and develop new ideas rather than get involved in the implementation phase. Continually engage in mental challenges that involve building complex conceptual models leading to logically flawless solutions. Because they are open-ended and possibility-oriented, an endless stream of new data pours in, making it difficult for them to finish developing whatever idea they are working on. Everything is open to revision. Consequently, they are at their best as architects of new ideas where there are endless hypothetical possibilities to be explored and no need for one final concrete answer. Their holy grail is conceptual perfection. May consider the project complete and lose interest when they have it figured out. To them, reality consists of thought processes, not the physical universe. Often seem lost in the complex tunnels of their own inner process. Seek work that allows them to develop intellectual mastery, provides a continual flow of new challenges, offers privacy, a quiet environment, and independence. Thrive in organizations where their self-reliance is valued and colleagues meet their high standards for competency.

Archaeologist
Architect
Artist
Biologist
Chemist
Computer programmer
Computer software designer
Computer systems analyst
Economist
Electronic technician
Engineer
Financial analyst
Historian
Judge
Lawyer
Mathematician
Musician
Philosopher
Physicist
Researcher
Social scientist
Sociologist
Strategic planner
Writer

ENTJ

Born to lead, outgoing, involved, fully engaged, ambitious, take charge, impersonal, hearty, robust, type A+, impatient, bossy, controlling, confrontational, argumentative, critical, sharp-tongued, intimidating, arrogant, direct, demanding, strategic, tough-minded, organized, orderly, efficient, long-range planner, objective problem solvers. Self-determined and independent. Skilled verbal communicators. Firmly believe that their way is best. Hold on to their point of view without alteration or compromise until some brave soul is able to convince them, through extensive argument and definitive proof, that another way is better. They consider all aspects of life to be the playing field for their favorite game, monkey on the mountain. Their energy is focused on winning, getting to the top, beating the competition, reaching the goal. See life and evaluate other people as part of this game. Assess others hierarchically, above them or below them on the mountain. Tend to look down on people who will not engage them in competition. Often generate hostility and rebellion from their employees and children. Show affection for others by helping them improve. Seek power. Learn by fully engaged discussion (also known as arguing). Are at their best planning and organizing challenging projects, providing the leadership, straight-ahead energy and drive to keep the momentum up, and efficiently managing people and forces to reach the objective.

Administrator	Military officer
Athlete	Mortgage banker
Consultant: management	Office manager
Corporate executive	President, CEO
Credit investigator	Program designer
Economic analyst	Sales
Engineer, project manager	Sales or marketing manager
Entrepreneur	Stockbroker
Financial planner	Supervisor
Lawyer	Systems analyst
Manager, senior level	Team leader

INTJ

Innovative, independent, individualists, self-sufficient, serious, determined, diligent, resourceful, impersonal, reserved, quick-minded, insightful, demanding, critical, argumentative debaters, may seem aloof to others, strategic, tough-minded, organized, orderly, efficient, global, long-range visionaries, planners, objective problem solvers. Self-determined and independent. Use resources efficiently. Do not waste their time on trivialities. True to their own visions. Can become stubborn when they are supposed to do things in a way that differs from their own opinions of the best methodology. Oriented toward new ideas, possibilities, and improving systems. Their motto is "Everything could use improvement." This includes processes, systems, information, technology, organizations, other people, and themselves. Many use education as a path to success and earn advanced degrees. Usually one of the first to buy the latest computer and upgrade to new, improved software and other technology. Show affection for others by helping them improve. Learn by in-depth study of the subject and by discussing and arguing. May not realize that other, more thin-skinned individuals do not interpret arguing in the positive way that INTJs do. Attain personal growth by confronting anything within themselves that could be ameliorated. Constantly stretch themselves in new directions. Highly competent. Read and understand both conceptual and practical materials. See both the forest and the trees. Excellent at planning, execution, and follow-through. They see the big picture, thinking and ably organizing the details into a coherent plan. Often rise to the top in organizations. At their best when they can conceptualize a new project and then push it through to completion; then do it all over again with another new project.

Administrator
Analyst: business or financial
Architect
CEO: high-tech
Computer programmer
Consultant
Curriculum designer
Design engineer
Designer
Engineer
Entrepreneur
Inventor

Judge
Lawyer
Pharmacologist
Physician, cardiologist, neurologist
Psychologist
Researcher
Scientist
Systems analyst
Teacher: college
Technician

ESFP

"Live for today. Face the consequences tomorrow." Warm, positive, friendly, popular, vivacious, helpful, generous, inclusive, tolerant, enthusiastic, gregarious, action-oriented, robust, zestful, spontaneous, flexible, energetic, alert, fun-loving, playful, impulsive, thrill seekers. Realistic, practical. A great deal of common sense. The focus is on people. Accepting, live-and-let-live attitude, go with the flow. Sunny disposition, love life. Laugh easily, even at themselves. Adventurous, fearless, willing to try anything that involves sensation and risk. Tuned in to and relishes the world around them. Smell the roses without stopping. Plunge in headfirst. Live in the present, spurred into action to meet today's needs. Seek immediate gratification, harmony, positive experiences. Avoid or repress unpleasant or negative experiences. Do not naturally plan ahead. Dislike routines, procedures, limits, conflict, and slow-moving, long-range projects. Learn by interactive, hands-on participation. Do best in careers that allow them to generate immediate, tangible results, while having fun harmoniously relating with other people in the center of the action.

Bus driver	Physician: emergency room
Carpenter	Police officer
Childcare provider	Producer: film
Coach	Promoter
Comedian	Public relations
Events coordinator	Receptionist
Fundraiser	Sales
Lifeguard	Sales manager
Mechanic	Small business, retail store
Mediator	Supervisor
Merchandiser	Teacher: preschool
Musician: rock and roll	Tour operator
Nurse: emergency room	Travel agent
Performer	Veterinarian
Physical therapist	Waiter/waitress

ISFP

Gentle, sensitive, quiet, modest, self-effacing, giving, warm, genuine, service-oriented, helpful, generous, inclusive, tolerant, people pleasers, considerate, respectful, loyal, trusting, devoted, compassionate, caring, supportive, nurturing, encouraging, serene, easygoing, fun-loving, open, flexible, realistic, practical, independent. Extremely observant and in touch, especially with the sensual world, both externally and within themselves. Savor the sweetness of life. A great deal of common sense. Accepting, live-and-let-live attitude, go with the flow. No need to lead, compete, influence, or control. Seek harmony. Do not impose their values on others. Find their own practical and creative way to do things. Often seek self-expression through crafts or hands-on arts. At their best in work that expresses their personal values and helps or provides a service to others. May forgo college for a practical education in the trades, crafts, or service professions.

Administrator	Electrician
Artisan	Forester
Beautician	Gardener
Bookkeeper	Luthier
Botanist	Massage therapist
Carpenter	Mechanic
Chef	Medical office personnel
Computer operator	Medical technician
Cosmetologist	Nurse
Craftsperson	Painter, potter
Dancer	Physical therapist

ESFJ

Gracious, amiable, affirming, gentle, giving, warm, genuine, cordial, kindly, caring, concerned, dutiful, reliable, punctual, polite, tactful, socially appropriate, thoughtful, self-sacrificing, nurturers, people pleasers, efficient managers, event planners, goal-oriented, helpful, cooperative, consistent, extremely loyal, traditional, rule-bound, uncomplicated. Perfectly in tune with other's needs and sensitive to nuances, they are the world's natural hosts and hostesses. Their presence contributes graciousness, harmony, fraternity, and fellowship to whatever they are engaged in. Both female and male ESFJs relate with people in a way that combines warmhearted "mothering" and caring, considerate "inn-keeping." So eager are they to please that they put other's needs before their own, ignoring their personal well-being as they care for the people most important to them. They seek harmony, avoid conflict, follow the rules, keep their commitments, ignore problems by pretending they do not exist. Sensitive to criticism. Need appreciation and praise. Particularly concerned with etiquette, "shoulds" and "should nots." Family and home are often their central passion. Value stability, harmony, relationships, and practical, hands-on experience. The day-to-day events in their lives are carefully planned and meticulously managed. At their best in professions that provide helpful, caring, practical service to others and do not require them to learn theories. They are particularly good at planning events, organizing people, and managing the day-to-day aspects of projects that deal with producing tangible results. When they learn an effective new method, it becomes standard operating procedure. Their extraordinary effectiveness comes from picking the perfect, tried-and-true procedure from their internal database at exactly the right time.

Bartender	Manager: office, restaurant, hotel
Caterer	Optometrist
Chef	Personal banker
Childcare provider	Real estate agent
Customer service representative	Receptionist
Event planner/coordinator	Sales, tangibles
Fitness coach	Secretary
Flight attendant	Small business, retail store
Hairdresser	Social worker
Host/hostess	Teacher: elementary school,
Innkeeper	special education, home
Maître d'	economics

ISFJ

Warm, conscientious, loyal, considerate, helpful, calm, quiet, devoted, gentle, open, nurturing, practical, patient, responsible, dependable, very observant, sensitive, holistic, inclusive, spontaneous, pragmatic, tactile, respectful, noncompetitive, sympathetic, painstaking and thorough, efficient, traditional. The most service-oriented of all the types. Very much in touch with their inner processes as well as the world around them. Seek harmony for themselves and all others. Serene, appreciative, in tune. Do not impose themselves or their opinions on others. Do not need to control. Find their own creative way to get the job done. Learn by doing. Uninterested in abstractions and theories. Use standard operating procedures only when they are the best method for reaching the goal. Often creative and highly skilled, but so averse to imposing that they are easily overlooked and their contributions go unnoticed.

Administrator: social services	Entrepreneur
Counselor	Guidance counselor
Curator	Hairdresser, cosmetologist
Customer service representative	Health-service worker
Dentist/dental hygienist	Household worker
Dietitian	Innkeeper
Educational administrator	Librarian

Manager: restaurant
Massage therapist
Media specialist
Medical technologist
Nurse
Occupational therapist
Personnel administrator
Personal assistant
Physical therapist

Physician: family practice or
  receptionist
Priest/minister/rabbi/monk/nun
Religious educator
Sales: retail
Secretary
Speech pathologist
Teacher: preschool, elementary,
  adult, ESL

ESTP

Outgoing, realistic, pragmatic problem solvers, action-oriented, robust, zestful, spontaneous, energetic, alert, direct, fearless, resourceful, expedient, competitive, spontaneous, flexible, gregarious, objective. Adventurous, willing to try anything that involves sensation and risk. Plunge in headfirst, then analyze. "Live for today. Face the consequences tomorrow." No tolerance for theories and abstractions. Short attention span. Typically have a laid-back attitude, and value individual rights and personal freedom. Do not naturally plan ahead. Prefer to deal with what life throws at them. Adapt to the present situation. React to emergencies instantly and appropriately. A passion for tackling tough jobs and winning in impossible situations. Football hero mentality. Break the rules more often than any other type. Often find themselves in trouble in strict bureaucracies. Dislike being tied down. Learn by doing; rarely read the manual. Want a big return for their investment of time, energy, money. Lively, entertaining, center of attention. The ultimate party-hearty souls. Always willing to put off mundane tasks for the thrill of something new and exciting. Often attracted to motorcycles, fast cars, powerboats, skydiving, and similar quick thrills, the new and the unexplored, tactile pleasures, high-risk sports. May enjoy working with their hands.

Athlete
Athletic coach
Auctioneer
Carpenter
Contractor
Entrepreneur
Explorer
Field technician
Firefighter

Fitness instructor
Heavy-equipment operator
Lifeguard
Manager: hands-on, day-to-day
  operations
Marketer
Mechanic
Military
Negotiator

News reporter
Paramedic
Photographer: combat or
  adventure
Pilot
Police officer or detective
Promoter

Real estate agent
Sales
Stunt person
Troubleshooter, problem solver
Truck driver
Waiter, waitress

ISTP

Independent, reserved, cool, curious, expedient, flexible, logical, analytical, realistic, spontaneous, action-oriented. Adventurous, willing to try anything that involves sensation and risk. Usually have a relaxed, laid-back attitude, value individual rights and personal freedom. Enthusiastic about and absorbed in their immediate interests. Constantly scanning and observing the world around them. Do not naturally plan ahead. Prefer to deal with what life throws at them. Adapt to the present situation. Follow the path of least resistance. React to emergencies instantly and appropriately. Live-and-let-live philosophy, laissez-faire approach to life. Dislike rules, being tied down, or imposing themselves on others. Often attracted to motorcycles, fast cars, powerboats, skydiving, and similar quick thrills, the new and the unexplored, tactile pleasures, high-risk sports. May enjoy working with their hands. Things or objective information are the focus, rather than people.

Ambulance driver
Athletic coach
Bus driver
Carpenter
Chef
Construction worker
Dental assistant
Diver
Engineer
Entrepreneur
Farmer
Field technician
Laborer
Lifeguard
Manager: hands-on, day-to-day
  operations

Mechanic
Military
Optometrist
Pharmacist
Photographer: news
Physician: pathology
Pilot
Recreational attendant
Secretary
Service worker
Stunt person
Surveyor
Technician
Troubleshooter, problem solver
Truck driver
Video-camera operator

ESTJ

Systematic, serious, thorough, down-to-earth, efficient, decisive, hardworking, dutiful, loyal, sincere, conservative, aggressive, in charge. Focused, controlled, and controlling. A strong sense of responsibility. Gregarious, active, socially gifted, partygoer. Make their points of view known. "Macho" or "macha." Often rise to positions of responsibility, such as senior-level management. Want their work to be practical, pragmatic, immediate, objective, have clear and unambiguous objectives, require follow-through and perseverance, involve facts, and produce tangible, measurable results. Natural managers and administrators. Type A personalities. Keep their commitments at any cost. Think from the point of view of "should" and "should not." Have difficulty appreciating and learning from other points of view. Work first, play later. Drawn to work in stable, structured, hierarchical organizations using standard operating procedures. Follow the rules. Seekers of security. They safeguard and maintain traditions and traditional values. A tendency to trample other people (usually unknowingly) as they plow straight ahead to accomplish their goals. A high percentage of military people have this personality type.

Athletic coach
Bank employee
Cashier
Chef
Computer-systems analyst
Contractor
Corporate executive (all levels)
Dietitian
Electrician
Engineer
Entrepreneur
Funeral director
Insurance agent, broker, or
　underwriter
Judge
Manager: retail store, operations,
　projects, restaurant, bank,
　government

Mechanic
Military
Nurse
Optometrist
Pharmacist
Physician
Police officer
Purchasing agent
School principal
Sales
Stockbroker
Supervisor
Teacher of practical material:
　math, gym, shop, technical

ISTJ

Systematic, serious, thorough, down-to-earth, efficient, decisive, hard-working, dutiful, loyal, reserved, sincere, conservative. A strong sense of responsibility. Very private, but learn extroverted social behaviors for the sake of practicality. Want their work to be practical, pragmatic, immediate, objective, have clear and unambiguous objectives, require follow-through and perseverance, involve facts, and produce tangible, measurable results. Often have type A personalities. Keep their commitments at any cost. Think from the point of view of "should" and "should not." Work first, play later. Drawn to work in stable, structured, hierarchical organizations using standard operating procedures. Seekers of security. They safeguard and maintain traditions and traditional values. A high percentage of military people have this personality type.

Accountant
Administrator
Bank employee
Bus driver
Chef
Chemist
Computer systems analyst, operator, programmer
Corporate executive (all levels)
Dentist
Dietitian
Electrician
Engineer
Entrepreneur
Farmer
Field technician
Government employee
Guard
IRS agent
Manager: retail store, operations, projects
Mechanic
Military
Operator: machinery
Pharmacist
Police officer
School principal
Speech pathologist
Surgeon
Teacher of practical material
Technical writer
Technician: lab, science, engineering

And if that wasn't enough information, here's another quick way to get some Clues about yourself.

Temperament

Like character and personality, you can think of temperament as pointing to over-arching themes that tend to show up within individual personalities.

We really like David Keirsey's work, which divides the sixteen types into what he calls "the Four temperaments." Since we really like his terms and concepts, we are borrowing them here.

INQUIRY 14

Temperament

Read each of the four temperament descriptions (below) and rank them from one to four ("most like you" to "least like you").

Temperament	Description	Rank
Artisan	The art and the craft of it. Unconventional, bold, spontaneous, and tolerant. Value freedom, boldness. Seek firsthand experiences and stimulation.	
Guardian	Serve and protect. Social and public institutions and law. Create and maintain peace and order. Hardworking and sensible.	
Idealist	Make the world a better place. Motivated to self-knowledge and self-improvement. Provide meaning to people's lives. Everyone should feel good and get along.	
Rational	Figure it out and solve the problem. Principled and rational. Value logic and objectivity. Interested in systems and how things work. Scientific.	

Temperament	Key Function Combos	Included Types
Artisan	The SPs (Sensing Perceivers)	ESFP, ESTP, ISFP, ISTP
Guardian	The SJs (Sensing Judgers)	ESFJ, ESTJ, ISFJ, ISTJ
Idealist	The NFs (Intuitive Feelers)	ENFJ, ENFP, INFJ, INFP
Rational	The NTs (Intuitive Thinkers)	ENTJ, ENTP, INTJ, INTP

Are they a match?

If they are—great! That is additional evidence that you are on track.

If they are not—great! Consider this new information and make any adjustments you like to your earlier conclusions about your best-fit personality type.

As always, consider what insights or ideas you got out of this Inquiry. What can you add to your Clues, Components, and Career Ideas lists?

Your time is limited, don't waste it living someone else's life.

—STEVE JOBS

CHAPTER 8

✦

NATURAL ROLES

No matter where you go, there you are.

—BUCKAROO BANZAI

We tend to think of ourselves—that person we call "me"—as a permanent, unchanging entity. Look a little more closely, though, and you may discover that there is more to you (and "me") than is obvious. We all play multiple roles. They are almost like different characters who take turns having lead roles in chapters of our lives. (These roles don't necessarily have any consistency or relationship among them. For example, a Mafia hit man may be an absolutely ruthless criminal at work and a loving and devoted parent at home.) Some of these may be temporary, or the result of circumstance. Others might be consistent, natural expressions of our character. We operate this way even as children. Think of kids you knew (or know) who were natural leaders, comedians, rebels, risk-takers, or artists—these roles, also called archetypes, stay with us for our entire lives. The kid who was the class president is likely to take on leadership roles in their adult life, and the class clown will probably always be a ham. Or, it may recede in later life and only appear after a couple drinks or with close friends.

Most of these roles have a genetic component: they choose you, not the other way around. For example, one of the roles described in this chapter is "risk-taker." This might seem like a random trait, but, as it turns out, scientists have linked risk-taking behavior in mice to a single gene. In experiments, those with a specific genetic structure were willing to walk along an unprotected walkway high above the ground, while those without it sought a safer, more secure path—like the men and women willing to walk unprotected on narrow steel beams to build the great skyscrapers, or extreme-sport athletes joyfully performing dangerous feats.

Since there is no single, unchanging "me," knowing your main roles is one of the best ways to know yourself and where you best fit in the world of work. After all, someone whose dominant roles are networker and marketer might fit best in a very different career than someone whose main roles are healer and animal lover.

Because we tend to go through life more conscious of *what* we do than *why* we do it, you may not have given much thought to the roles you play. We all take ourselves for granted, so it's going to take looking at yourself with new eyes. Your challenge in this chapter is to sort out your own unique collection of roles, how you function in the more dominant roles, and how roles combine.

There is no simple formula for turning roles into careers that fit you. Please remember that this Inquiry provides another kind of access to who you are; some more Clues and puzzle pieces about how you and the working world will best fit together.

INQUIRY 15

My Natural Roles

Part I

Read through each group of natural roles and the provided descriptions. Look for those roles you most identify with. There may be many groups that you don't identify with at all, and others in which you identify with several. Look for roles that are closest to your way of thinking, approaching life, or behaving. Consider the nuances and flavors between roles. Pick those that speak most to you.

> **Example: Maria.** *Maria identifies closely with the adviser and counselor group. She loves listening to people, using empathy and understanding to help them feel comfortable, and offering them suggestions. Her friends regularly come to her when they have "relationship problems." Looking through the whole group, Maria most comfortably identifies with the therapist, shoulder-to-cry-on, empathizer, and sage roles. They all have the warm, human-touch quality that is important to her. She doesn't identify with the more formal roles of consultant, trainer, or teacher. (Counselor is close, but is a word she wouldn't normally use, so she didn't include it as one of her top roles.) Maria may or may not choose to pursue a career as a therapist. She might also make a great manager or community development specialist. Whichever career track she follows, she will be happiest in a role and work environment that allow her to have warm social interactions with others and be encouraged and rewarded for providing them with empathy, a strong shoulder, and some wisdom.*

It's also important to remember that our relationship to various roles will differ in importance and strength, both generally and at different points in our lives. To help you consider all of the options and narrow them down later, you will see numbered circles before each role. Mark the appropriate circle for each role depending on its strength. Strong, clearly dominant roles get the ③ checked. Less dominant, but still important roles get a ②. If you are not completely sure whether or not a certain role is part of your repertoire, give it a ①. If it plays no part in your life, mark that ⓪.

Example: Richard. *Two of Richard's strongest roles are teacher and trainer. He has never had the formal job of "teacher" before, although he has thought about it and thinks he would be a good one. Richard loves to learn about business and sales techniques. He has had several sales jobs, with mixed success. He likes the idea of sales and the earning potential, but what really excites him is learning the best sales methods and thinking about how to improve them and teach others. He naturally pays attention to methods and techniques and is quick to come up with creative ideas and insights. He has read several books, and taken more than a few courses on business strategy and sales techniques. He always analyzes the trainers in these courses, admiring their skills and critiquing their performances. This has, at times, created problems for Richard at work. Hired to sell gadgets and widgets, he ends up spending a lot of time thinking about, and explaining to others, how and what they should do better or differently. This has included sharing his ideas with the owners of the companies. Richard's strongest roles include teacher, trainer, and critic. While he identifies as a salesman, this role is secondary to the others. Richard might have more fulfillment, more consistent success, and a lot less frustration in roles and positions that allow him to use his teacher, trainer, critic nature more directly.*

Natural Roles—Descriptions

Social Roles

This diverse group of roles all address ways of being when interacting with others or in groups. Which of these resonate with you? Our descriptions are meant as aids only—your mental pictures and interpretations of each role are more important. If you can think of a closer or better term, write it in.

⓪ ① ② ③ **High Class—Old Money:** Strong sense of privacy and strive to avoid the limelight, money is passed down through generations, highly invested in protecting assets, strong emphasis on education and culture, tend to lead very insulated, privileged lifestyles, the cost of protecting the old is little innovation.

⓪ ① ② ③ **High Class—New Money:** More likely to spend on experiences, such as travel and adventure, and invest in new technology and innovative products, showy, continually show symbols of success. Often more ambitious, more open to new ideas, and much more willing to take risks than old money. May pretend to be everyman in their dress and behavior

⓪ ① ② ③ **Go-to Person / Center of Influence / Community Builder / Organizer / Host(-ess).** These roles are focal points in the community. Are you resourceful, dynamic, responsible, and like to have your finger on the pulse of what goes on around you? Do you reach out, include, organize, help, and rally those around you? Pillars of the community and those who seek to build up or unite those around them. Leadership positions where you can interact with, and be needed, by a community of people might be a great fit.

⓪ ① ② ③ **Charmer / Influencer.** It's your smile, your good looks, or your approachability. You are someone who attracts others. Perhaps you like to impact their opinions and choices. You may enjoy getting people to bend to your will or power. Then again, maybe you love to make people feel wanted, love to be loved, or are simply huggable! Make sure that you can use your charm and good graces in your interactions with others. Sales, organizational leadership, politics, and advocacy work are good fits.

⓪ ① ② ③ **Comedian / Class Clown / Prankster / Wit.** The consummate jokester. The comedian thrives on making people laugh, cry, or think about things differently. They see the humor and absurdity in everyday life. They make us laugh at ourselves and our "foolish" ways. Some are court jesters, a role that gives them special permission to reveal the truth that most of us don't see, caught up in trying to be politically (or otherwise) correct. If you have a strong role in this group, you may not want to work in a highly formal or conservative environment. Being able to be yourself, and make people around you laugh, will help you feel comfortable and accepted.

⓪ ① ② ③ **Insider / Secret Holder.** You know the inside scoop, the real deal, the insides, outsides, and secrets of the organization. You are trusted with secrets and with the thoughts and ideas of those around you. You could use this knowledge gained through your relationships for good or for evil.

⓪ ① ② ③ **Miss or Mr. Popularity / Networker / Extrovert / Life of the Party / Social Butterfly / People Person.** Know what is going on with everyone? Do you love to arrange social events or throw parties? Do you know everyone? Does everyone know you? Are you comfortable in almost any social situation? PPP: popular party person. If you are always on the pulse of who and what is going on, are always talking on your phone, or are meeting someone for coffee after you finish this chapter—you might look to this group for one of your universal roles. Think twice before agreeing to work remotely or in a highly technical or analytical role. You may not find the social interacting you need.

⓪ ① ② ③ **Introvert / Observer.** Solitude, privacy. Do you prefer your own company to that of most others, or get anxious or exhausted interacting with others? Have just a few close friends? Don't easily fit in with social roles? Maybe you do better work on your own, or prefer activities that require quiet or freedom from interruption. You may notice things others miss or be an excellent listener. You welcome plenty of time to attend to your own thoughts and activities, and would probably find it exhausting or intimidating to have to engage with strangers or regularly work on group projects.

⓪ ① ② ③ **Outsider / Weirdo / Black Sheep / Orphan.** Whether or not you have peace of mind about it, you do not find it easy to fit in with the mainstream. Feel like the oddball in your family? Not a high school cheerleader, basketball star, or head of student government? Whether or not others know it about you, you regularly feel a bit different or separate from your fellows. Embrace it—and find a workplace and role where you can let your freak flag fly!

Explorers & Adventurers

Explorers and adventures love to experience new places, things, or ideas. It might be a physical thrill, an intellectual novelty, or landing on a new planet. You want to be stimulated and excited.

⓪ ① ② ③ **Wanderer / Traveler / World Traveler / Nomad / Gypsy.** Not everyone who wanders is lost. Want to see where the road takes you? Always choose the road less traveled? Ready to let serendipity guide you? Perhaps a portable field might answer your call or choose a career that lets you work wherever in the world suits you today.

⓪ ① ② ③ **Adventurer / Explorer / Risk-taker / Thrill Seeker.** A little adrenaline with your new experiences? Jumping out of a helicopter or escaping a lethal trap with Indiana Jones? Adrenaline junkies and thrill seekers wrestle alligators—they are also found on Wall Street, riding roller coasters on Sundays, and working out in the field seeking ways to combat malaria.

⓪ ① ② ③ **Pioneer.** Takes on finding a new way. Often comfortable with what scares everyone else. Early adopter. Reach out into the wild and build something.

Heroes & Warriors

⓪ ① ② ③ **Hero / Dragon Slayer.** The hero arises in many forms. The true hero begins as an ordinary person, called to a mission beyond his or her present capacities. Out of dedication to the goal or mission, the hero undergoes difficulties and emerges transformed by the experience. Many tales handed down to us these days express this theme. The character Frodo in *The Lord of the Rings* is the perfect embodiment of this role in modern literature. The hero's journey can involve an adventure in the external world or an inner quest for wisdom or personal transformation. The hero's quest always involves overcoming those very weaknesses or inner demons holding the him or her back. Heroes need work that allows them to face dragons and grow. They need challenges that they can overcome.

⓪ ① ② ③ **The Golden Child / The Chosen One / Savior.** Take on extraordinary missions or actions. Neo from *The Matrix* and Anakin Skywalker from *Star Wars* had destinies that only they could fulfill. If you have a strong role in this group, you need a career or position that allows you to shine.

⓪ ① ② ③ **Warrior / Soldier / White Knight / Black Knight / Samurai / Ninja / Fighter / Mercenary.** There are also many genres of "warrior." Most warriors takes a stand and fight for something. The adversary can be anything: other warriors, an injustice, a disease, a shortcoming of society, a personal weakness, a belief system, an unfulfilled goal. The warrior is willing to do what it takes to reach the goal, no matter what obstacles arise, and no matter how uncomfortable he or she feels. Warriors go to battle. Men and women drawn to defend their country on the battlefield embody the physical warrior or soldier, willing to put life on the line for a cause. Others manifest the warrior in fighting for social injustices, or on the proverbial battlefield of the competitive business world. Some warriors, like the ninja, are specialists who develop extraordinary skills. Others, such as the chivalric knight and the honorable and loyal samurai, follow strict codes of conduct. These roles might be full of physical or mechanical feats, or they may possibly be involved in business, technical, or financial wars.

Athletes & Extremists

⓪ ① ② ③ **Athlete / Extreme Athlete / Competitor / Marathoner / Olympian.** Athletes are high achievers, dedicated to countless hours of effort and sacrifice. Committed to excellence and greatness, they strive to surpass others. Athletes need to work hard and meet challenges. They need measurable goals and outcomes to know how they did. Some athletes strive to surpass their own limits. Others need to measure their ability or achievement against those of others. Similar to the warrior group, great-fit work for these roles requires clearly defined goals or challenges, effort over time, and clear measures or events from which you receive tangible feedback about your performance. Corporate America is full of high-action, challenge-filled measures in which an athlete can excel.

⓪ ① ② ③ **Perfectionist / Stickler / OCD.** Expect nothing but perfection from yourself or others? Are you intolerant of people who place their apostrophes in the wrong place? Do you have to have things a certain way? Perfectionists can have one area of focus, or many. If you identify as a perfectionist, is there a particular thing about which you are adamant? If so, note it down with this role. For example, Abby is rigorous and unforgiving when it comes to grammar and punctuation, but . . . she is easygoing about neatness and other types of organization. Her bedroom and desk are both messy. Abby is a stickler/perfectionist—grammar and punctuation. She would make a great technical writer or editor, but not necessarily a great house cleaner or organizer. Perfectionists should be wary of work environments or positions with a lot of time pressure. You will probably prefer producing quality over quantity—even if it takes more time to produce. You will do better in positions where meticulous and high quality are prioritized.

⓪ ① ② ③ **Addict / Workaholic / Extremist.** Addicts lack balance and control in their relationship to a substance, activity, or idea. They often feel like they can't help themselves, or must do or have their drug of choice. This can look like alcoholism or opiate addiction, but it can also look like working twelve hours every day and neglecting your family. Some addicts, like alcoholics in recovery, still identify as addicts, but work to feel and behave in healthy ways. Extremists are addicts that lack balance in their ideas or opinions. They can forgo reason and compromise for their position.

⓪①②③ **Fan Girl (Boy) / Devotee.** *Doctor Who, Star Wars,* or ?. If you study, quote, obsess about, attend, watch, purchase, and/or explain the virtues of a particular person, show, musical artist, or product—you may qualify for the Fan Girl (Boy) or Devotee role. If you identify in one of these roles, you may want to prioritize work with a subject matter of strong interest to you.

Thinkers & Evaluators

⓪①②③ **Lifelong Learner / Student.** You love to learn and learn more. You watch instructional videos, you take online courses, you read nonfiction books. You could happily be a student for the rest of your life. You may have multiple degrees. You are curious and find many subjects interesting. Great-fit work for you will include constant opportunities to learn new things and add to your repertoire of subject matter knowledge or skills. Then again, you may just be avoiding the real world.

⓪①②③ **Thinker / Brain / Intellectual / Scholar / Researcher / Philosopher.** Just picking up new information is not enough. You want to reflect on it, analyze it, extend the idea, or check the facts. You put effort into your considerations and thoughts. You like to understand things on a deeper level.

⓪①②③ **Analyst / Problem Solver / Puzzler / Strategist.** If you regularly feel compelled to figure it out, you may have a strong role in this group. Analysts use systematic, mathematical, or logical approaches to tasks in their life and work. Whether or not they have a strong natural gift for analytical reasoning, they are examining the task or problem in an effortful way. They tend to give more credence to logic than feelings and believe that life can and should be organized and rational. Not necessarily as logical as the Analysts, Problem Solvers seek out problems, be they intellectual puzzles, mechanical breakdowns, or a loved one dealing with heartbreak, they will find concrete solutions. Strategists find ways to achieve goals and overcome obstacles. They pay attention to how to make something happen.

⓪①②③ **Intuitive / Leaper to Conclusions.** Instead of thinking problems through step-by-step, Leapers can see to the heart of the matter accurately, without relying on a logical thought process. They might find others to be plodding or slow to understand. They are often amazed that they can see through to the heart of the problem or situation before other people. If your focus is on people, perhaps a career that allows you to intuit what's going on with others would fit. Many extraordinary nonfiction writers use this ability to draw conclusions that allow the reader to understand their point easily. Many of the most extraordinary inventions and designs were created by these people.

⓪ ① ② ③ **Critic / Critiquer / Skeptic / Freethinker / Out-of-the-Box Thinker / Devil's Advocate / Contrarian.** This mix of thinkers and evaluators don't easily go along with the status quo or main stream. "Yeah, but . . ." may be a regular comment. Taking a different perspective, finding fault with, seeing the illogic, and questioning the facts are regular habits of this group of roles.

⓪ ① ② ③ **Judge / Jury / Moral Authority / Auditor / Editor.** Consider the facts or materials provided and pass judgment. Judge and jury decide guilt or innocence. Moral Authorities know what others should be, or shouldn't be, doing. Auditors investigate the facts and look for foul play or inconsistency. Editors review, revise, and correct.

Politics & Law

⓪ ① ② ③ **Attorney / Lawyer / Debater.** This group of roles builds their case and argues the point. They may use facts and precedents or emotional appeals to make their points. You may have a position or specific interests to argue for. Or you may just like to point out the faults, mistakes, or shortsightedness of others. The goal is always to win.

⓪ ① ② ③ **Ambassador / Diplomat / Peacemaker / Peacekeeper / Bridge Builder / Mediator / Negotiator / Connector.** Can't we all just get along? More focused on finding a workable and middle ground than Debaters, the Diplomat group seeks compromise and peaceful relations.

⓪ ① ② ③ **Advocate / Protester / Voice of the People / Public Defender.** This group might stand up for the disenfranchised or those without a voice. Human rights, social justice, fairness, opportunity, and inclusion are all hallmark concerns for this group.

⓪ ① ② ③ **Politician / Influencer-Persuader / Lobbyist / Dealmaker.** Politicians and Influencers like to promote their ideas and projects and like to win people over to their point of view and agendas. Whether lobbying for national or corporate policy or winning the family over to go to the vacation destination of their choice, these persuaders love getting people to see things their way, win others over, or getting people to change their minds. Dealmakers make it happen.

⓪ ① ② ③ **Cop / Sheriff / Law Enforcer / Legislator / Rule Follower.** Laws and rules are there for a reason. They are important. Someone needs to keep order. The common good depends on this.

⓪ ① ② ③ **Spy / Secret Agent / Mata Hari.** Like to work in the shadows? Gather intel and information on the sly? Does corporate espionage sound like fun? You like the behind-the-scenes workings of things. Strategy and intrigue make it all more interesting.

⓪ ① ② ③ **Conservative / Liberal / Progressive / Capitalist / Socialist / Anarchist.** If you have definitive political views or party affiliations, have a bumper sticker on your car, or have offended someone with your social media posts, you may have a strong role in this group. Even if you keep your opinions to yourself and believe that "politics and religion" should not be discussed in polite society, you wouldn't be happy in a work environment in which the majority of people voiced strong political views that disagreed with yours.

Rebels & Mischief Makers

⓪ ① ② ③ **Rebel / Revolutionary / Non-Conformist / Challenger / Rule Breaker / Maverick.** Naturally buck the system, bend the rules, strive to be different, or consciously break the rules. Rebel energy often helps society break out of habits that no longer work. Social activists and critics, scientists, comedians, artists and poets, visionary leaders, and change agents who move the world to see things anew or challenge the status quo might fit here. Matt Groening, creator of *The Simpsons*, is a great example of an artistic, comedic member of this group.

⓪ ① ② ③ **Troublemaker / Trickster / Pirate / Rogue.** Like to walk on the wild side and cause trouble, a little or a lot. Whether you are playful about it, or more goal-oriented, you identify as someone who likes to create a little chaos or work outside of societal bounds.

Artists, Performers, & Storytellers

⓪ ① ② ③ **Artist / Creative / Artisan / Craftsperson.** Explore, create, express, build, innovate, and communicate. Some have specific media or subjects, others mix it up, or move from media to media. Your legacy is your creations.

⓪ ① ② ③ **Performer / Actor / Star.** Be onstage, hold a microphone, be the center of attention, hold court, or receive thunderous applause, seek a public platform, motivated by the engagement and reaction of the audience, or dream of fame and fortune.

⓪ ① ② ③ **Musician / Singer / Composer / Conductor.** Music is your love and your joy. Use your voice or other instrument to tell stories, or evoke and express emotion.

⓪ ① ② ③ **Storyteller / Communicator / Writer / Author / Poet / Novelist / Blogger-Vlogger / Podcaster.** Crafters of words and tellers of tales, whether conveying information, excitement, lessons, or beauty. You love to use words, language, or stories to communicate, share, or educate others.

⓪ ① ② ③ **Designer.** Designers develop and create physical, visual, or digital displays and objects. There are many types of designers—including interior designers, website designers, multiplayer online game designers, curriculum designers, and clothing and jewelry designers. What all designers have in common is an interest and ability to communicate or organize ideas or objects in a way that is both attractive and functional.

Leaders & Managers

Leaders come in many shapes, styles, and characteristics. Some leaders inspire; others rule by force or fear. Some leaders are born into their role; others earn the respect of others through deeds and actions.

⓪ ① ② ③ **Leader.** A leader directs, commands, organizes, or manages others.

⓪ ① ② ③ **King / Queen.** Without much effort, some people carry an air of authority, confidence, clarity, vision, or majesty. They are recognized by others as natural leaders. As if born with royal blood, they have natural authority.

⓪ ① ② ③ **Prince / Princess.** Deserving, entitled, expecting to always be considered as special. Some may be attention-seeking, arrogant, and rude. Others are brave, selfless, and risk-taking. Princes and princesses have some sense of privilege or inherited wealth or power. How they handle that privilege varies.

⓪ ① ② ③ **General / Lieutenant / Sergeant.** Command others. Their job is to generate results.

⓪ ① ② ③ **Elder / Father / Mother / Clan Leader / Patriarch / Matriarch.** Guiding with experience and wisdom, these leader roles are concerned with the future of the family or group. Many of us can claim this as one of our roles. One need not have children to be deeply living within this role. We know young girls and boys who are delightfully involved as mothers to their friends and sometimes to their parents. You may be a mother, or a father figure to your dog or cat, your friends, or colleagues at work. It is all about who you are being in your interactions with other people. They may not recognize you as such, but take a look. See if you, like many others, inhabit this role and way of being.

⓪ ① ② ③ **CEO / Boss / Director / Delegator.** These roles come directly from the world of business. They have unique characteristics. A CEO has the final say on all and is responsible for everything. Usually not hands-on. They set the culture, priorities, and future of their organization. The CEO has other leaders and their subordinates to attend to their area. A Boss expects you to do what you are told. A Director coordinates and decides who does what and when. A Delegator is keenly aware of what needs to get done—and assigns others to complete necessary tasks.

⓪ ① ② ③ **Manager / Supervisor / Team Leader.** A Manager attends to the daily operations of their area or department. A Supervisor may focus more on personnel. Not necessarily a natural authority or visionary leader, they get the job done. The Team Leader is usually more personally involved with their team, and may seek not only to guide but to empower and develop her or his team as they achieve their goals. Whether in the workplace, at home, planning a vacation or dinner party, these roles bring order to chaos, set the agenda, plan the project, orchestrate the activities, and manage the resources to make it all happen.

⓪ ① ② ③ **Center of Influence / Role Model.** These two roles lead, but less directly. People look to a center of influence to know what to do. Role Models lead by example. People follow their manner, deeds, and actions because they have experienced them firsthand and respect them.

⓪ ① ② ③ **Entrepreneur / Small-Business Owner / Freelancer.** Some people are happier working outside of the traditional company and corporate hierarchies. Innovative by nature, the Entrepreneur builds businesses from the ground up. They make use of a wide range of natural talents, calling on multiple abilities to create something that didn't exist before. They take pride in being able to do it on their own, counting on their own resources, talents, and know-how. Independence, self-direction, and creative problem-solving are hallmarks of these noncorporate roles.

⓪ ① ② ③ **Worker.** Not everyone wants to be the boss, or believes they can be. Some people, like a Worker Bee, are perfectly happy trading their time and effort for a fair wage. Others, like the Indentured Servant, may dream of independence and status, but feel that they must earn their way up from the bottom to get it.

Advisers & Counselors

⓪ ① ② ③ **Adviser / Consultant / Coach / Strategist.** The Coach role assists a talented, committed person in reaching a goal. Forty years ago, Nick invented the field of "Career Design" and the term *career coach*. He was one of the very first coaches in a field other than sports. He thought the term *career counselor* was insufficient, implying the provision mostly of information and advice. A coach, on the other hand, figures out what it will take for you to reach your goal, elicits your strengths, assigns appropriate tasks, and makes sure you get to your goal. You do the work, whether that means practicing your sport every day or moving toward some important personal goal. A relationship with a coach is a partnership between you and your coach.

⓪ ① ② ③ **Teacher / Trainer / Presenter / Tutor / Professor.** These roles all have an educational aspect to them and are typically found delivering acquired information or knowledge to groups. These days, however, a professor may not do a lot of teaching; instead being involved with research and writing all those necessary papers.

⓪ ① ② ③ **Counselor / Therapist / Shoulder to Cry On.** The Counselor provides advice and information, such as a lawyer, psychologist, the more humanistic physicians, and some of the best professors. They rely on a deep well of knowledge and years of experience to give you the best advice. Therapists work with people needing some form of help, who are suffering from some problem. A Shoulder to Cry On may take a less formal or advising stance, being a support and comfort for friends in need.

⓪ ① ② ③ **Guide / Empath / Sage / Guru / Wise Woman or Man.** The Guide communicates wisdom, based on their personal mastery of a subject that comes from a lifetime of experience or realization. Guides transmit principles, get to the heart of the matter, and are often the most creative contributors to their field. Empaths are sensitive and feel or intuit the emotions and intentions of others. Sages and Gurus embody inner wisdom and knowledge earned and realized over much time and experience. Sages and Gurus may live on a mountaintop, or they may have their own YouTube channel.

Builders & Producers

⓪ ① ② ③ **Builder.** A builder plans and builds—a home, a business, or a community. They take ideas and construct tangible objects and services.

⓪ ① ② ③ **Architect / Engineer / Designer.** This group of roles design and work out how to take an idea and make it a reality. They attend to how things fit together and function. Some may focus more on beauty or form, others specialize on more efficient or effective function. Architects and Designers focus on translating ideas into designs. Engineers create and/or manage the specific physical reality of how things work and how to make them work better.

Helpers

⓪ ① ② ③ **Right-Hand Person / Companion / Copilot / Sidekick.** The ultimate "right hand" who gets the job done. Their strength, dedication, loyalty, and supportive nature are often the real backbone of an organization. Vice presidents, chief operating officers, general managers, executive assistants, and secretaries often say they are not interested in being the main person out front, but thrive as the one who makes it all work behind the scenes. Companions or Sidekicks might have more of a giving nature who find joy in serving or pleasing others.

⓪ ① ② ③ **Helpers.** Compassionate and generous of spirit, Helpers give their time, energy, and love to others. They are found in many forms and roles. They are often in the background making sure that things work, or that others are taken care of or appreciated. They can be gentle and intentional, like someone who trains service and guide dogs, or they can be bold and fierce, like a military soldier liberating an occupied city. Helpers are fueled by making a difference for others, by making lives easier, or by reducing suffering. They are sometimes underappreciated or unacknowledged members of communities and organizations; if you are a Helper, see if you also identify with some version of Hero.

⓪ ① ② ③ **Handyperson / Fixer.** Fixers and Handypersons are pragmatic, versatile, and focused. If something is missing, broken, or a problem, you can rely on them to fix it. They may be mechanical, like a plumber, or they may be persuasive and strategic, like Winston Wolf in *Pulp Fiction*.

Scientists & Investigators

⓪ ① ② ③ **Scientist.** Scientists are logical and rigorous explorers devoted to increasing human knowledge and effectiveness. Long ago, a scientist was a discoverer. They applied curiosity and method to an unknown and their product was a breakthrough. Nowadays, many scientists are more engineer than pure scientist. The breakthrough has already been made, and it is their job to figure out how to use it, improve it, package it, describe it, or contribute to the marketing of it.

⓪ ① ② ③ **Doctor.** Doctors apply science to understand, fix, or cure the body or mind. There are humanistic doctors who chafe at the very short time they are allowed to work with patients or find a unique individual solution to this situation. There are technical doctors who are essentially super highly trained technicians. Hopefully, they are the women and men who read the journals, stay up-to-date on new ideas, and work with enthusiasm and curiosity. This is the kind of doctor you want to find to treat you. There are creative doctors who can't help but improve the methodology. There are robotic doctors who have found a method and stick with it, without updating their work by reading technical journals.

⓪ ① ② ③ **Inventor / Innovator / Experimenter.** These roles imagine, design, or build new methods, ideas, or products. Not satisfied with how things are, they are the builders of better mousetraps. Inventors and Experimenters are innately hands-on. Nothing is more fun than building something new than trying it out to see if it works.

⓪ ① ② ③ **Futurist / Visionary.** Futurists focus on, imagine, or plan for the future and the changes it will bring. Visionaries see into the future and have original ideas and wisdom about what the future will or could be like.

⓪ ① ② ③ **Investigator / Researcher / Finder / Detective.** This group seeks answers and explanations. They are concerned with the what, why, and how of things and won't stop until they get to the bottom of it. Some detectives solve homicides; others seek a cure for cancer. What all Investigators have in common is a nose for a good clue and a mind that can't help looking under the surface to figure out the truth. They constantly pay attention to their environment with a critiquing ability that allows them to discover clues that might not be obvious to others. Detectives, scientists, inventors, mystery writers, counselors, lawyers, and crime scene investigators may embody this trait.

⓪ ① ② ③ **Journalist / Reporter.** Journalists investigate, interview, and dig around. Then, they share their uncovered truths and explanations with others. Real journalists are bold, committed, and unstoppable. What we call journalists today are often reporters who feel constrained by their position. Reporters are the eyes and ears of the news media. At their best, they function as journalists.

Natural World

⓪ ① ② ③ **Environmentalist / Ecologist / Conservationist.** Proactive and focused on protecting or managing natural resources, the environment, or the world. There is often a scientific or educational aspect to these roles. These folks strive to positively impact the natural world through policy or action.

⓪ ① ② ③ **Nature Lover.** In sync with the world and nature. They have an emotional and intimate relationship to nature. Seeing the interconnectedness of it all, feeling a personal and deep relationship with their environment and with nonhumans.

⓪ ① ② ③ **Hunter / Survivalist.** As a sport, hobby, or way of life, Hunters and Survivalists are skilled at acquiring necessities and thriving in the natural world. They understand how the natural world works and enjoy being in sync with the mechanics and workings of it to achieve their goals.

⓪ ① ② ③ **Gardener.** Cultivates and nurtures life, health, or well-being with plants, flowers, and trees.

⓪ ① ② ③ **Steward.** Caretakers who have been entrusted with the management and well-being of something—be it natural resources, a property, or an organization. Often concerned with the responsible use and protection of natural environments or other vulnerable entities.

Intuition, Healing & Magic

⓪ ① ② ③ **Caretaker / Nurturer / Caregiver / Nurse.** This medically oriented group of healers has heart and attends to those who are ailing or in need. They often provide physical or mental assistance or support, and are typically focused on well-being and health. They may be particularly drawn to being there for people at critical or significant times of life—birth, crisis, and death. They give generously of themselves to those in their care.

⓪ ① ② ③ **Healer / Medicine Man or Woman / Shaman.** A holistic or natural approach to healing, using their ability to restore physical, mental, or spiritual health. They may use a variety of methods—traditional medicine, alternative therapies, or spiritual practices. These roles involve a deeper level of sensitivity and perception using energies, emotions, and information that may not be readily apparent to everyone. They may provide physical care and nurturing, like a hospice nurse or social worker, or just prioritize knowing that what they do helps others.

⓪ ① ② ③ **Wizard / Witch / Enchanter / Enchantress.** This group works with nature and magic. Wise practitioners of magic. They are friends of the earth and use nature-based magic. Enchanters and Enchantresses practice magic, often using beauty and seduction as their tools.

⓪ ① ② ③ **Intuit / Psychic / Empath / Mystic.** This group has a heightened sensitivity to the energies and emotions of others and the world around them. They tend to rely heavily on their intuition or gut feelings. They can sense things others cannot and have a sense of knowing without concrete evidence. Counselors, therapists, life coaches, energy workers, and many creative professions.

⓪ ① ② ③ **Magician / Illusionist / Conjurer.** This group creates illusions that seem to defy the laws of nature. They use their skills and knowledge to create illusions that entertain and amaze their audiences. Careers in the performing arts, or creative writing, are obvious options for these roles. Any position in which you are rewarded for coming up with creative and out-of-the-box or fantastical solutions might fit you.

Spiritual & Religious

Some people are sensitive about their religions or religious beliefs. Please take no offense in the groupings in this section. Roles are grouped because they have a common aspect—not because they are the same.

⓪ ① ② ③ **Religious or Devout** _____. If there is a faith community or belief system that you hold dear and as part of your personal or social identity, acknowledge it. If it influences your values, life goals, the type of work you would find acceptable or respected, it may be a strong role for you worth considering in your career design.

⓪ ① ② ③ **Priest / Rabbi / Minister / Monk / Nun / Yogi.** These individuals are often considered to be leaders or guides in their respective faiths, and they may serve as teachers, healers, or counselors to their communities. They are often respected for their wisdom, knowledge, and devotion to their faith. They all share a common dedication to their faith and a desire to help others on their spiritual journey.

⓪ ① ② ③ **Humanitarian.** Dedicated to helping others and making the world a better place. They actively engage in promoting human welfare and social reforms, and their work often centers around reducing suffering and improving the lives of others.

⓪ ① ② ③ **Old Soul / Seeker.** These roles focus on personal growth and self-discovery. An Old Soul has a deep sense of wisdom, understanding, and inner peace. They are often seen as being more spiritually mature than their peers, and may have a strong connection to the past, to tradition, and to the timeless wisdom of the ages. A Seeker, on the other hand, actively searches for meaning, purpose, and truth in their life. They are often driven by a desire to explore new ideas, experiences, and ways of being in the world.

Specialists & Tech

⓪ ① ② ③ **Expert / Specialist.** These roles are respected for their expertise and are often called upon to share their knowledge and insights with others. They see the value in taking the time and effort to develop a high level of knowledge, skill, or experience in a particular field or subject. They are considered authorities in their field.

⓪ ① ② ③ **Jack-of-All-Trades / Generalist.** The opposite of experts and specialists, they prefer to learn a little about a lot of things. Small-business owners may be specialists if they have a highly technical product or service, but are usually Generalists. A small-business owner needs to think about marketing, accounting, product choices, business strategy, hiring and management, and a host of other things.

⓪ ① ② ③ **Old-School.** Not old-fashioned, but proud to prefer doing things the way it used to be done, those with a strong Old-School role believe the tried-and-true is the better way. Work environments and positions that pride themselves in traditional or legacy practices, and those without fast-changing technologies, may be a good fit for those strong in this role.

⓪ ① ② ③ **Geek / Nerd / Techy Person.** A strong interest in technology, science, or other similar pursuits. These people often discover their work identity before college. They are one of the only groups for whom deciding on a career may not be a complex decision-making process, since they already are aware of their talents.

⓪ ① ② ③ **Gamer / Coder / Programmer / Computer Whiz.** This group shares a strong interest in technology and their proficiency in using computers and other digital devices. Gamers may be passionate about gaming and enjoy competing with others or exploring virtual worlds. Coders are skilled and detailed language and logic experts who manipulate code and syntax to create magic. Programmers often have a network or systems approach to working with software. A Computer Whiz may possess an extraordinary talent and is knowledgeable in their area of technology.

⓪ ① ② ③ **Hacker.** The bad boy (or girl) of the computer-programming universe, the Hacker can infiltrate, diagnose, or troubleshoot highly technical, complicated, or furtive code. White-hat hackers are like the heroes in a cowboy movie. Black hats usually have personality flaws that lead them to enjoy destroying or controlling existing systems. The Hacker is an interventionist, highly sought in the world of cybersecurity and software design and testing.

⓪ ① ② ③ **Academic / PhD.** The quintessential experts, PhDs dive deep into a specific topic or subject and add to the body of knowledge there. Along with Academics, they are committed to pursuing knowledge and understanding in a rigorous way that requires years of focus and effort. These days, the educational world has changed so much that there are many fewer opportunities for a tenure track in a university or college. Many PhDs seek other kinds of employment, often in the business or scientific world.

Antisocial Roles

Much of what is commonly considered antisocial may be just pushing the boundaries of what is known or accepted; and that is the engine that moves humanity forward. The roles in this category are different, however. They have no intention of making a contribution to society. Their impulse is narrow, in service to the ignoble in humanity or to cause intentional harm.

⓪ ① ② ③ **Sellout.** At one time or another, each of us plays this role. Whether or not it is a dominant role for you depends on how much time you devote to playing it. Sellouts make choices they know are based on expediency, what's easy rather than right, cashing in their values and dreams for money, power, comfort, security, or status. Common expressions of this role occur when you choose a career you don't enjoy, or marry someone you don't love for security or status. Selling out damages not only you but also the fabric of life around you.

⓪ ① ② ③ **Criminal.** This role is somewhat different from the everyday use of the word. Most people in prison fit the common definition: someone who commits acts against the law. But not all fit the role described here. The Criminal role includes people without much moral or ethical concern about the damage they inflict on other people as they pursue their own advancement, power, or wealth. They may have antisocial or psychopathic tendencies or simply not care how their actions affect others. The bad guy in the movies, the Mafia hit man, and the mercenary soldier of fortune fill this role wonderfully, but so do some perfectly respectable citizens who happily rob you with a fountain pen. Computer-virus creators fall into this category. Wherever you find hired guns, you also will find people playing the Criminal role: some lawyers, lobbyists, politicians, senior corporate managers, financial finaglers, and so forth.

⓪ ① ② ③ **Bully.** The Bully dominates others through force—either physical force or just a dominating personality focused on getting his or her way no matter what.

Part 2: Who You Are to Others

It can be helpful to get input from others about how they see you. Ask a couple (one to three) people who know you well to look over this exercise. See if they agree with the choices you made. Are there any roles they would add for you? Tell them to be completely honest and a little critical. If you question why they picked certain roles for you, ask them. Their input may help you see aspects of yourself more clearly.

Once they have given you their answers: What were the similarities and differences between your choices and others'? Did their input influence your perspective and choices at all?

Part 3: Zeroing In on Your Dominant Roles

Once you have gone through this chapter and marked your roles, and asked others for their opinions, go through the list again. Work to narrow your list down to the main players. Pay special attention to the ones marked as ③, but if your attention keeps going back to certain others, you may want to consider them as well. Then review your choices. Make a list of your top choices—the natural roles you relate to most and which have the strongest influence.

Remember: you are looking for roles you actually play as a regular and significant part of your life. The younger you are, the less likely it is that you will have had much actual experience playing some roles. In that case, what to look for is the connection, the recognition, the sense of familiarity.

Part 4: Combos and Conflicts

Combos. How are your main roles expressed in your life? For instance, you probably have one or more roles that influence the major choices in life. Are some of your biggest goals or common concerns and behaviors shaped by your main roles? For example: the Rebel may have trouble working in a traditional office setting or following directions, but the Critic may find fault with almost everything or constantly think about how things could be improved.

You may find that your roles work in combination with one another—Leonardo da Vinci might select Painter, Sculptor, Scientist, Polymath, Life-long Student, among others, but no single one describes all of him. He was a famous genius, with a very wide range of extraordinary gifts and talents. Only when you consider all of these roles together do you get more than a glimpse of his life. And, if one part of the combination varies, that creates an entirely different and distinct personality. (Can you see how great-fit work for someone with a Presenter–Charmer–Influencer-Persuader–Politician combination of roles might differ substantially from someone with a Presenter–Professor–Thinker–Father combo?)

That may be the case with you, too. Do your very best to get down to the pieces that create the full picture of you—two or three of them.

Now look back at your list of dominant roles and consider them in combinations or as a group. Amend your list to include combos that make sense to you.

Note: Sometimes your roles will seem to conflict. You may strongly identify with two that seem to be at odds with one another (e.g., a parent wanting to prioritize having a family and being available to them, and a workaholic feeling just as strongly about achieving goals outside of your home life). This might seem like an unreconcilable conflict, but there are two things you can do:

1. Dig in deeper and look for the biggest, strongest, most compelling roles, ones that will help to describe what sort of work will be the best fit. Can you prioritize your top roles, with number one being the strongest? You may have roles that are important to you, but that you do not want to express in your career. For example, one of Nick's strong roles is Nature Man. He grew up playing in the woods, had many wild-animal pets, and is a sucker for a good nature show on TV, but he never wanted a nature-centered career (though he tried organic farming and homesteading for a few years, long ago). Now he lives in a forest, where he sees and interacts with wild animals that eat his flowers every day, which satisfies the role.

2. You can also look for a creative way to reconcile the conflict and create a conflict role. Let's go back to the parent-workaholic example to see how.

Example: *"My work allows me to work to results and not hours; I can manage my own schedule to be available for my family,"* or *"My work allows me to work remotely, work as much or little as I like, to my own schedule." Contract or freelance work may facilitate this.*

Example: *"In my chosen field or career path, I will not be penalized or become obsolete if I step away from the workplace for periods of time."* This third example is a bit tricky. What it may rule out is fields or roles with fast-changing technologies or policies. It might be easier in fields or roles in which you can update or bring current a credential or certificate—like teaching or project management. Something in which you have demonstrated that you have the relevant skills or knowledge.

Part 5: Natural Roles—Clues, Components, and Career Ideas

Review the Natural Roles you chose as significant for you. Any particular habit, approach, or mannerism that stands out as soooo true for you?

See if you can create some Clues (insights, descriptions, preferences, or opinions) out of these ideas and add them to your Clues list.

E.g., Clue: *"I really hate bullies and people who take advantage of the vulnerable. Great-fit work for me would allow me to look out for, protect, or empower the little guy."*

Create a Component out of your chosen Natural Roles.

E.g., Component: *"My work allows me to express myself in my Natural Roles: Adviser, Scientist, Introvert, Nerd,* Star Wars *Fan, and active-outdoorsy Birder."**

*Now, we've kept the *Star Wars* Fan and Birder roles in this Component intentionally. They may not play out directly in a specific career choice, but . . . they are clear and dominant roles. Let's say, for example, this is your Component. You want to be able to be yourself at work—if everyone you worked with thought sci-fi fans were crazy, it might be difficult for you to feel accepted. A great-fit workplace would allow you to live somewhere that you can go birding regularly (and maybe start your workday a little later during migration season).

Career ideas? (Add them to your list.)

How about any Yeahbuts? (Add 'em to your list.)

CHAPTER 9

✦

SOCIAL ORIENTATION

Nigel is a former high school teacher who currently works at an Apple Genius Bar. He left his old job because he disliked the bureaucracy of education. When asked how his day goes now, he responded that it's often relaxing and enjoyable; he spends his entire day helping clients understand and troubleshoot their technical needs and problems. For Nigel, a workday filled with answering the questions and solving technical problems for a bunch of strangers is a great day. Nigel is an Extroverted Maestro.

For someone else, a day spent having to talk to others about something technical and detailed would be a living nightmare. They might find it stressful and exhausting. While this may sound like an extrovert vs. introvert distinction (which it is!)—there is a little more to it than that.

Human beings differ in how they relate to, and like to interact with, other humans—something we are going to call their *social orientation*. We'll discuss it more after you do a quick and fun Inquiry.

INQUIRY 16

Social Orientation

Below you will find a series of paired statements. Read each pair and mark the one that better describes you (better = more likely, on a typical day). This quick self-assessment should give you a glance at your leanings and tendencies as a social being. To help you identify and remember these multidimensional traits, we've coined terms to describe two overarching social orientations: Tribal and Maestro.

Tips for responding: Remember to consider how you naturally are—not how you think you should be. Don't quibble with the wording—simply mark the option that rings truer for you. If both statements describe you equally, mark both. If neither describe you—skip it. But . . . if you find you mark neither or both for many of them, change your method and be more rigorous about picking one over the other for as many as possible.

☑	Column A	or	Column B	☑
	I am generally on the same wavelength as others.		I am on my own, individual wavelength.	
	I prefer to contribute as part of a team.		I prefer to do my own thing in my own way.	
	My choices are similar to friends.		I have my own personal style.	
	I am one of the gang.		I float among different groups.	
	I listen to the same types of music as my friends or peers.		My taste in music is quite different from my friends or peers.	
	I can usually tell what someone else wants or needs.		I don't know what someone wants or needs unless they tell me.	
	I listen to and watch media on a wide variety of popular topics.		I have a few topics that I am really interested in and pursue.	
	In most ways, I'm a lot like other people.		I consider myself unique and different from others.	
	I'm not a deep diver into interests.		I tend to dive deeper into my interests than others.	
	I am attracted to team sports or activities.		I am attracted to solo sports or activities.	
	I prefer to collaborate on ideas with others.		I prefer to work on my own, individual ideas.	
	I see myself more as a jack-of-all-trades, doing a bit of many things.		I see myself as more of a specialist, doing a lot with fewer specific things.	
	I pay attention to and watch popular TV shows and movies.		I seek out and watch TV shows and movies that fit my interests.	
	I dress in a way that is similar to my friends and peers.		I have my own sense of style.	
	I fit in with most people.		I can fit in if I work at it.	
	I'm good at working closely with others.		I prefer my own projects.	
	I have strong ties to family.		I am the black sheep of the family.	
	I actively participate in more than one group, association, or community.		I don't actively participate in more than one group, association, or community.	

☑	Column A	or	Column B	☑
	I prefer to learn from someone else's established wisdom and experience.		I prefer to come up with my own ideas and understandings.	
	I keep up-to-date on popular opinion and trends.		Who cares about popular opinion?	
	I can take or give orders or directions easily.		I don't easily give or take orders or directions from others.	
	I identify with a particular religious or spiritual denomination.		I don't identify with a particular religious or spiritual denomination.	
	Sometimes I wish I stood out more from the crowd.		Sometimes I wish I were a bit more "normal."	
	Go along to get along.		Take the road less traveled.	
	My dreams of the future are similar to my friends and peers.		My dreams of the future differ from most others—theirs don't fit me.	
	Total marks TRIBAL		**Total marks MAESTRO →**	

Scoring Your Social Orientation Type

Because you had the option of marking neither or both of each pair, to properly calculate your percentages of Tribal-ness and Maestro-ness, you need to make a slight adjustment.

To Calculate Your Relative Percentages of Tribal and Maestro

1. Count the total number of marks you have in both columns: _____ TOTAL

2. Divide the "Total marks TRIBAL" by the total (#1, above): _____

3. Multiple that number by 100: _____ (% Tribal)

4. Divide the "Total marks MAESTRO" by the TOTAL (#1, above): _____

5. Multiple that number by 100: _____ (% Maestro)

For example: Winnie had a total of 27 checkmarks in both columns. She had 20 marks in Column 1 (Tribal). She had 7 marks in Column 2 (Maestro).

1. 27 TOTAL

2. 20/27 = .74

3. .74*100 = 74% Tribal

4. 7/27 = .259

5. .259*100 = 26% Maestro

____% TRIBAL   ____% MAESTRO

Tribal-Maestro

Tribal types and *Maestro* types tend to differ on a set of personality dimensions. These dimensions include **social intelligence, a need for belonging, a need for uniqueness, extroversion, introversion, and generalist or specialist preferences.**

Understanding how you naturally prefer and orient yourself socially will be very helpful as you determine the type of work you will do, your specific role, and a great-fit workplace environment.

The Tribal Orientation

Most people (about 75 percent) fit the type that we refer to as Tribal. As children, Tribals often have a lot of friends and participate in teams and activities. While not necessarily social or outgoing fundamentally, **Tribals pay attention to, seek out, and trust the wisdom of the tribe,** even if they do not realize it. They are also **natural members of groups and communities** and tend to be most successful and satisfied working with and through other people as members of an organization, group, or "tribe." Like a member of a flock of birds or a herd of gazelles, they move with the flow of the group. They are tuned in to what is important to the collective, and derive and shape their own points of view, goals, and values from it.

Because they are **on the same wavelength** as others, many Tribals **naturally understand human nature** without specialized training. They tend to naturally have some degree of **social intelligence**, which is often referred to in the working world as *soft skills*. Tribals tend to pay attention to and naturally understand how to work and interact with others. Some Tribals are great at reading other people and getting in sync with them. They naturally understand human psychology, knowing how to motivate and direct employees effectively. In the workplace, this ability can be the key to success; most exceptional sales managers and supervisors are Tribals.

(Teachers, counselors, and politicians also often find success in careers facilitated by social intelligence.) These abilities also help Tribals fit into the culture of an organization. Because they care about playing well with others, Tribals tend to interact well with others, collaborate, compromise, take direction, and socialize in beneficial and advancement-oriented ways.

Akin to naturally attuning to others, Tribals also tend to have a strong **need for belonging**. This often-undistinguished need for belonging fuels people's desire to be liked, and feel a part of, work culture and social life. Many people considering a career change come to us because they feel undervalued or like a misfit at work. Their need for belonging is not being met! Most Tribals are happiest when they are contributing to the larger goals of an organization and feel valued and respected.

Many Tribals are also **Generalists**. Generalists often have knowledge about many topics and a variety of interests, skills, and hobbies. They consider what is needed in the organization and community, and like to be able to competently succeed with a wide variety of tasks and projects. Many Generalists describe themselves as "liking variety" or as "a jack-of-all-trades." Some Generalists may be bored, or feel pinned down, with work that is highly specialized or narrow in scope. Roles that allow a variety of tasks and responsibilities may be better.

You will often find happy Tribals in most roles in business, management, personnel, high school teaching, training, supervision, sales, advertising, public relations, administration, banking, homemaking, etc.

All Maestros belong to tribes. All Tribals have independent thoughts and needs.

The Maestro Orientation

Only about 25 percent of the population identifies as a Maestro. Maestros have tribes, care about others, and are capable of getting along well with them. As children, they often delve deeply into specific interests and hobbies. They often recognize at an early age that their perspectives are different from the group's, and largely stay on that separate path. The fundamental differentiator between Tribal and Maestro is that **Maestros are less attentive to, and place less value on, the wisdom of the tribe than Tribals do.**

Relative to Tribals, Maestros may have less natural ease and ability to pick up on the nuances of human behavior. They may not seem to care as much about the intentions, needs, or ideas of others. While individuals vary, many Maestros are less concerned with the opinions or concerns of others, or are simply bad at communicating it. Some Maestros are more focused on process or function than on people. Others care deeply about getting along and are pained by their inability to get things right or to fit in easily. Ever meet someone who seems kind and really tries, and is just . . . unavoidably awkward? The quintessential TV nerd that gets beat up by the good-looking bully and goes home to play with his action figures? Probably a Maestro.

Maestros also care about contributing to the greater good, but are generally less concerned than Tribals about their social position. There is **less of a need for belonging,** and they may prefer to limit their social chatting time during the workday. They may be less capable at the people-managing functions inherent in most leadership roles. Maestros often prefer to be individual workers with plenty of time to develop and work on their projects.

Maestros are also characterized by a greater **need for uniqueness.** While they do not hold a monopoly on this trait, Maestros overwhelmingly seek to innovate, create, or produce something original, or be seen for their individual contribution and value. They excel when focusing on the mastering of a particular discipline or skill; many a happy Maestro's success is the result of extensive or specialized training or talent in a chosen field. What might be overly detailed or extensive for a Generalist Tribal will be the gift to a Specialist Maestro. Many do well when people seek them out for their expertise. They most enjoy being appreciated and valued for the unique contribution they make, while Tribals will be more pleased by the successful direction of the group at large. Maestros usually gravitate toward careers that put them on a raised platform or will aim toward the highest level possible within their career or field of interest. If Tribals sense and follow a wavelength, Maestros are the ones who create the wavelength.

Which Are You?

Few people are 100 percent Tribal or 100 percent Maestro—most are a combination of the two. Knowing where you fall on the Tribal-Maestro spectrum is very useful in picking a career that fits you, but it also tells you a great deal about why your present work may fall short.

If you don't quickly identify as Tribal or Maestro, here is a quick gut check to find out, at least, which side of the spectrum you are naturally gravitating toward. Tribals and Maestros tend to answer the question "What do you do for a living?" differently. Tribal responses often mention the tribe (i.e., where they work): "I work at Galactic Communications," or "I'm a manager at Acme Fireworks Company." Maestros, even when they respond similarly, answer from a different place. Their answers are more statements of their individual identity: "I am a scientist," "I am an artist."

How would you immediately answer that question?

For a Maestro, being proud of their role, and feeling that their work is the right self-expression, can be critically important. Ideally, Maestros should choose a subject area they are passionate about and spend their lives mastering it. If you are a Maestro and are not doing something that you are passionate about, or deeply interested in, you had better get to it. You will probably never be satisfied until you do. The good news is that it is never too late to get started.

For Tribals, things are a little more flexible. Change is easier to engage with and accept. Even though the workplace has become so highly specialized, Tribals are able to move from job to job based on factors other than specialized knowledge. In other words, they learn as they go. Their ability to manage, administer, market, or supervise is more important than technical knowledge.

One thing we've noticed by working with tens of thousands of clients is that for Maestros, the status or social position of a particular job or career may be an important consideration, whereas Tribals might prioritize finding their right tribe and workplace culture. Maestros may be more prone to consider the extent to which their job or career matches their best and truest self. Tribals tend to prioritize feelings of community. This is why, when they're younger, Tribals are less likely to choose a specific career to follow—they are more reflective, and need a baseline formed out of experience and context. When they look back, they frequently say that what was most valuable was something other than the specific subject matter learned in the classroom.

Young Maestros, ideally, go to college or training programs to start learning a specialty that takes time to gain mastery of and will hold their attention for years. If possible, a young person with a Maestro personality should select a career direction early—and should hold firm when confronted with outside pressures to go down a path they know is not right for them. If they are not passionate about the subject matter, they will not be able to proudly say, "I am a . . ." and will have a hard time staying the course.

Reality

In reality, careers do not line up neatly on one side of the line or the other, fitting either Tribals or Maestros. They don't need to. The point is not to rule certain career options in or out based on the result you get, but to consider your true nature and seek opportunities and options that allow you to be your best you!

For example, while a great majority of happy and successful retail store owners are Tribals, a Maestro with a raging passion for radio-controlled model airplanes, sewing, or mountaineering equipment might love owning such a specialty store that could allow them to indulge in their passion or interest and provide them with customers constantly seeking their expertise. Similarly, a Tribal with a strong aptitude for mathematics and numbers might make a brilliant college professor teaching high-level courses, contributing to the betterment of students' educations and the institution at large.

There are also ways to adapt a job you already have in order to highlight either your Maestro or Tribal tendencies. An administrative assistant with a Maestro personality, for instance, might successfully master some specialized aspect of the job and become the office expert on the word-processing software. By doing so, other employees will come to them for problem-solving and instruction, a role that suits their personality better than the usual work assistants perform. A Tribal project manager in a physics lab might strive daily to connect to others and create a strong team and collaborative work environment in an otherwise clinical and impersonal discipline.

Extroversion and Introversion—Revisited

In chapter 7, Inquiry 12: What's My Type?, we explored a distinction between introversion and extroversion. You responded to statements and determined your trait preference between the two.

While it may be useful shorthand to think of yourself as an extrovert or introvert, in truth **everyone is a mixture of both** of these traits. People with an extroverted preference value and enjoy time alone and introverts can enjoy and crave concerts and the company of others. The key is to figure out what the right balance of extroverted and introverted activities are for you.

Let's say the right balance for you is right in the middle—50 percent extrovert and 50 percent introvert. And at your job, you are spending most of your time alone, on a computer or doing other independent activities. Over time, you will likely develop a desire for more people contact. You may start feeling lonely or depressed. On the other hand, if your workweek involves a constant flow of meetings and conversations with others, you may feel exhausted and crave to spend your free time at home, curled up on the couch reading or watching TV at the end of a long day. You will feel a loss of energy and fulfillment if your work does not allow you the proper balance of social and reflective activities.

If not immediately obvious to you, a good way to estimate the right balance of social (extroverted) and reflective (introverted) activities for you is to look back through specific times of your life. What combination of activities (friends, family, work, part-time, hobbies, sports, volunteer work) gave you a great balance of energy? Do your best to turn your insights into percentages. For example: "A great workweek for me would allow me to spend about 60 percent of my time in extroverted (people and outward-facing) activities and 40 percent of my time in introverted (reflective, thoughtful, mentally-processing) activities." Then consider how you could achieve this balance at work.

Combining Tribal-Maestro and Extroversion-Introversion

Let's get crazy now and look at how combining both scales can provide you with a sense of what careers might fit you. The descriptions below may not describe you perfectly and the examples may not include careers that interest you. But, from these simplified guidelines, you should be able fit these concepts together with your sense of yourself.

Introverted Tribal. People with this combination like working as a part of the human beehive, often as a part of an organization, but they are happiest in a quieter part of the beehive, where they can mainly work internally rather than spending most of the day interacting with other people. Because they are more introverted, they do their best work either alone or with a small group of people they know well. Modern office-cubicle settings may be suited to some Introverted Tribals: they excel at project-based work that allows them to contribute to the whole by working in a semiprivate space where they can still sense the hum of other Tribals rubbing their wings together. Even though they may not interact with others as much as their Extroverted Tribal office mates, they know that at any moment they can grab a cup of coffee and collaborate with a buddy around the corner. They are the true unsung heroes. Tribals serve as the backbone of organizations. Professionally, they fit with many different jobs in organizations, wherever they can contribute to the goals of the organization in a way that allows them to spend a considerable portion of their day working internally.

If you score as an Introverted Tribal, particularly if you are very introverted, you may feel that our description of Tribals doesn't apply to you. You may not feel that you are on the same wavelength with other people. You may not want to be part of a group. Still, your score suggests that even if you wind up practicing in a specialized area, you will most likely be happiest working for an organization rather than being out on your own. There are, for instance, plenty of perfectly happy introverted computer programmers who score as Tribals. Examples: managers of projects that involve more planning than direct supervision, administrators, underwriters, lawyers working within a corporation, orchestra musicians, business owners who prefer to work behind the scenes.

Extroverted Tribal. They are happiest spending their workdays interacting, talking, and socializing in a part of the beehive where there are plenty of other bees to rub wings with. Their Tribal side drives them to be a member of a community; their extroverted side has them interacting much of the day within that community. They are nonstop, people-oriented, shiny happy party people in all those beer and Coke ads. Getting things done with and through other people most of the day is how they prefer to work and play. They may ask themselves, "Why write when I can talk to someone?" Examples: marketing-oriented CEOs, sales representatives, hosts, greeters, people managers, executives, spokespersons, promoters, supervisors, day care providers, recreation therapists, nurses, advertising account managers, marketing presenters, K–12 teachers, and personal trainers.

Introverted Maestros make up a large percentage of the people we think of as "professionals." They are experts who work internally in their chosen discipline, thinking and problem-solving in their area of specialty. Introverted Maestros prefer to do a whole project or job with their attention mostly on their inner world. Some are inclined to be scholarly, scientific, or professional, and occasionally eccentric. They perceive and do things their own way. Many Introverted Maestro physicians work with patients all day, but direct much of their attention internally, figuring out what is broken and how to fix it. More examples: scientists, engineers, college professors who most enjoy the research and writing, artists, specialist physicians, attorneys, dentists, inventors, technicians, analysts, accountants, consultants, master craftspeople, writers, and many computer-industry professionals.

Extroverted Maestros. They are experts or masters in a particular area, at their best performing their mastery in front of others. Not only do they see the world in a highly personal way, but are compelled to use their talent, knowledge, and wisdom in an extroverted manner—they are performers. When geared to take a lead role as an expert, they direct, advise, and guide others in their field of mastery. As entrepreneurs, they are often visionary leaders, with special technical competence, who develop a loyal following of people they have enrolled in their vision. Examples: college professors who love the classroom, seminar leaders, spokespersons for technical subjects, politicians, actors, comedians, performance artists, physicians in high-contact specialties, charismatic leaders, consultants, trainers, orchestra conductors.

When choosing your future career or next step, consider your combination of Tribal and Maestro elements and how they might impact your satisfaction in your role and work environment. Picking something that does not fit increases the risk of winding up in an unsatisfying career.

INQUIRY 17

Social Orientation—
Clues, Components, and Career Ideas

Look back at your responses and calculations for Inquiry 13.

1. What were your percentages of Tribal and Maestro?

    TRIBAL _____ MAESTRO_____

    (If the math is irritating—this is a Clue! And just rough it out: "Mostly Maestro, Mostly Tribal, right in the middle, etc.")

2. Considering introversion and extroversion, what combo type do you most identify as?

3. Look back over the whole section for Clues. Add whatever you find to your Clues list.

4. Ask, "Is there anything I am willing to choose as a definite component?" Add anything you choose to your Career Components list.

5. Do any new careers/jobs come to mind? If so, add them to your Career Ideas list.

CHAPTER 10

+

NATURAL TALENTS

The important thing in life is to have a great aim and to possess the aptitude and the perseverance to attain it.

—JOHANN WOLFGANG VON GOETHE

Take a duck. Drop it in a pond. Even if it was raised in the desert and has no swimming experience, it will be instantly at home in its new environment. In a matter of minutes, it will happily be doing what ducks do—exhibiting natural mastery of paddling around the pond. It would be hard to find a more suitable candidate for pond life than a duck, even one with no previous swimming experience. That's because ducks are designed for the environment they inhabit. They have an ideal set of natural abilities and talents for their job. They have webbed feet, bills shaped for obtaining the special foods available pondside, and hollow feathers that act as a raft to keep them floating high in the water. They have a waterproofing system that keeps them dry and a layer of down to keep them warm in near-freezing water. All the beasts of the field and the birds of the air are perfectly equipped for the highly specific way they go about making a living. Over millions of years, Mother Nature (and evolution and natural selection) have helped the best-suited candidates for each niche survive.

Human beings differ in one aspect from many other animal species. While successful members of a given animal species have a pretty darn similar set of natural talents—giraffes have long necks to reach the highest leaves, beavers have wide, flat tails for swimming and patting down mud, and bees dance to share information with their hive—successful human beings have a more diverse range of natural talents and abilities. While there are small differences between individuals, essentially each giraffe is pretty much like all the others (at least to outsiders). On the other hand, every person is a unique individual, different in many ways from all the others. Each of us is genetically dealt a specific hand of talent and ability cards. Our cards give us a knack for playing certain roles in the working world with natural ease and mastery and not-so-much ease in others.

Natural talents are different from acquired knowledge, skills, and interests. Your interests can change. You can gain new skills and knowledge. But your natural, inherited talents will remain with you, largely unchanging, for your entire life. Most of what we usually think of as special talents, such as music, writing, math, science, business management, are each actually constellations of deeper, more elemental abilities that, when well combined, play together in harmony like instruments in an orchestra.

Many of us have spent a lot of time and energy working on and improving talents that are not in our wheelhouse—not naturally ours. This is, at best, quite inefficient. A better strategy is to learn how to play the hand you have been dealt brilliantly and to your best advantage. To do this, you need to understand what they are. The better you understand your natural gifts and talents, the easier it is to match them to roles and opportunities in the real world and the more likely you will be to have a satisfying and successful career.

Let's use an example. Suppose you need an operation and want to pick the best possible surgeon, someone with a real "gift." Obviously, factors such as quality of training, commitment to excellence, and length of experience are important. But since you are looking for someone who is truly excellent, you want a surgeon who combines excellent training and experience with natural talent. How could you tell that a person possesses that blend?

First, you would want someone with high spatial ability, a talent for thinking in three dimensions. How would you feel about going under the blade of a surgeon who viewed your body as an abstract philosophical concept? Wouldn't you prefer someone who naturally understood how things fit together? You would also want your surgeon to be a natural in something called diagnostic reasoning. This is a talent for being able to leap to accurate conclusions based on just a few clues. If something went wrong during your operation, the surgeon would use this talent to figure out what to do quickly. Other natural talents you'd want your surgeon to have would be an ability to focus for a long period of time and superb eye-hand coordination. Some people have minds that move quickly, restlessly, seemingly at a hundred miles an hour. These folks are great at improvising, but have difficulty concentrating on one thing for long periods of time. Their brains are just zooming along too quickly. They have "high idea flow." You would want a surgeon who naturally and easily kept attention and focused on the task at hand—someone with "lower idea flow." You would also want someone with "great hands." Manual dexterity is an innate gift. If you had a choice between a surgeon with superb, average, or low hand dexterity, which would you pick? There are several more pieces to the puzzle of what constitutes the natural talents of a great surgeon. But, hopefully, now you have a sense of what we mean by innate talents.

Getting to the Source of Career Difficulties

The difference between a career that is just okay and one that really *soars and sings* depends on fitting together *many* elements, all of which are important and addressed throughout this book.

The most obvious problems that people face (and you know this because it is what they complain about) are issues like: a crappy boss, low pay, long or rigid hours, stress, and boredom. What people (you included?) might not realize is that **some of these problems are *symptoms* rather than causes.** The obnoxious boss and the long hours are usually just the tip of the iceberg; what stands between them (you?) and a truly satisfying career may be more complex. When you are willing to simply put up with work you don't totally hate, then solving the obvious problems may be all that matters. But when it is important to have a great fit between you and your work, you have to deal with the whole iceberg.

It is from real people and their real experience that we know this. Over the forty-plus years that Nick owned and ran Rockport Institute, he and a small group of expert coaches (including Monica) worked with many thousands of clients who swarmed there, seeking help and wanting to change their jobs and occupations. They, one after the other, described their problems, concerns, and dissatisfactions. Consistently, they reported that they were *bored, didn't fit in, weren't challenged,* and *were stressed out.* Less clear was *what* was boring, *how* they didn't fit in, and *why* they were stressed out. It became increasingly apparent that a major contributor to feelings of job and career misery was a mismatch between one's abilities (natural talents) and their work.

What happens when there is a mismatch between your talents and your work? For creatures other than us humans, the answer to this question is *extinction.* For humans, because we are so adaptable, we survive, but at a terrible cost. The bottom line—the further you get from fully expressing your natural talents and abilities, the less likely it is that you will enjoy your job. And, sometimes, having only one thing out of whack can ruin the chance for career satisfaction.

When important abilities go unused, people become bored with their work. When the job requires talents they do not possess, people find their work frustrating and difficult.

When someone performs less than optimally at work, his or her supervisor often makes inaccurate assumptions. The supervisor thinks the problem is that the employee isn't *motivated,* isn't *smart enough,* or has some sort of *attitude problem.* The supervisor doesn't understand that what's really going on is that the employee's innate talents don't fit well with his or her job. They may try to correct the situation with additional training or other suggestions—but these well-meaning attempts may make things worse. What would happen if your old-fashioned gas-powered car's fuel pump was broken, but you misdiagnosed the problem and began to adjust the carburetor? You would then have both a broken fuel pump and a carburetor problem. The misdiagnosis can lead to further frustration for everyone.

The workplace has no monopoly on difficulties caused by talent mismatches.

Imagine a bright high school student with a wild, fast-flowing imagination and a talent for powerful, critical thinking. Some kids with this combination may join the debate team, a perfect outlet for these talents that can be a great deal of fun and a major contribution to self-esteem. Others, just as worthy, just as gifted, will make a different set of assumptions. They may get rightfully bored in Miss Peabody's drone-it-right-out-of-the-book history class. To preserve their personal dignity, they may decide that "school obviously is not for them" or "they are not clever" and may opt out of school or a mainstream society that doesn't see how gifted they are.

It is important to identify your unique set of natural talents and abilities and know where and how to use them.

Nature vs. Nurture

Throughout the twentieth century, waves of debate shifted back and forth over whether or not intelligence and success were innate (genetic) or the by-product of environment and upbringing, which in turn created a lot of unfair classification, prejudice, and outright dismissal of different types of students and coworkers. (It also became the cornerstone of various political and social conversations relating to education, sexuality, and more.) *Nature vs. Nurture* requires people to declare themselves in one camp or the other. Our work and our approach don't fall within either camp. For our purposes, it doesn't *really* matter if it is in your DNA or your early upbringing. By the time you are in late adolescence, you have developed a brain with a certain wiring and certain patterns of processing information. Your brain wiring may not be complete until your mid-twenties (this is true!), but . . . you have a significantly structured set of aptitudes and abilities. These are what we call *natural talents*.

IQ vs. Multiple Intelligences

Until recently, the theories of intelligence that dominated scientific thinking boiled down to slightly different versions of one single premise: some people are smart, and some people ain't. Intelligence was thought to be measurable on a single scale, like a thermometer. Your IQ (intelligence quotient) was a certain number, and you could take a test to tell you if you were of average intelligence, or below or above average.

While this single measure may be helpful for some purposes, this narrow interpretation of intelligence does not recognize the enormous range of human abilities and individualized differences and gifts it can contain and offer. We hold with experts like Harvard psychologist Howard Gardner, whose excellent book, *Frames of Mind*, outlines seven different types of intelligence that people possess to greater or lesser degrees. Dr. Gardner argues that each person has a unique cognitive profile that comes from differing strengths in these intelligences.

Breakthroughs in neuroscience and psychology have shifted the way we understand the human mind and how it works. With new technology and brain scans, scientists are able to see how different brains respond during different activities and when different talents are used. Data, theory, and new technology all support the theory that individuals differ in their strengths and natural talents.

Instead of thinking of yourself as falling somewhere on a single "intelligence" line, think of yourself as having a unique collection of smaller, more specialized "intelligences" (or talents) that sets you apart.

Natural Talents

You have a very practical reason for learning more about innate abilities and talents: winding up in a career that you love. To help you get closer, let's redefine *talent* in a broader and more useful way.

Talent: an innate capacity for doing something well.

When someone stands out in any particular area, we say they have a "gift." We think that each person has their own gifts. Your gifts are made up of several innate abilities playing together in harmony. By identifying the natural abilities that you have, and don't have, you can harmonize your way into career choices that make fabulous use of your talents. Some people have a natural gift for music, athletics, invention, interpersonal relationships, etc. These gifts are just as real and just as important as the combination of abilities that are generally thought of as intelligence—that of certain types of academic ability. There is even a variety of academic abilities or intelligences—it is rare for someone to be both a math whiz and an imaginative creative writer.

Bottom line: wherever it came from, you have a unique set of talents and abilities—your own brand of intelligences. If you can identify yours, you can use that information to help you make extraordinary choices for yourself and your career.

So, What If You Have an Innate Talent and Just Don't Know About It?

This is a conundrum. Maybe you have the innate talent to become a great musician, but never have had the opportunity to learn to play. Or you started learning an instrument, but early lessons were so contrary to your learning style that you abandoned the instrument before discovering your talent.

Realistically, it would be quite difficult to try out and to experience every type of task or activity to find out if you loved it and found you had a natural gift for it. We have no overarching solution for this and, sometimes, luck, timing, and circumstance leads you one way or another, but there is a conservative—and, we'd say, better—way of assessing ability. You know you have an ability to do a thing because you have done it and it worked out well for you. Look for Clues and consider related activities. You can think of the building blocks (aptitudes or abilities) for an activity and whether or not they fit yours. And you might have to be willing to experiment or try out some new stuff.

An example: You love music and have always been attracted to multiple genres of it, but your family isn't musical and they never put you in music lessons. You're good with your hands. You can immediately tell when someone plays a wrong note. The other day, you were walking down the hall and heard some music playing. You opened a door and there were several violinists and cellists playing. You were mesmerized. You thought of some alternative ways they could have concluded the piece you just listened to. Clue, clue, clue, clue, clue. While you may never have held a violin or played slide guitar in your life . . . if you are observant and open-minded, you may have noticed a lot of evidence that you have some innate musical ability or talent. Find a way to dip your toe into the stringed-instrument pool. You have to play to win!

Anything you have a natural knack for is a talent, an aptitude, a kind of intelligence to be appreciated and considered as a possible piece of the puzzle in designing your career.

What About Learned Skills?

Nowadays, we are encouraged to learn specialized skills, which are built up through long practice and acquired skill. Skiing is a good example of this: you can be talented at it and have an innate ability to lock in, but it didn't quite come from nowhere. You will have had to have spent hours, days, years on the slopes to master it technically. It requires time, commitment, and practice. Unless you were raised next door to a ski slope and skied constantly, it would be unlikely that you would ever get much beyond the intermediate level unless you had a natural gift for the sport.

In general, people enjoy doing that which they do well naturally. Usually, if you are spending many happy hours engaged in a hobby or certain activity, you are probably expressing a natural talent. If you have become highly skilled at something you were not forced to learn or do, it is fairly safe to assume you are expressing a natural gift. The learning curve is shorter and steeper for those with natural talent. A math whiz with natural talents with math and spatial reasoning might soar through an accelerated calculus class, earn an A, have fun with it, and still have time for friends.

An intelligent friend with little natural talent with mathematics might hire a tutor, spend three hours each night on homework, and still only pass with a B–, frustrated and tired.

So, the way to really get your work life flying is to choose a career for which you have exceptional natural talent and then put in the time and energy to become a real master. Talent and acquired skill are an unbeatable combination.

Don't Hit Your Head on the Metal Flagpole

Humans are so darn adaptable! We dominate the earth partially because of our ability to make do with whatever life throws at us. We find a way to ignore it, change it, or work around it. We can survive extraordinary trials and situations. We can work with people we don't like or respect who don't like or respect us. We are quite capable of continuing for years spending eight hours a day bored out of our minds. We can find a way to survive a lot of pain and misery.

Our versatility comes with a price. In the working world, each of us is able to fill a wide range of jobs and survive in almost any organization; given sufficient intelligence, the average human can do just about anything with reasonable competence. We can go to work and be decent at things we don't enjoy and aren't particularly good at.

Consequently, people accept the daily discomfort of a career that does not really fit their talents. They tend to put up with unsuitable, ill-fitting careers because they don't realize that their suffering is unnecessary. Monica, an avid bird watcher, has seen woodpeckers land on a metal flagpole and start tapping away, looking for supper. Each time, it took only a few seconds for the bird to realize that it was in the wrong place and fly off. We human beings put up with careers that are, in some ways, as ill-suited as the metal flagpole is for a woodpecker. We can get by. We can survive. But **if you want your life to really soar, you have to find a way to match your natural abilities with your work.** Otherwise, you will keep banging away at the metal flagpole with an empty stomach, wondering why you keep getting migraines.

An Elegant Fit

You don't need anybody to tell you who you
are or what you are. You are what you are!

—JOHN LENNON

It is an obvious, empirical truth that when people are doing something they enjoy and do it extremely well, they get more done and they do it better. When someone is able to perform at a level of mastery, it is usually a function of making use of acquired skills and experience in conjunction with a strong foundation of natural talent. What is most important is the role of natural talents. People who are both highly successful and continue to love their work, year after year, spend most of their time at work engaged in activities that make use of their strongest abilities. They spend very little time performing functions for which they have no special gift. Their lives are concentrated on doing what they do best. Their talents are perfectly matched with what they do.

You are probably someone with a big, sensitive career antenna who unerringly made the perfect career decision early on, or you would not be reading this book. So you are faced with a question: How can you go about doing the best possible job of matching your talents and your work? How can you come closest to duplicating what the people who have succeeded in finding a perfect match for their talents have accomplished?

Self-Assessing Your Natural Talents Is Tricky

If someone presented you with a survey that asked you to rate yourself in a wide range of different areas of ability, you could most likely do a very accurate self-assessment—there are experiences, over the years, that have given you a good sense of what you are good at and not good at. (For example: you've gone through enough years of gym class to know if you have an affinity for physical activity and strength.) You might have a harder time, though, accurately assessing the talents and abilities that would allow you to perform brilliantly in some jobs, only competently in others, and less well in the rest. Few of us have done more than scratch the surface with regard to recognizing and appreciating our unique profile of talents within a career space because we only enter that world at a certain point in our lives. What you know of your talents is based only on what you have done before.

If you are in mid-career and plan to choose a new career direction, you probably do not want to limit yourself to choices suggested by what you have learned from your previous experiences. It makes sense to look at a broader and deeper range of possible career options than would be evident by simply reshuffling the deck.

Often, people are most proud of skills they possess that took a great deal of effort to develop. At the same time, they may take for granted the things they are best at doing because these things come so naturally and easily to them. If you met a fish who could play the piano, it would most likely be extremely proud of its skill, especially since it doesn't have hands. The fish would probably not consider its gift for swimming and breathing underwater as anything special because these talents come so naturally to it. All of these influences tend to confuse the picture we have of our innate abilities.

A Constellation of Talents

The question "Who ought to be boss?" is like asking, "Who ought to be the tenor in the quartet?" Obviously, the man who can sing tenor.

—HENRY FORD

Another problem when self-assessing is that what we think of as our talents are usually collections of innate abilities working together, rather than the individual talents themselves.

For example, people say John Lennon was a genius, an extraordinary natural talent. But if you think about it, he had many individual talents and personality characteristics that combined, like stars in a constellation, to create that larger gift. On a basic level, he had the inherent, underlying musical aptitudes needed by any reasonably competent musician: tonal memory, which is a memory for complex melodies; an accurate sense of pitch; and a great sense of rhythm. He also had the soul of the true revolutionary artist, always true to his vision, never compromising. He had a great sage heart constantly giving everything he had and a streak of rebelliousness and playful cynicism. He had a great gift for language, for subtle wordplay. He had an ability to communicate from the core of the most profound aspects of life, while taking it all lightly. He never lost a sense of wonder. He had a lightning-fast imagination and wit. He could pierce to the heart of people and issues and situations, see them clearly and from a perspective unlike anyone else's. He had a marvelous collection of individual traits that combined into genius. You do, too.

Be like John Lennon and find a way to have all of your abilities play together in perfect harmony. And get paid for it.

The Cards in Your Hand

When people say they are good at math, or working with people, or writing, they are not describing a single ability, but several aptitudes working in concert. We see the loaf of bread, not the ingredients. If you think about it, there are only a few things to do with a loaf of bread: make sandwiches and French toast, or wait for it to get stale and use it as a doorstop. But if, instead, you consider uses for the combination of the basic ingredients—flour, yeast, salt, and water—the sky is the limit! Depending on how you combine those fundamental ingredients, in what proportions, and what else you add to it—you can make things as diverse as crackers, baguettes, cakes, popovers, empanadas, and, of course, pizza. On the shelves of your supermarket there are thousands of items made from these core ingredients.

Think of yourself as a band, a collection of instruments (talents) wondering what kind of music to play. If you have tubas and a big bass drum, you might be a marching band. If you have violins and a selection of woodwinds and brass instruments plus tympani, you might be an orchestra. If you have a banjo, mandolin, stand-up bass, and acoustic guitar, you might be another kind of band. It's up to you to find out what your main instruments are and how they might combine.

Throughout our lives, we play various combinations of these cards in our work and elsewhere. These combinations are what we recognize as our talents and strengths. Recognizing and understanding the individual "cards" allows us to combine them in new ways rather than limiting ourselves to replaying the combinations we have used successfully in the past. This is especially useful for people considering heading in a new direction.

The best way to understand your innate abilities in a way that helps you design a well-fitting career is to get down to the deepest level, to the basic abilities that combine to make up your unique profile of talents. And the one way to do that well is to go through an in-depth career testing program. The value is not just in understanding individual pieces of the puzzle, but knowing how they combine. When you mix personality traits into the recipe, there are hundreds of different profiles, each perfectly suited to some careers and less so to the great majority of jobs.

Professional Career Testing Programs

Programs that test innate abilities are very different from the kinds of tests traditionally given by career counselors. Most people who have taken old-fashioned career interest tests say they contribute little to their ability to make life-work decisions. Programs that test abilities give you an edge in making excellent career decisions. Going through a testing program that measures natural talents and abilities is such a powerfully effective tool that we recommend it to all of our clients. Time after time, clients who have taken our career tests have shared that they are amazed by how much they learned about themselves. New entrants into the job market feel more confident in what they're good at, and what they're looking for; mid-career clients quickly realize why certain aspects of their work was such a mismatch. Again and again, we've heard "I wish I had done this years ago." And "Why don't they require this in schools?!" They feel much better prepared to pursue education and careers that fit them and their natural gifts. Clients of all ages learn how to use their talents in harmony to create a future that is both challenging and engaging to them.

On the internet, you can find a number of websites and companies that provide some form of career testing. Some of it is free. There are only a few that provide a high-quality, comprehensive career testing program. We suggest that, should you choose to invest your time, effort, and money in career testing, you be very discerning in your choice.

When selecting your program, there are three things you should look for:

1. Make sure that they are providing objective measures of a range of aptitudes and abilities (not just "self-report" assessments).

2. Make sure that you are provided with more than a computer-generated report. A one-to-one coaching conversation with an experienced coach, who can help you interpret your testing results with you, is key.

3. Avoid standardized or highly prescriptive interpretations. The traditional approach looks at the high scores and prescribes careers typically associated with those scores. One thing we have discovered over the past forty years is that no one is "typical." Just because you score high in three things that emergency room nurses should be high in doesn't mean you should be an emergency room nurse. What if you can't stand to be around sick people?

We recommend going to an organization with a highly personalized, holistic approach, communicating results to you in a way that makes sure you can look back and see for yourself how the various talents and combinations have shown up in your life so far. Your own recognition and sense of certainty about what is most important is far more useful in defining definite components than information alone. This is expert, customized work. Expect the cost of a good testing program to be between $500 and $2,000. With the right company and an excellent coach, it will be worth more than ten times that investment.

There are only a handful of competent companies who can provide the expertise and individualized attention that Monica's company, Career Matters, does. She provides an objective battery (aka set) of Career-Relevant Aptitude Tests as well as an in-depth coaching service. Nick's former company, Rockport Institute, no longer provides individualized coaching and testing services, but now focuses on training effective career coaches.

Natural Talent and Ability Self-Assessment

Now that we've familiarized you with the ideas behind natural and learned talents, it's time for a couple of Inquiries. *Inquiry 18: What Comes Naturally to Me* is a simple self-assessment of your perceived strengths. After it, *Inquiry 19: Natural Talents and Abilities Self-Assessment* will provide some basic information and insights about your natural gifts. It roughly resembles the objective tests that Career Matters– and Rockport Institute–trained coaches provide.

INQUIRY 18

What Comes Naturally to Me?

In this Inquiry, you will take a look into what you now perceive as your natural gifts.

1. Write down everything that comes naturally to you, for which you seem to have a "knack." Include everything, both work-related and otherwise. Don't include those areas where you think you have developed a skill but have no real natural talent. (For example, as a boy, Nick swam competitively on a national level. It would seem, at first glance, that he was a talented swimmer. Actually, he made it to the nationals because he happened to be on a great team with a great coach and because his dad forced him to go to a very rigorous team practice every morning. He worked hard and built competency, but had no natural thrill, love, or ability as a competitive swimmer.)

2. List the areas in which you feel you are a "natural." What were you known for in school? What do you excel in at work? What do you enjoy most? What work activities do you not consider as work but as fun? What projects have you enjoyed? What hobbies are you passionate about? What do you spend your time at work wishing you were doing?

3. What do other people say you are especially good at? Ask your partner, your boss, your parents, and others who may have different points of view from yours. Include personality trait strengths as well. They are also elements of your "talent profile."

4. Look back over this Inquiry for clues. Add whatever you find to your Clues list.

5. Ask, "Is there anything I am willing to choose as a definite component?" Add anything you choose to your Career Components list.

6. Do any new careers/jobs come to mind? If so, add them to your Career Ideas list.

*Few people think more than two or three times a year. I have made an
international reputation for myself by thinking once or twice a week.*

—GEORGE BERNARD SHAW

INQUIRY 19

Natural Talents and Abilities Self-Assessment

This Inquiry provides a way for you to assess your natural abilities. Read the
following descriptions of talents and abilities and rate yourself in each talent
area. Don't rush. Spend some time looking back over your life to see how
much evidence you find for each talent/natural ability.

1. Rate your talents and abilities. To help with rating yourself in the natu-
    ral talents listed below, remember situations that came easily and natu-
    rally to you at work and in the rest of your life, both in recent times
    and in the distant past. After reading about each ability, check one of
    the circles to rate yourself in that ability: ① for low, ② for midrange,
    ③ for high. If you're not sure, check the circle with the question mark.
    Don't guess. If you aren't sure, check the circle. Don't worry about how
    many categories you checked. After you've finished assessing your tal-
    ents, further instructions will tell you what to do next.

Problem-Solving Talents

①②③❓ Diagnostic Reasoning

Diagnostic reasoning is a gift for quickly seeing a relationship between seemingly unrelated facts, or forming an accurate conclusion from a few scat-
tered bits of evidence in one big step instead of many. It is especially useful
in situations where there is no way to logically solve the problem, where an
accurate diagnosis must be made without having all of the facts available—
like scientists, who often create new theories from hypotheses and limited
concrete information. Newton used diagnostic reasoning when he discovered
gravity on that fateful day when the apple fell on his head. A physician, too,
might use this ability to quickly and accurately pinpoint the illness at the root

of a group of symptoms. A critic uses it to critique a movie or restaurant, to come to a conclusion that unifies many individual impressions.

Diagnostic reasoning is a powerfully active ability, but it can cause as many problems as it solves. People with this talent need to have a constant flow of new problems. They may have a fascination with learning a new job or skill and then get bored as soon they have it figured out and are not presented with a new problem to sink their teeth into. When high scorers have a career that does not use it regularly, diagnostic reasoning keeps on running and critiques whatever gets in its path—the workplace, the boss—and all too often turns to self-criticism. In many careers, this ability is a liability. For example, in traditional corporate management and other careers that place a premium on maintaining the status quo, the diagnostic problem solver's drive to ferret out unworkability, get to the heart of every problem, and bring these problems, along with suggested solutions, to the attention of senior management, who didn't even recognize there was a problem, is usually considered to be unwanted boat-rocking and complaining.

> *Career fields that use diagnostic reasoning: physical, life, and social sciences; emergency medicine and all medicine specialties that present a constant flow of new, nonroutine problems; consulting of all kinds; litigation and criminal law; investigative journalism; forensic science; critiquing professions (comedy, art critic, food critic, social satire); political pundits, op-ed columnists; innovators (inventors, entrepreneurs, all design fields); troubleshooting technical problems; persuasive fields such as advertising and marketing, product buying; quality improvement; copyediting, coaching.*

①②③❹ Analytical Reasoning

People high in analytical reasoning ability think systematically and logically. They can easily organize information within a set of existing rules and theories, and solve problems by organizing concepts, information, or things in a logical sequence. They bring order to chaos, analyze, systematize, organize, prioritize, synthesize, categorize, schedule, plan, and boil down information to the most important components.

Analytical reasoning is the most used and trusted problem-solving talent in our computer-centered world, and is an absolutely essential aptitude for careers in the business, technology, engineering, computer, and technical editing spaces. (Scientists and engineers use mathematical equations to make sense of data, while executives plan and implement new strategies. Writers use the ability to organize ideas and information.)

> *Career fields that use analytical reasoning: business management, engineering, science, mathematics, law, social science, research and writing, editing, planning, strategizing, accounting, finance, technical writing, computer programming, journalism.*

Specialized Talents

①②③❓ Spatial Visualization Orientation

Each of us is born with our own natural way of understanding the world around us. Some of us easily understand the physical world of objects and how they relate to one another, and some of us don't. The spatial/nonspatial scale provides some important basic information about how you experience and understand your environment, how you perceive the world, and what you understand and work with most naturally and easily. Deciding on a career without being aware of this important distinction has caused untold havoc in the careers of millions of people.

NON-SPATIAL   TANGIBLES   SPATIAL (3D)

People with a high spatial aptitude are comfortable working with and around three-dimensional objects. They understand how things fit together and what happens when they move or change. They are able to create images of 3D objects in their mind and consider what the object would look like if it moved or rotated. People who are low in spatial visualization aptitude are less able to picture dynamic, shifting objects in their mind—they need more reference points, or physicalized examples.

It is often easiest to understand this aptitude by considering examples of preferences and activities in the real world. High-spatial people might like to build things or fix or modify objects beyond what an average person will do. Can you take apart a computer and put it back together in a more effective way? Can you look at the trunk of a car and know roughly how many shoe-boxes would fill it? You may be high-spatial.

A simple way to estimate your level of spatial ability with IKEA furniture:

- If you don't feel the need to look at the directions for putting together a piece of IKEA furniture—and it turns out great—you are likely to be high spatial. You are apt to quickly notice and learn how things fit together in the physical world.

- If you follow the step-by-step directions for building the IKEA furniture and there's a slight lean, you may have a moderate spatial aptitude—what we call *tangible*. Those of us with a tangible level of aptitude are pretty good with simple 3D problem-solving, but you wouldn't want us to be your neurosurgeon and we may not easily comprehend the physical nature of a black hole.

- If you wouldn't even *try* to put together a piece of IKEA furniture—because you just know it would be a disaster—then you are probably non-spatial. Non-spatial folks tend to avoid activities that require more than the most basic fixing, building, or manipulation of objects. Non-spatial folks are not typically attracted to high-spatial subjects like mechanical engineering or architectural design.

①②③❓ Spatial Orientation

High-spatial orientation is an aptitude for visualizing in 3D. People with this talent are usually happiest in careers where the work is mainly concerned with thinking about or working directly with "things" (objects), especially where they spend significant time solving three-dimensional problems. Both a biologist and an architect spend most of their time at work thinking about three-dimensional objects, even though they may not come in physical contact with the actual objects. Architects without a natural talent for perceiving and working with three-dimensional reality would, in time, almost certainly grow to dislike their careers. Most people with this talent would experience a profound lack of fit with careers that are not spatial.

In the field of medicine, surgery is spatial, as are other specialties such as radiology, where it is important to think three-dimensionally. Most medical specialties fit someone who is either in the tangible part of the continuum or somewhat spatial. A dermatologist spends their day with real, tangible skin, but he or she does not need the degree of spatial ability a surgeon does.

Businesses appropriate for a spatially gifted person include such things as landscaping and construction management. Even though the manager of a construction company performs many of the same functions as any other businessperson, much of the construction manager's day involves three-dimensional thinking.

> *Career fields that use spatial orientation: some medical specialties, forensic science, physical therapy, chiropractic, dentistry, speech pathology, architecture, most engineering disciplines, physics, microbiology, organic chemistry, robotics, computer architecture, computer game design, microelectronics, most design fields, hairstyling, farming, culinary arts, sports (gymnastics, golf, basketball, football, and many others), construction, kitchen and bath design, auto mechanics, carpentry, navigating, battlefield command, manufacturing, dance and choreography, special effects in film, sculpture, and other fields that require an ability to mentally visualize in 3D. Careers that fit people with a tangible orientation are sometimes appropriate for spatial people as well.*

①②③❹ Tangible Orientation

A tangible orientation, in the middle of the continuum between spatial and non-spatial, often suggests work involving the physical (tangible) world that does not require continual 3D problem-solving. Detectives use this ability to pull together real-world facts and evidence to solve a criminal case. Most medical specialties do not require thinking in 3D and may be a good fit for some people with a tangible orientation. Antique dealers choose and surround themselves with objects. Criminal attorneys and prosecutors depend on physical evidence and a chain of tangible events. Some people in this range, especially those with humanistic personality types, enjoy careers that do not involve the physical world, but concentrate on the practical application of fields such as psychology. In recent years, real world–oriented neuroscientists have moved the understanding of human behavior forward far beyond the contributions of traditional theoretical, non-spatial psychologists.

> *Career fields that use a tangible orientation: computer programming, IT and network engineering, database design, electrical engineering, industrial engineering, wildlife biology, zoology, botany, naturalist, some medical specialties, nursing, web design, display design, product development and brand management, cosmetology, business management*

in manufacturing and product distribution, retail store and restaurant management.

①②③❓ Non-Spatial Orientation

To many, life occurs mainly as concepts that have little to do with three-dimensional reality. This ability is the opposite of spatial talent. Those scoring high on the non-spatial scale are especially gifted in understanding nonphysical, conceptual reality. When spatial people look at a house, they usually concentrate their perceptions on the structural, physical aspects of the house, whereas the non-spatial person may think mainly about the lives of the people who live in the house, its value as an investment, the feeling it projects, or any number of nonphysical perceptions or concepts about it. People with an MBA use this ability to run and improve business operations. Most lawyers test as non-spatial; constitutional lawyers fit on the far end of the non-spatial scale. Sociologists work with ideas about group behavior, and economists construct conceptual models of consumer trends.

We've met trained surgeons and engineers who tested as non-spatial who said they had to work extremely hard to perform even moderately well. Some left their field for fear of making a major mistake or becoming ill themselves from high stress.

Career fields that use non-spatial reasoning: all business disciplines: marketing, advertising, public relations, finance, accounting, human resources, sales, management; social sciences: economics, sociology, psychology, political science, demographics, actuarial mathematics, statistics, politics, cultural anthropology, gender studies, social history; humanities: philosophy, religion, language, literature, diplomacy, international relations, public policy; counseling, psychology, organizational behavior; journalism, publishing, editing, poetry.

①②③❓ Abstract ___ ①②③❓ Mixed ___ ①②③❓ Concrete ___

Some people are naturally result-oriented and driven to seek concrete results. This is obviously an important trait for anyone in a "get the job done" business. Others are perfectly happy to cogitate forever on abstractions. People who score on the abstract end of the scale are usually happiest in work that is theoretical or concept-oriented. Their work does not need to produce tangible results in the world of physical reality. For example, many economists are unperturbed when their predictions about trends turn out to be inaccurate. Their interest is in a reality so abstract that their thinking does not need to refer directly to any practical aspect of reality. When you combine this scale with the spatial/non-spatial scale, you get some excellent clues as to what sorts of careers would fit you best.

Someone with a spatial talent could be concrete, which would be appropriate for an engineer or someone in construction, or they could be abstract, like Albert Einstein. A non-spatial person could be oriented toward producing results, like a stockbroker or corporate manager, or they could be abstract, like a philosopher or Jungian psychologist. Of course, there are many other possible positions on these scales. Career difficulties are almost a certainty if you and your work do not mesh well in these important areas. Doing business with people whose profiles do not mesh with your expectations also causes untold grief. For example, many people who become psychotherapists are non-spatial abstracts. A therapist with this profile might be helpful to someone seeking more understanding or a sounding board. They would not be of much help to someone seeking to produce real concrete changes rapidly.

Here is a grid that combines natural abstract/concrete talents with the spatial/non-spatial continuum to show sample career paths:

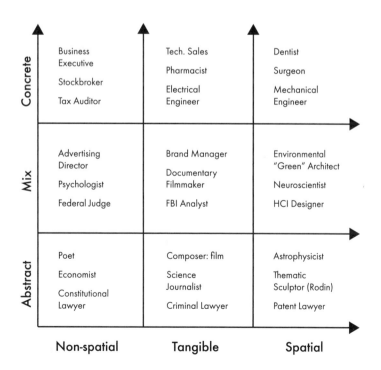

	Non-spatial	Tangible	Spatial
Concrete	Business Executive, Stockbroker, Tax Auditor	Tech. Sales, Pharmacist, Electrical Engineer	Dentist, Surgeon, Mechanical Engineer
Mix	Advertising Director, Psychologist, Federal Judge	Brand Manager, Documentary Filmmaker, FBI Analyst	Environmental "Green" Architect, Neuroscientist, HCI Designer
Abstract	Poet, Economist, Constitutional Lawyer	Composer: film, Science Journalist, Criminal Lawyer	Astrophysicist, Thematic Sculptor (Rodin), Patent Lawyer

①②③❓ **Rate of Idea Flow**

Have you noticed that some people never seem to run out of new ideas, plans, or things to say? Idea flow involves the rate at which your mind generates thoughts and ideas. It is a gauge of the quantity, not the quality, of those things. (Like water coming out of a faucet, there could be a tremendous flow of polluted water or just a trickle of the tastiest water you've ever had.) A fast flow of ideas doesn't mean that you necessarily have brilliant thoughts or ideas; it means they come quickly.

People with high idea flow are especially prolific at coming up with spur-of-the-moment ideas. They have minds that move quickly from one thought to another, from one idea to the next. They often have trouble concentrating on one thing for too long, especially if they aren't particularly interested in the task at hand. They have more difficulty than other people in concentrating on repetitive tasks—in school, they often have trouble keeping their attention focused on the professor who drones on and on. Many high-idea-flow people have a gift for improvisation and enjoy conversations that move from subject to subject. They are often good at thinking on their feet and responding quickly. It's interesting and worthwhile to note that introverts sometimes don't notice they possess this ability because it operates inside their heads. In the arts, a modern artist who painted spontaneously and quickly, like Picasso, would be a good example of quick idea flow. At the other, low-idea-flow end of the spectrum would be an engraver, who would benefit from a mind that naturally and easily focused for long periods of time.

People with a lower rate of idea flow can be just as creative as people with a fast flow—their ideas just come more slowly, or they think of them more carefully. People with lower idea flow can concentrate their energies on a particular task for a longer period of time, a helpful trait in business, science, and other process-oriented fields. (Thomas Edison experimented with hundreds of filaments before he came up with one that led to the light bulb. Someone with high idea flow might have given up and gone on to other projects.)

Your position on this scale is a good indicator of how much "flow" you need in your work during the course of each day. People with high idea flow feel more at home with, and are usually better at, work that lets thoughts continue unimpeded most of the time. Low-scoring people usually enjoy work that involves focus and concentration. As with the other abilities, there is no good or bad score—just a powerful clue about what sort of work would fit best.

Career fields that use high idea flow: advertising, marketing, comedy, acting, emergency medicine, teaching, consulting, improvisational music and arts, cartooning, newspaper journalism, TV and radio media, sales.

Mid-range idea flow: business management, design engineering, architecture, some sales, project management.

Low idea flow: dentistry, surgery, banking, accounting, auditing, insurance, computer programming, house painting, engraving.

①②③❓ Interpersonal Intelligence

There are several kinds of interpersonal or social intelligence. You may have a gift for one or more of them. One form is the ability to accurately perceive and understand others' moods, motives, and intentions. Someone with this talent has a kind of interpersonal X-ray vision that enables them to read other people, even if their subjects are attempting to conceal their true thoughts and feelings. Some people have a variety of this ability that works only with individuals, one-on-one. This is an extremely useful ability for counselors, salespeople, employment interviewers, managers, and police detectives. Others have a gift for understanding and affecting groups. The best politicians, seminar speakers, religious leaders, and teachers possess this "group reading" aptitude. A third form of social intelligence is an ability to get along with others. Some people possess all three varieties of social intelligence. Truly excellent managers have a gift for all three. They can "read people like a book." They pick up subtle signals that allow them to manage individual employees with sensitivity arid to understand the ever-changing dynamics of the group they lead. They also get along with people easily and naturally.

Career fields that use interpersonal intelligence: film directing, acting, screenwriting, creative writing, psychology fields, counseling and coaching fields, nursing, physical therapies, childcare, teaching K–12, mentoring, diplomacy, training, organizational development, people management, marketing, sales, advertising, humanities, social sciences, public policy, politics.

①②③❓ Intrapersonal Intelligence

This is your degree of access to your inner life and feelings, a natural ability to perceive and understand your own moods, motives, and behaviors. Some people have almost no access to their inner life. They can distinguish pleasure from pain, but are completely unaware of the constantly changing flow of the tides of their inner life. At the other end of the spectrum are people who are aware of every subtle emotional nuance and who can call upon these distinctions to guide their actions and choices. This keen intrapersonal intelligence is found in the best poets, novelists, actors, painters, therapists, and mentors.

> *Career fields that use intrapersonal intelligence: poet, playwright, novelist, musician, fine artist, actor, journalist, mediator, counselor, coach, therapist, teacher, professor, social scientist.*

Sensory and Perception Abilities

①②③❓ Intuition

Intuition is an imaginative way of perceiving the world around you. While your five senses see factual detail, your intuition sees the nuances or shades of meaning. For intuitives, the world is full of possibilities, and exploring new ideas, people, places, and things is what gives life its zest. They love to seek what's possible in the future; they aim to understand whole systems rather than just the parts. This is the aptitude used by scientists to raise new questions and think outside the box. Poets employ intuition to create metaphors and playfully manipulate the commonsense meaning of words. Actors use it to imagine the inner life and motives of the characters they portray.

> *Career fields that use intuition: physical sciences, life sciences, social sciences, humanities, abstract arts, poetry, acting, filmmaking, advertising, marketing, design, psychology, investigative journalism, media studies, entrepreneurs, trend forecasters.*

①②③❓ Sensing

Whereas intuition is an internalized ability, sensing is a factual way of perceiving the external world. Strong sensors trust literal details perceived by their eyes, ears, and sense of touch more than the vague impressions and hunches that come from intuition. Rather than giving their attention to speculating about possible futures, sensors jump in and get the job done. They feel at home with practical ideas and things.

> *Career fields that use sensing: engineering, medicine, dentistry, business administration, dance, physical therapy, cooking, cinematography, sales, accounting, landscape architecture, information technology, broadcast journalism, social work.*

①②③❓ Visual Dexterity

A high score in visual dexterity indicates a gift for working quickly and accurately with the clerical tasks and the pen-and-paper details of the working world—editing, accounting, secretarial work, banking, and law. If you have a high score in this aptitude, you won't necessarily have a passionate love affair with paperwork, but you will be good at getting it done quickly. Those with high scores are terrific proofreaders and extremely detail-oriented—sometimes to their detriment, making sure every t is crossed and i is dotted. People with a high score often "miss the forest for the trees," dividing life into pieces and parts, thereby missing the "big picture." Most physicians, too, are very high in visual dexterity, tending to look at ailments of the body as specific symptoms caused by the malfunction of a specific organ, instead of a broader systemic issue. (As a result, physicians with an interest in preventive medicine or with a more holistic mind-body interpretation of illness usually score somewhat lower in this measure.)

> *Career fields that use visual dexterity: accounting, auditing, banking, biotechnology, business management, computer programming, finance, forensic science, informatics, language translation, law, legal research, library science, medical research, microbiology, nanotechnology, public administration, publishing and editing.*

Memory

①②③❓ Associative Memory

This is an aptitude for learning vocabulary in other languages and memorizing by association. It can be used to learn foreign languages, technical jargon, or computer languages. It is also a useful ability for politicians and others who need to easily remember the names of many people. If you have a low or mid-range score in this ability, it does not mean that you cannot learn languages; it will just take longer for you to memorize vocabulary. A very low score suggests that you should avoid work that involves heavy doses of memorization, such as computer programming.

> *Career fields that use associative memory:* acting, ad copywriting, computer science, curriculum design, consulting, creative writing, education/teaching, humanities, journalism, language, law, medicine, museum docent, physical sciences, life and social sciences, politics, sales, training and development.

①②③❓ Number Memory

A talent for number memory suggests a gift for remembering numbers and details easily. It is useful in accounting, banking, tax law, and statistics. People with a very high score are usually gifted at remembering a vast range of encyclopedic facts and details, and are terrific at games like Trivial Pursuit. This ability is useful to tax lawyers, inventory workers, and all others who need to commit to memory a vast quantity of detailed information.

> *Career fields that use number memory:* accounting, allied health, anesthesiology, auditing, banking, bioinformatics, business journalism, business management, computer science, engineering, finance and investing, financial planning, information technology, library and information science, mathematics, management information systems, nursing, retail sales (e.g., auto parts, grocery cashier), physical and earth sciences, sports journalism, statistics, tax law.

①②③❓ Design Memory

Design memory is the ability to memorize visual information and tangible forms in the world around you. It also plays a role in navigating. Many people who are high in it quickly learn their way around a new city, and see how pieces add up to a larger picture.

Career fields that use design memory: architecture, adventure guide, antique appraiser, archivist, botany, chemistry, dance and performance arts, dentistry, earth sciences, engineering, graphic arts, fashion design, filmmaking, forensic science, interior design, industrial design, law enforcement, mechanical engineering, materials science, microbiology, patent law, aircraft piloting, physical science, medicine (especially surgery), tour guide, sports coaching (playing field strategy), surveying, taxi and truck driving, visual arts.

Other Specialized Abilities

①②③❓ Mathematical Ability

People who display a natural talent for math may have a mix of several natural abilities working together. For example, mathematics used to solve 3D problems such as geometry and advanced calculus (used in engineering fields) engages a combination of high analytical reasoning, high spatial reasoning, high number memory, and a logical temperament, the perfect recipe of strengths for math talent. Adding intuition to this mix of talents can suggest the ability for abstract mathematics such as differential calculus used in theoretical research fields in the physical and life sciences.

Career fields that use mathematical ability: actuary science, architecture, computer science, engineering, financial engineering and investing, marketing research, mathematics, physical sciences, earth sciences, economics, operations research, statistics and probability.

---

①②③❓ Language Ability

The natural talent for learning and using language involves a mix of several natural abilities working together. People with high associative memory and high analytical reasoning tend to learn languages easily. Adding in some musical talent provides the mix of abilities necessary for speaking a second language with perfect inflection.

> *Career fields that use language ability:* acting, screenwriting, print journalism, languages, law, poetry and literary arts, literary agents and editors, social sciences and humanities, politics, publishing, technical writing, scientific writing and research, science journalism.

①②③❓ Artistic and Musical Abilities

People who display a natural talent for the arts have a mix of several natural abilities working together. Each artistic expression (music, performance art, dance, and plastic and other visual arts) engages a different set of innate abilities. In all art forms, from the classical and traditional to the contemporary and improvisational, different talent combinations tend to pull the artist in the direction that comes easily and naturally.

> *Career fields that use artistic and musical abilities:* acting, advertising and commercial arts, architecture, computer video game design, dance performance arts, most design fields, filmmaking, film editing and production, film scoring, film special effects, graphic arts, music composition, musical performance arts, photography and photojournalism, literary arts, sound engineering, speech therapy, visual arts, website design.

①②③❓ Body Kinesthetic Ability

People who excel at gymnastics, athletic sports, dance and performance arts, and martial arts have just the right mix of kinesthetic talents for their specific field of performance. Other fields that require regular use of kinesthetic talents include modeling, acting, circus performing, exploring, diving, search and rescue, and law enforcement. This is, perhaps, one of the more complex ability groups of the set because it involves a number of factors including muscular-skeletal makeup, heart-lung capacity, mental-sensory perception, and other traits. A world-class cross-country skier, for example, needs larger lung capacity than a top-notch tennis player. A dancer has a very different build than a wrestler or a gymnast. Someone who excels at swimming the butterfly would find the broad chest and shoulders that is such an advantage in that sport a disadvantage in bicycle racing because it would create wind resistance.

> *Career fields that use body kinesthetic ability: acting, dance and performance arts, farming, fashion modeling, law enforcement, firefighting, heavy-equipment operation and construction, military, paramedic/ EMT, sports, search and rescue, trades.*

1. Now that you have rated each of these skill sets as they pertain to you, transfer your self-assessments to your notebook or the grid below by checking the box that you think best represents your strength in each area. If you're not sure of your strength in a certain area, check the "Not Sure" column to remind yourself to look for more clues about that ability. Think about the abilities you think may represent strong natural talents. Spend some time paying attention to your activities, noticing which talents you use often and what you do well. Also, notice what you do not do well naturally.

Natural Talents and Abilities	High	Mid	Low	Not Sure	Definite Career Components
Diagnostic Reasoning					
Analytical Reasoning					
Spatial Orientation					
Tangible Orientation					
Nonspatial Orientation					
Abstract Orientation					
Concrete Orientation					
Rate of Idea Flow					
Interpersonal Intelligence					
Intrapersonal Intelligence					
Intuition					

Natural Talents and Abilities	High	Mid	Low	Not Sure	Definite Career Components
Sensing					
Visual Dexterity					
Associative Memory					
Number Memory					
Design Memory					
Mathematical Ability					
Language Ability					
Artistic and Musical Ability					
Body Kinesthetic Ability					

2. Look back over this Inquiry. What insights did you have about yourself? Add any insights to your Clues list.

3. Were their certain abilities, or descriptions, that you see as significant to you? Any talent or aptitude that great-fit work for you would use? Or avoid? Add anything that stands out as key to you in your Career Components list.

4. See any interesting new job or career ideas? Any pop to mind? If so, add them to your Career Ideas list.

** If you have completed this chapter as well as the Inquiries in **Chapter 7—Personality and Temperament** and **Chapter 9—Social Orientation**, you may enjoy checking out **The Type and Talent Indicator** in the back of the book. It uses the results of the inquiries in these three chapters to suggest possible careers.

WHAT I DO

Throughout the next two chapters, we will explore two important elements in the Career Design process—subject matter and job function.

This section will focus on *what you are interested in* and what you would like to spend your time *doing*. Inquiries in both chapters will provide you with sets of options to consider. Great-fit work will hold your interest over time and will allow you to regularly engage in tasks and activities that allow you to use your natural talents and abilities, develop skill, and provide you with outlets of self-expression.

For sheer workability, the lists are limited and fairly mainstream. Use the provided examples as guides. If you think of, or come across, other options or ideas—write them in! *This is your Career Design.* Our provided lists and options are there to help train you on what sort of things to consider and to help you identify some key options.

Unlike many other things in life, the younger you are, or the more stable your life has been, the more difficult these sections may be for you—simply because you have less time and less variety of experiences.

If you are not familiar with something you see, or don't know much about it, do some quick research! Search engines are your friends. Who knows what you might stumble across when you look a term up. It's also okay to imagine what something would be like or if you would enjoy it. Reality being, you might have to try a thing out to know for sure, but, just because you've never done it doesn't mean you couldn't do it or wouldn't love it. Don't edit ideas out too quickly. Use your Clues and Career Ideas lists as gathering places for those wild and bold thoughts and ideas. It's all fair game!

CHAPTER 11

+

SUBJECT MATTER AND INTERESTS

Let yourself be drawn by the stronger pull of that which you truly love.

—RUMI

Have you ever met someone who, as long as you've known them, has had a singular and unique interest? Maybe as a kid, they knew everything about a particular topic or subject. They were an aficionado of 1970s muscle cars or of grandfather clock mechanics. Maybe you were that kid or that teenager—someone with a clear interest (or obsession) a bit different or more extreme than your peers. Not the normal kid fascination with dinosaurs or superheroes, but an all-out interest in black holes, segmented worms, or ancient Japanese swords. An interest that didn't go away when the possibilities of dating began to consume much of your attention.

People vary in the variety, number, and intensity of interests they have. Some of us have one strong interest over our lifetime, others go through phases—picking up and putting down interests seasonally. Some people live for uncovering new interests and some never need more than they've always had. If you are someone with an interest that clearly and obviously surpasses all others, and you *know* that great-fit work for you must include that interest, fabulous! Create a Career Component, something like "My work will involve Amazonian dart frogs," and you can skip the rest of this chapter. Your subject matter is handled.

But, if you don't have quite this level of clarity in certainty, you might fit into one of a few other categories:

1. You know that it is really important for you to be interested in your work's subject matter—you can't engage unless you care about it.

2. You find many things interesting and don't have a particular need to have a career focusing on a topic or subject currently interesting to you. And it might be really cool to incorporate your personal interests into your career.

3. You have hobbies and interests that you love, and you prefer them to be separate from your work life. You don't want to muddy the waters of enjoying your interests for their own sake.

4. You are not particularly concerned about the subject matter of your work. You are more interested in the specific tasks and activities your career involves (addressed in the next chapter, "Job Functions").

Subject matter tends to be one of the most important factors in a career search for a few notable groups:

- Those who have a hardcore, longtime fascination or interest in a subject.

- Those making formal education or training decisions. Which program to enter? What major to declare? If you are about to spend $100,000 (or much more!) for a university program—the subject matter and program you enter should be important to you.

- Those who have acquired a lot of specialized training or education in a particular area. After you just spent eight years getting a PhD in nineteenth-century Russian literature, subject matter may again be a clear and important Career Component for you (or not); or you may discover there are no jobs available.

- Those with a lot of work experience, subject matter knowledge, or mastery in a certain field or industry. If you know that you would not sleep at night if you weren't leveraging your twenty years of experience, you might strategically choose an alternative focus for your work.

- Those who are values-driven (see chapter 12) and want their work to impact a field or problem of importance to them.

- Those who want a substantial career change and want to avoid repeating the past. If you have been bored out of your mind for the past fifteen years, or haven't felt like your work was meaningful (further addressed in chapter 13), identifying fields that light you up might make a difference.

Not everyone designs their career based on the subject matter. For many of us, subject matter is more flexible, or of less importance, than our *Job Functions* (chapter 12) or *Values* (chapter 13).

Here's an example: When Nick was in the process of choosing his career, many long years ago, he did not have one specific subject interest, but he had made several definite choices and commitments about his future work. They were:

1. "I will never work for another company again."

2. "My work will put me in the forefront of developing a field that is encumbered in old ideas and is in dire need of creative, breakthrough work."

3. "I won't go into a field like medical research because it is full of supercompetent people, and I am not at all competitive."

4. "It is a field that I can spend a lifetime exploring, expanding, and contributing to without getting bored."

5. "As a result of my work, many thousands of lives will be transformed, and, as a result, will live happier, more fulfilled lives."

Leading up to the time when he created the field of Career Design and Career Coaching, and before he started writing books and things, Nick hadn't thought of work as an interest. His passions were: his organic farm, Buddhism, sailing, positive psychology, and nature. And, after a lot of thought and research, he identified one field that would enable him to fulfill all of his commitments—Careers and Jobs became his field of choice. It fit his definite Components. This is how the Career Design field entered his career design. A subject matter interest grew out of a series of desired functions.

This is fairly common: like Nick did, people start identifying key pieces of importance within the career framework, and then investigate and look for other features and factors that fit those pieces. Adding the new pieces to your Career Design, they point in a definite direction, and then you become interested in that focus.

So, now it's your turn.

Let's identify topics, subject matters, or issues that you know you find interesting. Even if you are very flexible about the specific subject matter addressed, having a short list of clear interests is helpful. Subject matter might tip the scale on your Career Choice or shorten and simplify future job searches.

The Inquiries that follow are designed to help get your juices flowing and provide a structure to help you. It would be overwhelming, and darn impossible, for us to provide a comprehensive list of subjects for you to consider, but what you'll find below can get you started. Be open-minded, and investigate and explore when something piques your interest. Look for Clues and Components along the way.

INQUIRY 20

My Interests

Please write down your responses to the following series of questions:

1. What topics, issues, fields, and subjects do you find interesting?

2. Think back to your childhood. What were your top interests? How was your room decorated? What did you play with? What was your favorite subject in school? What was your favorite way to spend time outside of school?

3. As a teen, what clubs, groups, or activities did you participate in? What were your favorite school subjects? What was your dream career? What did you spend your time doing outside of school?

4. What hobbies, activities, clubs, volunteer positions have you participated in? Sports, recreation, crafts, home repair, gardening? Anything you really would like to pick up again?

5. What subjects have you studied? Formally (college, tech school, etc.) and informally (online classes, seminars, self-taught, etc.). What were your favorite classes or subjects?

6. Thinking about your work experience, what topics, subjects, issues, or problem types do you, or have you, enjoyed? What have you wanted to do more of? Learn more about?

7. If you were considering going back to school or to get more training, what subjects would you pursue?

8. What do you wish you had more time to do? What would you like to learn more about?

9. What types of books, magazines, or online articles do you read? Any particular subject matter or genre?

10. How about other forms of media? What podcasts do you listen to? You-Tube videos do you watch? What websites do you have bookmarked on your computer?

    Now look back over your list of responses. What subjects or topics do they suggest? Make a list of those that you identified. Bonus: Ask people who know you well. What do they think you are most interested in? They may remind you of something or notice something insightful that you missed. If they do, add it to your list.

Hopefully from this exercise you've been able to build a list of subjects that you find interesting. Maybe they've been in your life for a long time, or maybe you've become interested in them more recently. Both are perfect. Now that you've had an opportunity to look for yourself and come up with a list of interests, we have an additional list of subjects for you to consider. Remember: Don't edit yourself. You are not limited to your past—what you have already experienced or what you know a lot about. If you find a subject interesting, even if you have very little personal experience with it—make a note. When you review all the subjects that catch your interest, you may see a common thread. For example, if you find dart frogs, crocodiles, and cobras interesting, herpetology may be worth further investigation.

INQUIRY 21

My Interests, Part 2

Work through the list of subjects below, marking your level of interest, and add helpful comments as you go. At the bottom, there are several rows for you to add in subjects not included in this list (such as those you identified in Inquiry 20).

   Tip: Use the Notes columns to add any specifics that matter to you. For example, under the subject "Languages" if you are only interested in the Spanish language, you might add "Spanish" to the Notes column. Similarly, if you are a big fan of Noam Chomsky, or specifically interested in how non-human animals use language, you could write a note about that.

Subject	Level of Interest			Notes
	None or low	Some	High	
Adventure				
Aging				
Animals				
Anthropology				
Anxiety & Depression				
Archaeology				
Architecture				
Artificial Intelligence				
Arts: visual, graphic, multimedia, etc.				
Arts & Crafts				
Astronomy: space, planets, sciences				
Beliefs				
Books & Literature				
Bugs, Spiders, Bees				
Business: strategy, growth, finance, management				
Careers & Vocations				
Cars				
Child Development & Child-rearing				
Cities				
Clothes: fashion, design				
Coding & Programming				
Coffee, Tea, Alcohol				
Communication				
Community Service				
Comparitive Cultures, Religions				
Computers & Information Technology				
Conservation				
Construction & Building				

Subject	Level of Interest			Notes
	None or low	Some	High	
Cooking				
Crime & Law Enforcement				
Culture				
Current Events				
Data: science, analysis, etc.				
Design: interior, graphic, etc.				
Dinosaurs				
Ecology				
Ecosystems				
Effectiveness				
Efficiency				
Engineering				
Entrepreneurship				
Environment				
Family				
Farms				
Film & TV				
Finance				
Fitness				
Food & Nutrition				
Forensics				
Forests				
Friendship				
Games				
Gaming: design, story, coding, tech				
Geography				
Goals				
Government & Policy				
Habits				

Subject	Level of Interest			Notes
	None or low	Some	High	
History				
Human Development				
Humor				
Improvement				
Innovation				
Investment				
Jewelry: design, craft, fashion				
Languages				
Law				
Leadership				
Learning & Education				
Libraries & Curation				
Lifestyle				
Love				
Machine Learning				
Marketing & Advertising				
Mechanics				
Medicine & Health				
Mental Illness				
Military: tactics, weaponry, leadership, organization				
Money				
Mountains				
Music				
Mythology & Folklore				
Nano and Quantum Mechanics				
Natural Resources				
Nature				
New Technology				

Subject	Level of Interest			Notes
	None or low	Some	High	
Performing Arts				
Personal Growth & Improvement				
Pets: care, training				
Philosophy				
Physical Health and Well-being				
Physics				
Planes				
Planning & Organization				
Plants & Trees				
Politics				
Preservation				
Problems: personal				
Project Management				
Psychology				
Public Safety				
Real Estate				
Recreation & Hobbies				
Relationships				
Religion				
Repair				
Restaurants & Bars				
Risk				
Robotics & Drones				
Rockets & Space Travel				
Safety & Security				
Sales				
School				
Science				
Seas & Oceans				

Subject	Level of Interest			Notes
	None or low	Some	High	
Self-care				
Sex				
Shopping				
Sleep				
Social Justice				
Social & National Policy				
Social Trends				
Spirituality				
Sports				
Storms				
Stress Relief				
Superpowers				
Talents & Abilities				
Technology				
Traditions & Rituals				
Trains				
Transportation				
Travel				
Virtual Technology				
Water				
Weather & Seasons				
Web Design & Mastering				
Writing: creative, technical, journalism, etc.				
Yoga & Mindfulness				

Take a look back at your designations. Is there anything that you are not interested in that you have been doing or that has been a part of your work? That might be an important Clue. Maybe you could be wild and crazy and create a Component declaring a future that does not include that.

An example: *Monica was in the real estate mortgage industry for eleven years. She was clear that she did not want to continue in that industry. A bold Component for Monica was "I will not work in the mortgage industry." An alternative, if more appropriate, could have been "I will not be in a sales role in an industry that is highly price competitive." In that Component, she is acknowledging and addressing one of the aspects of that business that she hated.*

Look back over your responses from Inquiries 20 and 21. What Clue(s) can you create about your strong interests? Add 'em to your list.

Are you ready to declare a Component—anything that you are clear that great-fit work would include or not? Go ahead and do so.

Remember, as you work through the Career Design process, you are not hammering any of your Clues into stone. You are not tattooing any of your Components onto your body. If and when new insights or ideas show up, you can modify your design (Clues and Components) to include the new information.

✦

CHAPTER 12

JOB FUNCTIONS

You are what you repeatedly do.

—ARISTOTLE

In the last chapter, you considered subjects of interest to you. Now you're going to shift your focus from the topic (e.g., microchips, human development, or sports)—to your role within it.

What Do You Want to DO?

No matter what your job is, you are paid to perform certain functions and produce specific results. Whether you are interviewing for a job, looking at a listing, or trying to create one from scratch, it is always helpful to have clarity about the main roles and responsibilities your future work would include: Are you planning and leading videoconference calls? Brushing sand off of bits of pottery and bone somewhere west of the Nile? Dancing onstage?

Your job functions should fit your talents and abilities and personality and what is most important to you. Nearly everyone who operates at a high skill level and loves their work spends their days performing functions that express their strongest talents. They do what comes naturally. If you are working in a field or industry of interest to you, and your day is filled with doing things you like to do, you are well on your way to having a career that you love!

Generalist or Specialist?

Specific positions vary in the number of functions and responsibilities they entail. In some jobs, you may have only one or two specific functions. In others, you may regularly perform a wide range. As a first step, think about which side of that spectrum you'd like to fall onto.

In chapter 9, on social orientation, we distinguished two types: Tribal and Maestro, and within those types we talked about generalizing and specializing. Surprise, surprise! They come into play again here.

As a reminder: those with a strong Maestro tendency tend toward specialization, seeking to focus on one of the interests and activities of most importance to them. They tend to appreciate work that allows them to deep dive into subjects and activities they choose, and find it more challenging to engage in, or stick with, tasks or responsibilities they don't value or enjoy. It is common that their career paths require many years of targeted education or training: lawyers, doctors, astrophysicists. A lot of Maestros are also attracted to self-employment, which allows them to do their own thing, the way they want to do it. (The twist being that the dynamic that attracts Maestros to independent businesses, the ability to focus on what they want to do, leads to the biggest problem they have—dealing with the large variety of functions they need to perform to make it work!)

Those with a strong Tribal social orientation may be, in some ways, less particular. They gravitate toward pragmatism and productivity—wanting to be good at what they do, and properly prepared, but also more willing and able to take on a wider variety of regular responsibilities. This kind of thinking makes them, typically, a Generalist. Some people call it a jack-of-all-trades. You often see highly developed Generalists successfully leading companies or running their own businesses, because they are (and need to be) proficient at a few different kinds of things within the workspace. A CEO, for example, needs to know about sales, marketing, and how to manage people, plus organizational structures, finance, and technology—and then, to carry out those functions on a more detailed level, they delegate the work to specialists.

People, Ideas, and Things

Not only do the Job Functions of specific positions and career paths differ in number, they also vary in focus. There may be a single focus area; or there may be two or more areas and other necessary functions. Some functions are *directly people-oriented*—customer service representatives, supervisors, therapists, and teachers. When conducting these functions, you are speaking with, working with, acting upon, or directly concerned with people.

Other functions are *idea- and data-centered*. Idea-centered functions include those working with or manipulating all types of data, information, or ideas. Songwriters, historians, editors, and data analysts fall into this category, all performing functions that heavily involve data/information/ideas.

Third, job functions can be *thing-focused*; i.e., careers that design, develop, test, and build objects. Surgeons, surfboard shapers, and landscape architects are all thing-focused careers.

Like types of intelligence, these job functions can group together and work in tandem within a specific role. For example, a journalist's primary function is writing news stories, an idea-centered function, but they may spend significant time in people- and data-oriented functions as well: interviewing, researching, fact-checking, and putting all of that information together into a story. We call those other elements "secondary," or "supporting," functions.

Being realistic about how these functions interact with one another is crucial to identifying, finding, and being happy with a career.

Many smart, hardworking, and caring people turn to the field of medicine, but not all of them turn to the right specialty or role. A general practitioner (GP), a surgeon, a radiologist, and a research oncologist may all have the same field of study and same medical degree (MD), but have substantially different job functions. A GP interacts more with people, a surgeon with technology and bodies, and a research oncologist's primary focus is ideas. These days, a psychiatrist is often more of an expert in the complexities of psychopharmacology than in therapy. The field of medicine, like many others, is vast and diverse. Paying attention to the job functions of a specific role is essential.

Do your research before you make your final career decision to make sure you are basing your choice on accurate information. We have worked with many frustrated physicians (to extend the prior example) who envisioned themselves as hands-on diagnosticians and healers. They imagine their work filled with warm, personal interactions with patients where they use their knowledge and training to provide care. Instead, some have found the reality of their job functions to be more mechanical—spending more time managing technology and databases than listening to individual patients. Many have also felt the burden of having to conform to health insurance companies and the paperwork and rules associated with it, limiting patient interactions. If you are considering a career in medicine, look closely at what each area of the discipline offers. If your primary wish is to have direct and personal interactions with people, the role of nurse practitioner or holistic practitioner *may* be a better fit for you than that of a general practitioner or surgeon.

Also be wary of choosing a career with interesting subject matter without considering the fit of the day-to-day activities. Just because you love carpets woven by nomads in the Persian deserts doesn't necessarily mean you will love selling them, or studying them, or weaving them. The trick is to find a way to have it all: work where you perform a set of functions you really enjoy, using your best talents in a career that fits with your personality and values combined with a subject matter that you care about.

Before you step into the next Inquiry, take a minute to consider the work you have done and the careers of people you know. Look for the central function, and look at what might be considered supporting ones. Think about whether the former is what you were promised when you started the job, or if the latter has come to define your workflow.

You are now are going to have a chance to get clear about which functions are your best and most natural forms of self-expression. This is an especially important

Inquiry because, if you can pin down the functions you will perform, you will have solved some big pieces of the puzzle: What do you do naturally, without being asked? What are the functions you just can't help doing when an opportunity is presented?

People stuck in careers that don't really fit often find a way to do what comes naturally, either at work or after work. Someone whose natural functions lean toward teaching, but is stuck in an assistant job, may find a way to function as an educator on the job or after work, seeking out opportunities to explain things to others, or helping kids with their homework. Another assistant with a gift for counseling may be the one everyone trusts to listen to their problems and advise them. Your activities and interests outside of work also provide Clues about what functions express you most naturally.

Some folks hate to "box themselves in" by narrowing the field to just a few functions; they say they want to perform a wide range—but almost everyone, no matter how creative, brilliant, or successful, does work that concentrates three or less. Even the multitalented Leonardo da Vinci concentrated his work into three areas over his extraordinary life: creating art, designing three-dimensional objects, and investigating the physical world. This doesn't mean you will not get to do many other things as significant parts of your work or your life outside of work. In fact, we suppose there is no reason why you cannot do everything in the following functions list, if you so desire. But use this Inquiry to pin down just a few major functions.

What are you being paid to spend your time doing? What specific tasks and activities are primary and active in the pursuit of your work efforts and goals? What job functions are central in your Career Design?

INQUIRY 22

Job Functions

1. Start at the beginning of the Job Functions list (below). Place a check-mark in front of the functions that come naturally to you or express what you do best. Even if you haven't done them, still mark them if there's interest—your future career does not need to be limited to what you have done before!

2. Some entries have several versions of a function on one line. If one or more really stands out, circle it.

3. If you think of something not listed—write it in. This will be especially helpful if you have a specific or niche job function in mind.

4. When you have finished, go to the end of the functions list, where the instructions will continue. Remember, this is just Nick and Monica's list. You may find that you have functions that are not listed below.

People-Oriented Functions and Activities: Primarily One-on-One

Problem-Solving, Providing Expert Advice

__ ①②③④⑤ Mentoring, one-on-one teaching, instructing, training, tutoring
__ ①②③④⑤ Counseling, coaching, guiding, empowering
__ ①②③④⑤ Healing, treating the diseases or problems of, rehabilitate
__ ①②③④⑤ Advising, consulting with
__ ①②③④⑤ Assessing, evaluating
__ ①②③④⑤ Diagnosing, analyzing, or understanding an individual's needs, mood, motives, responses, behavior, etc.
__ ①②③④⑤ Using intuition or nonverbal clues to understand individuals
__ ①②③④⑤ Observing, studying behaviors
__ ①②③④⑤ Other _____

Supporting, Enabling, Hosting, Entertaining

__ ①②③④⑤ Encouraging, supporting
__ ①②③④⑤ Providing emotional support
__ ①②③④⑤ Promoting, being an agent for others
__ ①②③④⑤ Listening
__ ①②③④⑤ Being understanding and patient with others
__ ①②③④⑤ Enabling, assisting other people to locate information
__ ①②③④⑤ Helping, serving, providing needs of individuals
__ ①②③④⑤ Assisting, caretaking
__ ①②③④⑤ Hosting
__ ①②③④⑤ Entertain, amuse, converse with
__ ①②③④⑤ Give pleasure to

__①②③④⑤ Using your personal charisma
__①②③④⑤ Other _____

Managing, Informing, General Administrative Activities

__①②③④⑤ Cultivating and maintaining relationships
__①②③④⑤ Selecting, screening, hiring
__①②③④⑤ Managing, supervising
__①②③④⑤ Giving instructions, providing information to
__①②③④⑤ Persuading, selling, motivating, influencing, enrolling, recruiting
__①②③④⑤ Interviewing
__①②③④⑤ Communicating verbally with
__①②③④⑤ Bring together, introduce
__①②③④⑤ Networking, building alliances and relationships
__①②③④⑤ Negotiating between individuals, arbitrating
__①②③④⑤ Other _____

People-Oriented Functions and Activities:
Primarily with Groups, Organizations, the Public, or Humanity

Problem-Solving, Providing Expert Advice to a Group

__①②③④⑤ Empowering, enabling a group
__①②③④⑤ Instructing, teaching, training a group
__①②③④⑤ Guiding a group through a healing process
__①②③④⑤ Diagnosing, analyzing, or understanding a group's existing or potential needs, mood, motives, responses, behavior
__①②③④⑤ Using intuition or nonverbal clues to understand a group or individuals in a group setting
__①②③④⑤ Consulting to affect a group or organization's productivity, behavior
__①②③④⑤ Advising a group, providing expertise
__①②③④⑤ Designing events or educational experiences
__①②③④⑤ Creating activities, games
__①②③④⑤ Other _____

Managing, Leading, Interacting with a Group

_①②③④⑤ Managing, leading a group, organization, or company
_①②③④⑤ Initiating, creating, founding a group of people or a company
_①②③④⑤ Supervising, captaining a group or team
_①②③④⑤ Team member such as a member of a work group, athlete, orchestra member
_①②③④⑤ Leading a group in recreation, games, exercise, travel, rehabilitation
_①②③④⑤ Negotiating between groups, resolving conflicts or disputes, bringing conflicting groups together
_①②③④⑤ Inspiring a group
_①②③④⑤ Facilitating, guiding a group
_①②③④⑤ Other _____

Influencing and Persuading a Group

_①②③④⑤ Persuading, motivating, convincing, or selling to a group
_①②③④⑤ Using personal charisma
_①②③④⑤ Networking with groups
_①②③④⑤ Communicating verbally with groups, public speaking, or communicating verbally through the media
_①②③④⑤ Communicating with people via art, music, writing, film, or other art forms
_①②③④⑤ Other _____

Entertaining and Hosting Group Functions

_①②③④⑤ Hosting, entertaining socially
_①②③④⑤ Amusing, providing entertainment or pleasure
_①②③④⑤ Performing, acting
_①②③④⑤ Presenting to people via TV, films, seminars, speeches
_①②③④⑤ Selecting, screening prospective members or employees
_①②③④⑤ Assisting, serving, helping
_①②③④⑤ Other _____

Information-Oriented Functions and Activities:
Primarily with Ideas, Data, Media, Knowledge, Wisdom, or Art

Creating, Designing, and Using Imagination

__①②③④⑤ Idea generating, creating, inventing, imagining
__①②③④⑤ Asking new questions, pioneering new ideas
__①②③④⑤ Brainstorming
__①②③④⑤ Drawing, painting, filming, photographing
__①②③④⑤ Creating original works of art, including music
__①②③④⑤ Creating visual or written presentations or presentations using other media
__①②③④⑤ Creating marketing materials, advertisements, promotional campaigns
__①②③④⑤ Creating activities, games, or other experiential learning activities
__①②③④⑤ Designing events or educational experiences
__①②③④⑤ Writing fiction, creative writing—poetry, essays, novels, scripts
__①②③④⑤ Performing, acting
__①②③④⑤ Presenting to people via TV, films, seminars, speeches
__①②③④⑤ Information engineering, database design, computer programming
__①②③④⑤ Information architecture, such as in website design
__①②③④⑤ Creating software or similar works
__①②③④⑤ Designing research experiments to make new discoveries
__①②③④⑤ Other _____

Problem-Solving, Researching, Investigating

__①②③④⑤ Diagnosing by seeing the relationship between clues
__①②③④⑤ Analyzing by perceiving patterns in data, events, or processes, or accurately evaluating information
__①②③④⑤ Seeing through masses of information to the central principles or most important facts
__①②③④⑤ Breaking masses of data down into component parts, analyzing
__①②③④⑤ Synthesizing: combining parts to form a whole
__①②③④⑤ Systematizing, prioritizing, categorizing, or organizing information

__①②③④⑤ Deciding what data or information to collect
__①②③④⑤ Conducting research to develop new ideas, theories
__①②③④⑤ Researching via observing behavior or phenomena
__①②③④⑤ Researching by gathering or compiling information
__①②③④⑤ Making decisions about the meaning of data or information
__①②③④⑤ Other _____

Reading, Learning, Mastering a Body of Knowledge

__①②③④⑤ Reading, learning, gathering information
__①②③④⑤ Interpreting other people's concepts, ideas
__①②③④⑤ Adapting information to suit another purpose
__①②③④⑤ Combining existing ideas or concepts into new ones
__①②③④⑤ Mastering a specialized body of knowledge, expertise, wisdom, lore
__①②③④⑤ Other _____

Critiquing, Evaluating, Making Recommendations

__①②③④⑤ Critiquing other people's ideas
__①②③④⑤ Critiquing works of art, such as in script reading, book reviews, film reviews
__①②③④⑤ Critical writing, such as nonfiction, journalism, and science writing
__①②③④⑤ Technical writing, such as in business, law, technology, medicine, public policy
__①②③④⑤ Judging, evaluating, or appraising information
__①②③④⑤ Using physical senses to evaluate information
__①②③④⑤ Process improvement, making systems more efficient
__①②③④⑤ Risk and opportunity cost analysis
__①②③④⑤ Making recommendations, providing solutions
__①②③④⑤ Troubleshooting, debugging, and maintaining software
__①②③④⑤ Editing to improve content
__①②③④⑤ Using mathematics, numbers, statistics, working with formulas to evaluate
__①②③④⑤ Other _____

Organizing, Planning, Improving, Other General Administrative Activities

__①②③④⑤ Organizing information, projects, or events
__①②③④⑤ Project management, setting goals and milestones, budgeting, status reporting
__①②③④⑤ Planning, strategizing, forecasting
__①②③④⑤ Translating, interpreting information to another language, medium, or style
__①②③④⑤ Copyediting to improve grammar, syntax
__①②③④⑤ Retrieving or finding information, researching, compiling information
__①②③④⑤ Entering data into a computer, data entry, word processing
__①②③④⑤ Comparing, proofing
__①②③④⑤ Accounting, bookkeeping, business mathematics
__①②③④⑤ Recordkeeping, storing, filing
__①②③④⑤ Other _____

Thing-Oriented Functions and Activities: Primarily with Objects, Tools, the Human Body, or the Physical World

Problem-Solving and Understanding Complex Physical Systems

__①②③④⑤ Understanding complex physical systems such as in the physical sciences, medicine, engineering, and technology
__①②③④⑤ Diagnosing and analyzing complex mechanical systems such as a mechanic, engineer, physician, or veterinarian does
__①②③④⑤ Repairing or improving complex mechanical systems
__①②③④⑤ Other _____

Creating, Designing, Inventing Physical Objects, Including Art

__①②③④⑤ Designing complex physical systems
__①②③④⑤ Creating new theories, understanding or interpreting physical systems
__①②③④⑤ Inventing, creating, designing original devices or objects
__①②③④⑤ Directing films or plays, choreographing scenes, storyboarding

__①②③④⑤ Creating works of three-dimensional art
__①②③④⑤ Other _____

Evaluating, Critiquing, Fixing, and Repairing Objects and Things

__①②③④⑤ Evaluating and critiquing physical objects, including food, art, design, or the human body
__①②③④⑤ Appraising and judging physical objects, including food, arts, design, or the human body
__①②③④⑤ Repairing or restoring things, maintaining
__①②③④⑤ Assembling
__①②③④⑤ Other _____

Crafting, Beautifying, Using Tools to Produce Objects

__①②③④⑤ Sculpting, shaping, tooling
__①②③④⑤ Crafting (combining artistic and motor skills to fashion things)
__①②③④⑤ Employing fine hand dexterity (as used by surgeon, dentist, craftsman, artist, musician)
__①②③④⑤ Precision use of tools
__①②③④⑤ Manufacturing or mass-producing objects
__①②③④⑤ Cooking, preparing, or displaying food
__①②③④⑤ Choosing, arranging objects artistically
__①②③④⑤ Utilizing eye for design, color, texture, or proportion
__①②③④⑤ Sensual acuity of sight, sound, smell, taste, or feel
__①②③④⑤ Other _____

Athletics, Performing Expertly with the Body, Manipulating the Human Anatomy

__①②③④⑤ Dancing or choreographing dance routines
__①②③④⑤ Using physical agility, fine sensory motor skills, strength, and dexterity in athletics and other fields such as law enforcement, firefighting, emergency medicine
__①②③④⑤ Using spatial visualization for gymnastics, figure skating, diving, and other sports that require visualizing body movements

__①②③④⑤ Performing stunts or other extreme physical feats
__①②③④⑤ Massaging, adjusting, touching, hands-on healing
__①②③④⑤ Other _____

Operating Machines and Equipment

__①②③④⑤ Operating an airplane, ship or boat, truck or car, motorcycle or bicycle
__①②③④⑤ Using large tools such as bulldozers and other construction machinery, tanks
__①②③④⑤ Constructing buildings or other large objects, such as bridges and roads
__①②③④⑤ Operating, controlling, or guiding machines
__①②③④⑤ Tending machines
__①②③④⑤ Fighting, using firearms or other weapons
__①②③④⑤ Installing
__①②③④⑤ Cleaning, preparing, washing, dusting
__①②③④⑤ Moving, storing, warehousing, carrying, lifting, handling
__①②③④⑤ Other _____

Interacting with the Physical World, Including Nature

__①②③④⑤ Navigating, orienteering, pathfinding, exploring
__①②③④⑤ Farming, gardening, growing, or tending to plants or animals
__①②③④⑤ Acute awareness of surroundings, physical environment, nature
__①②③④⑤ Using street wisdom, acute alertness to threats to survival
__①②③④⑤ Hunting, trapping, fishing
__①②③④⑤ Other _____

After you have made your first pass, go back over the functions again.

1. Examine all the ones you marked and rate your estimated natural ability for each by marking the numbered circles. One ① is the lowest rating; five ⑤ is the highest. This will be easier if you have a lot of experience with the Job Function. It will be more difficult for things you haven't. If you do not have a history with a Job Function that you are keen on,

look for evidence that you would be good at it—your experience with similar problems, tasks, or activities, your interest and success in related classes, and results from an objective aptitude test. Especially if you are a young adult or have had little variety of work experience, you may not be able to discern a natural talent for something unfamiliar. That you have a strong pull toward the activity is helpful. Sometimes, you may need to make your best-effort guess about a thing.

2. Next, narrow down your top functions to a maximum of ten. You are whittling down to your top functions based on your sense of fit, appeal, and talent.

3. Then narrow the ten to somewhere around five final, most important, most fitting functions. Get to the real essentials. If you have many functions marked and have difficulty selecting a few, it may be that you do not want to toss out things you like to do or give up on having work with diverse activities. You don't have to surrender anything, just find the ones that describe the major activities you will do every day. The things that dominate what you spend your time doing.

4. Look over your selections. Are there any themes or clusters of similar functions? Do most of your highest-rated functions involve people, information, or things? Are there any clusters of functions in a specific subcategory, such as "Problem-Solving," "Providing Expert Advice," or "Managing, Leading, Interacting with a Group"? (If one section dominates, that's a pretty good Clue that your work should concentrate in that area.) One way to begin narrowing things down is to look for clusters of functions that work together. If you selected a group of activities that can operate as a series of steps in a process, you can group them into a single function. For example, a cluster of functions such as using intuition or nonverbal clues to understand individuals, observing behaviors, listening, assessing, diagnosing moods and motives, and making recommendations can be grouped under a single combined function such as advising or counseling. Perhaps a group of functions from different categories combine in some way, such as running a particular kind of business. Another way to reduce the number of your selections is to imagine performing them for several hours each day forever. Do any of them lose their appeal when put to the volume test? Push yourself to get past the romance of functions that may sound good for only a few hours a week or less.

5. See if you can pick one or two of your final five as your primary function or functions. If you can't, don't worry—just go to the next step.

6. Are any of your final five functions obviously secondary or supporting functions? For example, someone who sells high-end audio gear may have selling as a primary function and teaching, advising, and learning about new gear as secondary.

Having difficulty sorting out what's primary and what's not? Try this:

1. List your final five.

2. Try out some playful scenarios. For example: imagine you died and woke up in heaven with an angel wringing her hands and saying she had made a terrible mistake—the person who was supposed to get run over by the truck was right behind you and wearing the same clothes. You get to go back to earth, and to make up for the confusion, you can pick four of your top five functions to use in whatever job you'd like. You have to drop or demote one of the five. Which one would it be?

3. Another approach is to simulate your workday. Create a pie chart to visually imagine how much of your day might make use of your top functions. The following example illustrates a workday breakdown of

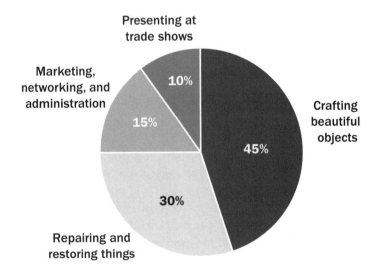

an actual career, someone who runs her own arts-and-crafts business. There are one primary function and three secondary ones. Notice that the primary function, crafting beautiful objects, comprises about half of the workday, and the secondary tasks and activities are support functions that are performed less often, but are just as important to the job. Create some experimental pie charts, simulating several possible workday scenarios by varying the percentage of time for each function. Explore different combinations until one clicks for you.

4. Once you've done that, look back over this Inquiry for clues. Add whatever you find. Then ask, "Is there anything I am willing to choose as a definite component?" Add anything you choose to your Career Design Components. Do any new careers/jobs come to mind? If so, add them to your Career Ideas.

WHY I DO IT

Now that we have the "what," we will spend time over the next two chapters delving into the WHY. Most of us work to earn money. Income is an important reason to work. It can strongly influence the choices we make. No reason it shouldn't. But **for those of us seeking a lifetime of satisfaction and success, the job provides more than a paycheck.**

Not only does great-fit work hold your interest over time, it allows you to regularly engage in tasks and activities that allow you to use your natural talents and abilities, and earn a paycheck. It also provides you with *a sense of purpose* and the feeling that *what you do matters*. Here you will focus in on what motivates you, calls to you, and provides you with a sense of *fulfillment*. You will explore the inherent sources of *motivation, engagement, and meaning* that, once identified, can provide you with a renewable source of energy and power. Here lies *the rocket fuel* for your career.

Section 3.3 has two chapters, each addressing WHY I DO IT through different lenses.

Chapter 13: *Values*
Chapter 14: *Passion, Meaning, and Purpose*

CHAPTER 13

+

VALUES

I will not let anyone walk through my mind with their dirty feet.

—MAHATMA GANDHI

You've already identified many factors that, combined well, will help you design a wonderful career. Piecing together your natural abilities and personality, subjects you find interesting, and the functions you want to perform—whether you realize it or not—your career design is more than half-finished! Take a moment and let that sink in.

While we have a few more subjects to explore before we start investigating specific jobs and careers in the real world, we are heading toward the point in the process where you will have to make some definitive choices. That can be scary, but remember: you are doing all of this exploratory and investigative work now so that you are well prepared for future career choices.

This chapter will help you better understand, fundamentally, what motivates you and what you need to feel fulfilled. By identifying your core personal values, you will be better able to evaluate and steer yourself toward work and work environments that fill you with a sense of satisfaction and success.

But first, we are going to do an Inquiry to refresh your brain on the work you have already done and look at your progress.

ASIDE 5

Progress Check

Let me tell you the secret that has led me to my goal. My strength lies solely in my tenacity.

—LOUIS PASTEUR

If you've worked through the entire book thus far, you've read twelve chapters and completed twenty-two Inquiries. You've created and added to three main lists—Clues, Components, and Career Ideas—that have served as gathering places for your insights, ideas, and design components. Update your lists now. You should find it informative, refreshing, and encouraging. Think of these questions as you do:

1. Do you remember when you started reading this book? When did you do your first Inquiry?

2. Do you remember what you knew you wanted when you began this journey? Do you remember how many items you had on your Clues, Components, and Career lists when you started?

Now look at your Clues, Components, and Career lists. How many items do you have on each list now? By far, the most important part of this project is your definite components. Everything else is just a way to define those components.

If you've been doing the Inquiries, but haven't updated your three lists with the "takeaways" from each Inquiry, go back and do this now. This may take a while, but is an important step.

If you have added new items to your lists, how many items do you now have on each?

Look at your Components list. Read each one and consider if there is a way you could make it more specific or measurable. Does each of them describe an element of great-fit work for you? Modify them as helpful.

Is a picture beginning to form? Is there anything that you know you still have to figure out? If you have a question, or questions, that you know you need to handle before you make a career choice, make a bold note of it now.

Whether or not the specific topic is covered in these chapters, get it answered for yourself.

Look again at the progress you've made! Think of what you were sure about when you began. Look at the Components and Career Ideas you have now. We still have some fun stuff to do, but you are over halfway there!

Needs, Wants, Preferences, and Values

Many career-counseling programs ask you to consider your values and encourage you to find work that fits your values. We certainly agree, but what do they mean by your "values"? Is wanting to bring a dog to work a value? Is earning a six-figure income? Is having job security? What about the way you think you should behave or how others should treat you?

Questions about values get tricky fast because we tend to lump our needs, wants, preferences, and values all together. Without getting too picky about differentiating them, let's quickly distinguish what we mean by each before we seek to identify your *core personal values*.

A Reminder: Needs, Wants, and Preferences Are Not Values

As part of your Career Design process, you are identifying Clues and Components—criteria that great-fit work, for you, would include. Many of your Clues and Components are based on your wants and preferences. If you would like to work for a company where you can bring your dog to work because you love him so much, that is a want or preference; bringing him because you have a visual impairment, on the other hand, is a need. Most of your Components will probably be best characterized as wants and preferences. You may value a six-salary income, really want your own office, and would really, really like to bring Buster the dog to work, and, by all means—add them to your Components list!—but these are not your core personal values. They may be manifestations of core values, but are not the driving force itself. We are getting to that.

So, What Are?

Aside from understanding how your natural talents and cognitive aptitudes shape what you are good at, there may be nothing more fundamental to your true nature, and more important to consider in your Career Design, than identifying your core personal values. They are your choices and decisions every day; living and working in ways that align with them help you feel fulfilled, and help you identify what might be missing when you are feeling unfulfilled. They underlie many of your preferences, impact how and when you feel fulfilled, and what is rewarding to you. They impact your political views and the friends and partners you choose. They fuel your motivation and opinions. They are at the heart of it. Of you.

When you identify your core, true values, you will start to see many things more clearly. You may better understand why you are drawn to a particular person, or why you have no tolerance for a particular trait or behavior. You may better understand why you never felt comfortable or at home at a particular job or company. You may even begin to see why you made certain choices and decisions and understand why they worked out (or didn't). It will also help you seek out roles and work environments that align with what is most important to you.

To have work that is inherently rewarding and meaningful for you, choose work and a work environment that closely aligns with your core personal values.

Before you begin this Inquiry, look back over your notes and responses from earlier in this chapter. Do you see any themes or common denominators? Keep that work in mind as you do this Inquiry. Your core personal values underlie many of them.

INQUIRY 23

Core Personal Values

Take a few minutes to read over the following list of values. These are universal values, and, across the globe, are important to people. You may notice that, looking over this long list, you value many of them.

Step 1: Put a mark in the "1st pass" column for all of the values that stand out to you as being significant and important to you. If you would use a different word to communicate an idea, write that word in. Don't worry so much about being "right" about your choices. You can always go back and update your list.

Value	1st Pass	Top 10	Proximity
Acceptance			
Accomplishment			
Achievement			
Acknowledgment			
Advancement			
Adventure			
Aliveness			
Ambition			
Art			
Authority			
Autonomy			
Avoid Pain			
Be Capable			
Be Challenged			
Be Charitable			
Be of Service			
Be the Best			
Beauty			
Belonging			
Build Something			
Caring			
Challenge Status Quo			
Choose Own Goals			
Civic Duty			
Cleanliness			
Comfort			
Community			
Competition			
Connection			
Conservative			

Value	1st Pass	Top 10	Proximity
Contribute to Others			
Control			
Cooperation			
Creativity			
Curiosity			
Daring			
Detachment			
Devout			
Diversity			
Do Good			
Do the Right Thing			
Empowerment			
Engage Fully with Life			
Enjoy Life			
Enlightenment			
Entrepreneurship			
Equality			
Excellence			
An Exciting Life			
Family Security			
Family Values			
Feel Good			
Financial Security			
Follow the Rules			
Forgiveness			
Frankness			
Freedom			
Friendship			
Fulfillment			
Fun & Laughter			

Value	1st Pass	Top 10	Proximity
Go for It			
Goodness			
Happiness			
Harmony of Rhetoric & Action			
Healthy			
Hedonism			
Helpfulness			
Honesty			
Honor Elders			
Humble			
Iconoclastic			
Inclusiveness			
Independence			
Influence			
Inner Harmony			
Intelligence			
Interesting Experiences			
Joy			
Lawfulness			
Leadership			
Legacy			
Loyalty			
Make Money			
Mastery			
Mature Love			
Meaning			
Membership			
My Way			
National Security			
Novelty			

Value	1st Pass	Top 10	Proximity
Obedience			
Openness			
Opportunity			
Peace			
Personal Development			
Pleasure			
Politness			
Preparedness			
Preserve Public Image			
Privacy			
Protect the Environment			
Quality			
Reciprocation			
Recognition			
Reliability			
Respect			
Respect for Tradition			
Responsibility			
Safety			
Savings			
Self-direction			
Self-discipline			
Self-esteem			
Self-expression			
Self-indulgence			
Self-respect			
Set Example, Be Role Model			
Social Justice			
Social Order			
Social Power			

Value	1st Pass	Top 10	Proximity
Social Recognition			
Spontaneity			
Stability			
Status			
Stimulation			
Strength			
Success			
Synergy			
Team Spirit			
Trusted			
Truth			
Uniqueness			
Unity with Nature			
Use My Talents			
Valued Member of Team			
Vitality			
Wealth			
Wisdom			

Step 2: You may have a lot of marks after completing Step 1. Now it is time to narrow it down. Think about people you admire—what traits or values do they represent? Think about people or situations you cannot tolerate. What values might be missing? Narrow down your list to the top ten to twelve most significant values for you.

Step 3: Pick your top five values and put them in hierarchical order. Now, you may ask: How do I do that? Well, values are hierarchical. People will usually sacrifice a lower, but still very important, value to protect or uphold a higher value. Some basically honest senior government officials have in the past resorted to lying when faced with a choice between loyalty to their administration and honesty. That's because loyalty, keeping their jobs, or some other value was higher on their scale than honesty.

Step 4: Create at least one strong Component from the insights you have had working through this chapter.

Can you see the difference in helpfulness between "My work aligns with my core personal values" and "My work aligns with my core personal values: creativity, independence, empowerment, integrity, and truth"? Only with the second, specific Component can you seek out or evaluate Career Ideas, Job Opportunities, or Organizations for potential great fit.

A Component-Making Tip: Being specific is helpful.

CHAPTER 14

+

PASSION, MEANING, AND PURPOSE

Accomplishing something provides the only real satisfaction in life.

—THOMAS EDISON

Why do you get up in the morning and go to work? Do you wake up with the same enthusiasm on workdays as you do on the weekend? Even if your career fits your personality and uses your talents fully, it won't be truly satisfying if you go to work if you only feel you are doing it because you have to. Working only to pay the bills can feel like a form of bondage. The chains can be subtle, invisible, and strengthened over time. If you are primarily dragging yourself to work each day to avoid facing the lash of the mortgage company or credit bureau, you are leading the life of an indentured servant. There are two practical ways out. The first is to make so much money that you can buy your freedom. The second is to choose a career you care about—work that matters to you and gives you a sense of meaning and contribution. Although you will still work to pay your bills and create workability in your life, you can start going to work because you want to!

No matter what you experience now, or have experienced in the past, you too can love what you do. Now, of course, we are not suggesting that every single day will begin with joy and eagerness—there will be days when you would much rather stay snuggled up in your warm, cozy bed or spend the day at the beach. There are days that will drag on or include tasks and activities that you would rather avoid. However, by identifying and choosing work that you are passionate about, you can be, more often than not, filled with a sense of excitement and enthusiasm for the day ahead.

We know what you might say: Is this actually realistic? It's called work, after all!

Although many of us already know what we care about and what we find interesting, we may have trouble making the journey from knowledge to actually *living our lives* as an expression of what matters to us. For many of us, having work and building a career around something that really matters to us seems like a *grand idea*, an ideal, something a few good-deed-doers do, or a pipe dream. And making it actually meaningful in today's world seems equally idealistic.

The reality is, you might not *need* your work to be meaningful. Not everyone does. You may instead be focused on doing work that you are trained and skilled in, that allows you to generate an income and the career stability to enjoy your life outside of work. You may feel no compulsion to strive to cure cancer or make the world safe for democracy. We each have our own ideas about what makes something meaningful and what meaningful work entails and to what degree we find it important. You may not feel the need to be fulfilled by your work. You may be perfectly content finding fulfillment in other areas of your life—family, community, hobbies, or outside interests. Still, why not get clear about this? Why not strive to have it all? Have pragmatic work that you are good at and provides you with a healthy income, that you also find rewarding and engaging?

We relate to meaningful work as something we could do if and only if we were willing to sacrifice everything else, give up our security, or let go of the opportunity to earn a healthy (or very healthy) income. But what if it's not an either-or situation? Let's see if we can bring the ideal of having meaningful work down to earth, where it can grow and flourish.

In service of you having it all, we will help you uncover your own understanding of what meaningful work means to you. We'll do this by looking at the subject through a variety of lenses: passions, meaning, mission, and purpose. Some may resonate with you more than others. Through each, look for clues about what great-fit, fulfilling work for you would entail.

Passion

No alarm clock needed. My passion wakes me.

—ERIC THOMAS

In chapter 11, "Subject Matter and Interests," you looked at subject matters that you found interesting and considered which of them you might build into your career. But what differentiates an *interest* from a *passion*? A matter of degree? Something intellectual vs. something emotional? Could be. Interest often refers to having a curiosity or attraction to a specific topic, activity, or area. **Passion often denotes having a strong or intense enthusiasm or desire for something.** It is more emotionally charged and characterized by excitement and joy. If the experience of feeling excited and energized about something is an indicator of feeling passionate about it, pursuing a career in which the field or your role aligns with your passions will help you feel motivated and eager to invest your time and effort in it.

No need to split hairs about which category something fits into (interest or passion)—we'll trust you to work that out for yourself. (But if something stands out for you, make sure you capture the information in a Component.)

Consider the influence of passion for someone working as a graphic designer. They might have a deep passion for creating visually appealing and innovative designs. In the workplace, this passion is evident through their enthusiasm. They willingly take on extra design tasks, participate in design competitions, and eagerly share their design ideas during team meetings, inspiring colleagues to engage more creatively. Can you see how this passion could lead to achievement, advancement, and success? Can you imagine how this person might feel, or react, if, instead, their job required them to audit tax returns?

Now consider someone with a passion for environmental sustainability. Might they be better off working as defense counsel for an international oil company, or working as an environmental advocate for an organization dedicated to reducing carbon emissions? In which workplace would you expect them to find their work deeply rewarding? In which role would you expect them to shine? To excel?

INQUIRY 24

My Passions

Start a new document, "Passion, Meaning, and Purpose."

Under the heading "Passions," write down everything you feel passionate about.

Do not limit your entries to areas you think you could turn into a career—if you are wildly passionate about some new technology, but do not envision it as a career opportunity, write it down anyway. Your passion may be for some specific subject matter, such as antiques, art, or history. It could be for a field, like mathematics, robotics, or engineering. It could be an activity, such as sailing, football, reading, or using spreadsheets to solve problems.

Look at your childhood and at yourself over the years. Have you had activities or subjects that have always been there? What are your favorite memories?

Look at yourself in school or at work. Identify any tasks, activities, or projects that you found particularly engaging and energizing. What were the best projects you have worked on? Look for passions there.

How about in your home life, with family, with friends? Hobbies, interests, and activities that you turn to for escape or for the pure joy of it?

Are there any causes, subjects, news items, or interests that fill you with joy, emotion, or ire?

You may have difficulty coming up with responses to this Inquiry. This could mean a few things. One, that you look at a job or a career in terms of function, not meaning. That is A-OK. But it also could mean that time and resignation have beaten your passions and interests into submission. That's less okay, for your sake. But if you think that's what's happened, there is a way to regenerate your sense of passion: pay more attention to what you enjoy, remember what you used to do that brought enjoyment, and experiment by trying out new activities. Plan one day or evening each week dedicated to those things. Your assignment is to have ten times as much fun as you usually do, without winding up in jail.

It also might be useful to ask yourself these questions: "How passionate must I feel about my work?" "Is it enough to be doing interesting activities?" "Must I also have a personal interest in the subject matter?" "If so, what interests, passions, and subjects might play a big part in my future career?"

Look back over this Inquiry for Clues. Add whatever you find to your Clues list. Then, ask yourself, "Is there anything I am willing to choose as a Component?" Add those to your Career Components list. Do any new careers/jobs come to mind? If so, add them to your Career Ideas list.

Your list of Passions could turn out to be a long list, or may just contain a few items or nothing at all. It is perfectly fine if you do not have any strong passions or if your passions seem to have no connection with possible future careers. Some people just feel more naturally passionate than others do. If you do not feel the raging exaltation of Zorba the Greek, that does not mean something is wrong. We will look through more lenses, and . . . you can always add to this list if/when you identify new items.

Meaning

When the sun rises, I go to work. When the sun goes down, I take my rest.
I dig the well from which I drink. I farm the soil which yields my food.
I share creation. Kings can do no more.

—ANONYMOUS, FROM CHINA, CIRCA 2500 BCE

Everyone wants to do work they care about and that makes sense to them. Even if they have to, no one *wants* to waste time doing impact-free, unproductive tasks just to pay the bills. Who would shuffle off to chip away at the salt mine if they could fill their workday with projects and activities of interest to them? Each of us has our own internal model of what matters and of what is interesting and worthwhile. It is highly personal and can be completely different from one person to the next. By "meaning-ful" you might mean working toward fulfilling your highest ideals and values, or you might be perfectly satisfied simply doing something you enjoy doing. Human beings find things of personal significance to themselves—meaningful and rewarding. Some of us will fight tooth and nail to defend our positions about those things. This enor-mous variety of perspectives is what makes us such a rich and varied tribe.

Meaning in work and life relates to the significance, value, or purpose one finds in their actions and experiences. It's about feeling that what you do matters. For some of us, this list consists of our highest ideals and beliefs, for others it may revolve around values or feeling useful or productive. A nurse might find his or her work deeply rewarding and meaningful because each patient that they work with provides them with an opportunity to make a positive impact. They may value their role and take extra time to comfort and educate the patient and provide support and understanding to families during difficult times. A coordinator for an organi-zation that provides education to underprivileged children might find meaning in their work organizing fundraising events and connecting with donors, with the end result of making and witnessing tangible improvements in the lives of the children they serve.

Because we each have a unique take on what is meaningful to us, you are the only one who can define this for yourself. No one else can decide this for you.

You Do You.

Sainthood Not Required

You could argue that spending the time and effort it takes to identify and pursue a career that you love, and that you would be great at, and that you find rewarding and meaningful, is inherently self-serving. And how wonderful that it is! Meaningful work can honor both your ideals and noble intentions and feed your own self-interest and prosperity. These two ideas are completely compatible. You do not need to choose between doing something that pays the bills and doing something meaningful. You are designing a future that allows you to have both workability *and* fulfillment. You *can* contribute to others, to the planet, and be of service—*and* save for retire-ment, buy a house, and go on great vacations. You just need to design your career and take relevant actions that allow for all of it!

Don't think OR, think AND.

A great goal is to take amazing care of yourself, to put yourself in a position to excel and prosper, and to do work that you find meaningful and rewarding. All guilt free! You do not have to spend the rest of your life feeling guilty because you did not choose to become Joan of Arc or Mother Teresa. Your goal is to make career choices based on what is important to you—to design and act as an aware and free agent.

Next, we're going to explore what is meaningful to you. Strive to answer as many of the questions in this Inquiry as you can. You are seeking to identify strong clues and definite components.

What Meaningful Work Means to Me

Start a new document or section titled "Meaning and Work."

First, answer the question "What do I mean by meaningful?" Take time to think about and thoughtfully respond to this question. Do you mean that you want to do something you enjoy? Work in a field in which you have an interest? Do you mean that you want your work to provide you with certain kinds of rewards or challenges? Do you mean that you want to do work that you believe in and think is important? Do you mean your work should make some sort of social contribution? A specific type of contribution? There are no right answers and no wrong answers.

List several (ten to twenty) specific examples of things that are meaningful to you. Include work-related activities or goals and not-necessarily-work-related actions or activities. "Meaningful" does not have to be "noble" or "idealistic"— just note down what pops into your mind. If making tons of money is meaningful to you, write it down. If being well respected in society is meaningful to you, write it down. If spending as much time as possible with your family is meaningful to you, write it down. (It is also very helpful to consider how important meaningfulness to you is, relative to other human needs and rewards. For some people, it is vitally important that the central focus of their work be a direct expression of their highest ideals—activists and advocates for the unhoused or disenfranchised typically fit into this category, prioritizing work that is meaningful to them above monetary or comfort concerns. Others find meaning in work that they find interesting and stimulating. They might forgo stability, money, or family time to be able to pursue their intellectual interests. Some scientists, extreme athletes, or adventurers might fit into this category.

Consider the relative importance of meaning to other rewards or human needs, such as: stability, status, money, sociality, family, flexibility, advancement opportunities, power . . . Where does "doing meaningful work" (as you define it) fall in your stack? Is it important that you make a direct impact or contribution in an area? What kind of an impact? How much of an impact? Could you be happy in a job that does not make a direct contribution to something you care about? Are you less concerned with this idea of meaning than you are in more pragmatic components?

Do you have any Yeahbuts that get in the way of pursuing meaningful work? Write them down.

Prioritize. Make a vertical list of the items you might consider meaningful enough to choose as a Component of your future work. Prioritize them so that the strongest contenders are at the top of the list and less significant items are below.

Now draw a line at the point that separates those things that would be meaningful enough to make a central Component of your work from those that wouldn't. Here's an example:

- Population control

- Educating children in a way that preserves their sense of wonder

- Educating children to be ready for the challenges of the future

- Publishing good books

- Producing educational television

- Creating technology to reduce stress

- Ecological balance

- Creating new tools and technology appropriate for developing nations

- Helping homeless people

- Helping families in trouble

- Marketing ecologically appropriate products

- Providing opportunities for people to reduce stress in the country

Look back over this inquiry for Clues. Add whatever you find to your Clues list. Ask, "Is there anything I am willing to choose as a definite component?" Add anything you choose to your Career Design Components list. Do any new careers/jobs come to mind? If so, add them to your Career Ideas list.

If your work must be meaningful, commit to that. If it must be one of the areas above the line, commit to *that*. Nail down as much as you can. What do you have to learn, consider, or decide in order to commit? If you are unable to go all the way to the point of commitment now, go on, do other parts of this book and come back here later. Work to develop more clarity and definition. Making decisions about other pieces of the puzzle may help you narrow it down further. For example, if you decide you are not willing to learn a completely new discipline, that might automatically cross some items off your list.

That's all there is to it. If you have wanted to find work with meaning, you may have identified it. It need not be the great mystery it sometimes seems. Some folks spend their lives searching for meaning when it was right there, within reach, all the time.

Mission

The most extraordinary people in the world today don't have a career. They have a mission.

—VISHEN LAKHIANI

If meaning is primarily an internal factor, mission is external. A career with a Mission is often an action-oriented extension of what you feel is meaningful or important to your job. The goal is not just fulfillment, but a tangible result. You may find *exploring the cosmos* meaningful, but *leading the first manned space voyage to Mars* is a Mission.

Defining a Mission focuses the mind and the effort. It gives you a specific objective to work toward and suggests the tasks to accomplish in order to achieve. This could look like a lot of things: winning an Oscar, inventing a new alternative energy source, making $10 million, building an environmentally friendly airplane fuel, or helping the European Union become financially solvent. Each of these has a measurable goal or outcome that is likely a tangible manifestation of something meaningful or rich with purpose. If you need a goal in mind to be in action—identifying a meaningful Mission is key!

Not everyone needs to define a goal (or Mission) to have meaning. Some of us would be perfectly satisfied to work in a particular field, concentrate on a personal interest, or use certain abilities without the need to produce some result in the world around us. Others of us *need* to have a clear result or goal in mind to work effectively and happily. *Exactly what am I aiming for? What is the goal? How will I know I have succeeded—what will be the tangible evidence?* These are great, Mission-minded questions.

Whether or not you naturally think in terms of having a Mission or achieving specific goals, declaring a Mission (out of your passions, interests, and purpose) is helpful. Whether you start with a Mission or end with a Mission, it will provide you with direction and focus. Enjoy this Inquiry.

INQUIRY 26

A Mission

On a scale of 1 to 5, how important is it that your work involves having a clearly defined Mission, directing your energy toward achieving long-term specific goals?

Who do you admire who has or had a Mission? What was their Mission? Why did they (or the Mission) make it on to your list?

What Mission(s) do you find exciting or inspiring? What would be a huge goal to reach for, a meaningful target to aim for?

Use this question to brainstorm. Write down whatever surfaces. Don't edit out things that seem beyond your reach or impossible for some reason or another.

Some examples: bring back art and music to the classrooms in your area; own five rental properties; travel to all seven continents; raise $5 million to disrupt the slaughter of elephants and rhinoceroses, have a number one hit album; generate a collaborative environment in the U.S. Congress, reduce the deforestation of the Amazon by 25 percent in the next twenty years; build a business employing one hundred workers, etc.

Which items are most fitting, most attractive? Which ones sing your song loud and clear? Go over your Missions list and categorize the items into A, B, and C lists (the A list being the best). Rewrite your list so that the A list is prominent or on top.

Consider those that are great in theory, but not really your cup of tea. Or that would be amazing for someone else to do. Be honest with yourself, but keep any items on the list that your eyes or mind keep returning to.

Ask yourself why you crossed out the ones you did. What is it about them that made you take them off the list? This is important information. It may help guide you to focus on which of the ones remaining best fulfill what is important to you. (Good Clues here.)

What are the elements that make the ones you just marked so attractive to you? Is it the subject matter, the furthering of an ideal, an elegant fit between aspects of you and the work the Mission would entail?

Can you narrow down your selection to one or more top candidates?

Do you need to do some research, talk with people, or otherwise find out more about any of your top contenders? If so, what do you need to do? Be specific. What do you need to know to decide or to further narrow down the range of possibilities? What questions do you need to ask and answer? Go do the research and come back here when it is completed.

Look back over this Inquiry for Clues. Add whatever you find to your Clues list. If there is anything you are willing to choose as a definite career component, add it to your Definite Career Design Components list. If any new career/job comes to mind, add it to your Career Ideas list. Ask yourself why that career appeals to you and see if that suggests more Clues. If you now know a career on your Career Ideas list does not fit, remove it. See if that suggests any Clues. Remember to keep recording and working with your Clues, moving them toward definite Career Components.

Purpose

Let the beauty of what you love be what you do.

—RUMI

Several years ago, Nick noticed something unusual about an older man who worked on the garbage truck that serviced his neighborhood. Come rain, shine, or particularly ripe offerings from his clients, he always had boundless enthusiasm and a smile for everyone he met along the way. As time passed, Nick's curiosity grew. Did this man love working outdoors? Was he just a naturally cheerful fellow? Or was he a bit of a lunatic?

Finally, Nick asked. The gentleman said that he had worked on a trash truck all of his life. When he was a young man, he had always thought that someday he would hang up his trash can and move on to something more in keeping with his dreams, but then, one day, he woke up middle-aged and realized that he would likely spend the rest of his life doing what he was already doing. He felt that his life didn't amount to anything. After a bout of self-pity, he realized that the reason he felt his life didn't amount to anything had nothing to do with working as a trashman. It was because his life had no purpose. He saw for the first time that he was just a cog in the wheel. Somehow, he realized then that he could create himself as something other than just a trashman. Our friend decided that he would dedicate his life to one thing, "to bringing a little ray of sunshine into the lives of everyone I meet."

He had found his purpose.

A helpful way to think about purpose is as *an ongoing commitment to a principle that guides our actions and gives our life direction.* Rather than a goal to be achieved, it is a place to come from. It is the *being* that informs the doing.

A person with the purpose of *bringing a little ray of sunshine into people's lives* would never say, "Well, I finally did it. I brought sunshine to five thousand lives. My job is finished. I'm retiring from the sunshine business." (Although that might be a great Mission!) Purpose becomes the organizing principle of your life or of a part of your life. Instead of checking with your mood or opinions to know what to do, you check in with your purpose. The trashman experienced the same moods that you and I do. But he didn't usually indulge in them. His actions were enlightened by his purpose.

> *The meaning of life is to find your gift.*
> *The purpose of life is to give it away.*
>
> —PABLO PICASSO

You are the only one who can decide what a life lived from purpose means to you.

Were you born with a purpose? Who knows. Our work with many thousands of clients suggests that people tend to fall into one of three camps:

1. The lucky ones with a God-given, or otherwise ordained purpose. From the start, it's been clear and obvious to them, and they are able to follow it accordingly.

2. Those who say they *want* to discover their true purpose in life, but haven't quite gotten there yet.

3. Those who are willing to consider that they get to create or choose the purpose they live from.

If you already know your life's purpose, the guiding principle that informs your words and actions, go ahead and write it down here:

Even if you are holding out and waiting to uncover your true purpose, you can live a purpose-centered life now simply by making the commitment to trying. Your purpose can be something lofty: advocating a worldview or faith or consciousness that inspires hope in a benevolent cosmos and leads to greater planetary well-being. Or it can be much more down-to-earth. You do not have to be Gandhi, Mother Teresa, or Martin Luther King Jr. There are people all around you right now who live from a purpose. They may never post it on their website or wear it on a T-shirt, but their actions and their work show it. It may be to teach your kids in a way that helps them preserve their sense of wonder, to make technology and resources available to everyone, to help people navigate complex systems, or to share with the world how wonderful your restaurant is.

To have a purpose for your work does not mean dedicating yourself to widely agreed-upon ideals. It doesn't necessarily mean resolving today's largest crises. Artists, civil servants, and sanitation workers can all live and work with a profound sense of purpose. The world is filled with many thousands of unknown people who, because they live from purpose, contribute in their own very special ways to our world. Ever meet a used-car salesperson dedicated to selling with total integrity? The one who turned the stereotypically manipulative sales relationship around and who stands up for and contributes to their customers? Want to bet on how trusted and successful they are?

Greatness is often born of the passionate dance between a rare talent and a noble purpose.

A fascinating thing happens when you live and work from a created purpose. Suddenly, you are able to transcend your own moods and complaints in a new way. You end up not being stopped by your past and your ego, but are able to stretch and reach beyond your own self-concerned limitations. Like our trashman friend whose experience of his work, and self, shifted in a moment, you get to say, *This is who I am and what I contribute.*

When we quit thinking primarily about ourselves and our own self-preservation, we undergo a truly heroic transformation of consciousness.

—JOSEPH CAMPBELL

The Benefits of Living from a Purpose

1. **Singleness of purpose is the most powerful way to move mountains.** Normally, folks do what is within their comfort zone, or at least within the limits of

what they think is possible. When your reference point is your purpose rather than your psyche, you seek solutions outside the boundaries you normally live within. You do what works rather than what you want and feel like doing. You become almost an unstoppable force of nature.

To illustrate: some of the best, most exciting, and most profoundly satisfying marriages we know of are dedicated to a purpose. Why does this contribute to having a marriage work? In most marriages, the quality of the relationship depends mostly on chance. There are precious few commitments that effectively shape the quality of the relationship into something truly extraordinary. It is so easy to let a me-first mentality erode what began as a passionate tango. Little problems tend to pile up in the dark. Uncommunicated things and unresolved transactions form walls that reduce intimacy. When a marriage is dedicated to furthering a purpose, it is imperative to keep it well-oiled and working smoothly if the relationship itself is to make a contribution. You discover that if you want the marriage to make a difference, you must give up playing all these little games that create friction and distance. Instead of hiding problems in the closet, you resolve them, in service of your purpose. A couple who has dedicated their marriage to "being a model for other people, including our children, of just how great a relationship can be" may find it easier to avoid getting stuck in the inevitable problems that arise because they keep referring to their purpose.

2. **You notice when things are not working much more quickly.** You tend to be awake and sensitive to how well you are playing to a degree that is nearly impossible otherwise. If you notice you are heading down a blind alley quickly, you can change course posthaste. The faster you are able to make course corrections in any journey, the better.

3. **Life becomes an exciting adventure.** Don't you love movies when heroes like Indiana Jones run through the jungle, leap, and swing on a vine across the bottomless chasm?! When you live with purpose, you feel like you are the one who is running and leaping. If you want to have a life of excitement, challenge, and deep fulfillment, jump. Give yourself to a purpose larger than you.

It is extraordinary to be able do something you care about, something meaningful. That is sufficient for most people who seek full self-expression in their work. Working from purpose is not better, loftier, or more important than anything else. But once people have outgrown the routine of survival-based living or have become passionately committed to a principle or contribute beyond their own ego, their lives and what's possible for them tends to expand exponentially. If that is what you are seeking, this chapter, and this section on purpose—and the following Inquiry—is for you.

How can I be useful, of what service can I be?
There is something inside me, what can it be?

—VINCENT VAN GOGH

INQUIRY 27

A Created Purpose

First of all, decide if you are willing to live from a purpose. You do not need to be selfless or humble to live from a purpose. Throughout history, most of the people who demonstrate the best examples of purposeful living have had big, healthy egos. The goal is for your purpose to be bigger than your ego— then it counts.

Brainstorm on ideas or principles that resonate with you.

Think of people you admire and respect. Did any of them take a stand and work to change, shift, abolish, grow, or create something meaningful? Not all people who achieve great things are guided by a purpose. Some are. Albanian-born missionary and nun Mother Teresa lived to bring happiness and love to the destitute. She promoted peace and compassion through her care for those who society ignored and neglected. Author Walter Meyer speaks and writes about anti-bullying. His purpose is to make the world better through his words. Make a list of the people you admire and respect. What purpose might they be living from? You can guess, or make one up, if you don't know.

Now think about what you are good at and what comes naturally to you. While not mandatory, working from a purpose that aligns with your natural talents and personality makes sense. Combine an authentic purpose with your talents and personality, and you have best chance of moving mountains. A talented writer and journalist might live from the purpose of exposing abuses of power. A whiz with numbers and finance might work from a purpose of helping others achieve financial stability. Write down any ideas that come to mind.

Now think about your values. Go back and review your work from chapter 13. For each of your top values, create a purpose that you could live from. For example, if one of your core values is community, you could create a purpose of "creating inclusive and supportive communities."

It also helps if you have a very strong natural passion for contributing in an area. Earlier in this chapter, you looked at what you are passionate about. The energy and attention that you naturally have for things you are passionate about can fuel actions and achievements. Review your earlier work in this chapter and create a purpose from each of the subjects or areas that you care about most.

Craft several purposes. Play with your ideas until you settle in on the right one. Remember, a purpose is not a goal. It is the expression of a principle. Craft the words so that they remind you that your purpose is a place to come from, not someplace to get to: "To be a great example to my children" can be a purpose. If you can invent it now, live it now, and from it can issue an endless stream of appropriate actions, then it could be a purpose. Play with several ideas (if applicable) until one stands out to you. Keep working on it until, when you write it or say it, you feel moved or inspired. Goose bumps are a good sign. So are tears.

Make a commitment to your purpose as a big part of your identity. For example, "I am a commitment to bringing together East and West through communication and media." "I am a commitment to people having careers that fit them perfectly so their lives will be creative, purposeful, and fun." "I am a commitment to using ethical salesmanship to get products to people that make a real difference in their lives."

Work out great ways you could express your purpose. What are different actions or ways that your purpose could be expressed in the real world? What are roles or careers that would be natural extensions of your purpose? From a clear purpose come potent actions. Sit down and figure out what roles would move things most powerfully in the direction of your purpose.

Create a Career Component from the purpose you created. If any new career/job comes to mind, add it to your Career Ideas list. Ask yourself why that career appeals to you, and see if that suggests more Clues. If you now know a career on your Career Ideas list does not fit, remove it.

This is the true joy in life, being used for a purpose recognized by yourself as a mighty one: being a force of nature instead of a feverish, selfish little clod of ailments and grievances, complaining that the world will not devote itself to making you happy. I am of the opinion that my life belongs to the whole community and as long as I live it is my privilege to do for it whatever I can. I want to be thoroughly used up when I die, for the harder I work the more I live. I rejoice in life for its own sake. Life is no "brief candle" to me. It is a sort of splendid torch that I have got hold of for the moment, and I want to make it burn as brightly as possible before handing it on to future generations.

—GEORGE BERNARD SHAW

WHERE I WORK

You have considered your aptitudes, personality, values, and interests. You have thought about the roles and functions you want to engage in at work and clarified work that you would find meaningful and fulfilling. You have only one topic left to consider in your Career Design—the characteristics, dynamics, and culture of organizations. Where would you thrive?!

Section 3.4 has one chapter—

Chapter 15: *Workplace Environment*

CHAPTER 15

+

WORKPLACE ENVIRONMENT

Workplace Ecology

When the subject of ecology comes up, it is usually in reference to environmental concerns addressing the nature and interactions of living things, each other, and their environments. While certain plants or animals may be more versatile and flexible about the type of ecosystems in which they can succeed, each ecosystem has unique characteristics and dynamics that allow certain species to thrive and others to fail. A saguaro cactus is likely to thrive in the dry and sandy New Mexican desert, but would have little chance in a waterlogged Louisiana swamp. A mountain goat, especially gifted to climb up steep rock faces, might lose their competitive advantage on the flat, grass-covered fields of Ohio. In a healthy ecosystem, the soil and the plant life and the insects and animals share a symbiotic relationship—all working together and providing for one another.

Companies and workplaces are their own version of an ecosystem. They vary in their physical characteristics, social dynamics, and leadership styles. They have differing degrees of formality, hierarchy, and uniformity. Some are large, active, and fast-paced, and others are slower and more laid-back. Some are super competitive, and others are not.

Now you, you unique animal, have your own blend of talents, traits, and characteristics—and should consider the type of workplace ecosystems in which you are most likely to thrive.

How do you know if your workplace ecology fits you? The immediate response might be *Well, I like it*. The people you work with are nice. The physical office is pleasant, and you enjoy being there. You might respect the decision-making processes of leadership and believe that you have the skills and chops to achieve and advance.

How do you know if your workplace ecology doesn't fit? Sometimes it's obvious— you can't stand the moneygrubbing, micromanaging egotist that is your boss. Or you hate wearing a tie to work every day; you would rather dress business casual. The stressors you notice and complain about are just the tip of the iceberg—beneath the surface there are other, more subtle environmental factors that affect your peace of mind, clarity of thought, creativity, and physical health. You may feel a growing unease and agitation on your commute to work, like you need to put on a mental suit of armor before you walk through the workplace door. You might be like an outsider and feel like you don't fit in. Or you might feel a chronic sense that you aren't in the know on the policies and future plans of the organization.

Most workplaces are a mixed bag of positives and negatives. You may like certain aspects and dislike others. This is normal. You can deal with it by simply accepting your fate with a shrug, and paying the price that your personal ecological disaster zone exacts. Many of us do this for a long time—until we just can't take it anymore. (That's not to say that it all falls on you. Usually, people are not inventing reasons to dislike their job. There is such a thing as an awful workplace. Toxic. Negative and exploitative. Unsupportive and churning through employees without regard for their well-being. If this is the case for you, figure out how to move out of there ASAP.)

One of the strengths of human beings is their adaptability—we can live from bread and water for months, survive social isolation, and be reasonably productive in poor-fitting jobs in workplace environments we hate. In career planning, the quality of the workplace environment is often the first thing to be sacrificed for the sake of other goals. Sometimes the traditional climb up the career ladder requires you to temporarily pay heavy dues—but for every person who temporarily puts up with an ill-suited environment as part of a clearly focused plan, there are ten who wind up permanently stuck, glued by stasis like flies on flypaper. People end up in these ecological cesspools permanently because they were not sufficiently committed to working in a supportive environment, or because they did not understand the impact an adverse work environment would have on the overall quality of their lives. It is one thing to pay some dues now for a wonderful future you have carefully planned. It is yet another to fool yourself that you are paying temporary dues when, in reality, you are just in a bad place.

When Nick founded Rockport Institute many years ago, he put every penny into research. That meant living at the office for a while. The office was in downtown Washington, D.C., four blocks up Pennsylvania Avenue from the White House. Whenever the president needed a pack of gum in the middle of the night, a whole fleet of vehicles would go screaming by just a few feet below Nick's window with the sirens going full tilt. There was a big, noisy student bar close by, and the young dudes would gather on his corner for late-night games of chest-thumping, hurling, and yelling. Nick used earphones, shades, exercise, and meditation to deal with that incredibly stress-provoking corner—but he just kept telling himself it was temporary. Many years later, he was sitting in an office overlooking a lake and flower gardens and listen to mockingbirds and wood thrushes sing. Was it worth it to put up with that terrible downtown environment in the beginning? Oh yes! Would he have gone berserk if he had not had a clear vision of where he was going? Oh yes!

We know a man who wakes up at 4:30 a.m., does the chores on his ten-acre country place, drives a two-hour commute into the city every morning, works a ten-hour day at a job he doesn't like, and arrives back home at 8 p.m. He enjoys his time in the country for two hours before he falls asleep and does it all over again. Nearly every weekend he brings a big pile of work home. Is it worth it? Speaking from the shade of his furrowed brow, he says it is. And if that's true, good for him. But we can't help thinking that he pays a hefty price for his few hours of pleasure. Instead of designing a career from the ground up that included living in the country and the time to enjoy it, he just added the farm on top of an already stressful career, thinking it would be the cure.

The point of considering your workplace environment is more than just hanging around in a place you like. It is to **identify a workplace ecosystem that minimizes negative stress for you and provides you with great-fit social and organizational structures.** Prioritize this and every day you will have maximum freedom and energy. You can attend to your tasks and responsibilities with focus. You can be yourself and feel supported as you develop skills and experience.

Designing Your Workplace Ecosystem

To design a career that fits, you need to consider both the physical and social environments of your work life. The physical environment ranges from the big geographical picture, where you live, to the micro—the noise level and the color of the paint in your office. The social environment includes everything from the socioeconomics of where you live to the customary mood of the people you work with (including you). To be your own human ecologist takes more observation than study. Your heart knows what fits and what doesn't. You could easily sit down right now and invent a workplace environment that would be perfect for you. On the other hand, many of us make unnecessary compromises because it seems too difficult and challenging to have it all fit together perfectly. As usual, it is a question of commitment. If it is important that you love your work, you will definitely need to make the environment just as important as the other vital pieces of the puzzle.

But, these days, you not only have to think about designing a career by considering the present workplace environments but also about what will likely take place in the future. Years ago, you may have had very limited career options. Geography mattered. Technology and a global economy have radically changed this. Not only are there more job and career options available than you will ever know about, but you may also now have the additional option of whether or not you ever go in to work. Remote and hybrid positions have further expanded the dynamics that you need to consider when designing your career.

So, what is the right workplace ecology for you? We are so glad you asked . . .

My Workplace Environment

Below, you will find a long list of questions that deal with workplace environment and culture. You may care very much about some aspects and have little preference for others. Answer as many questions as you can. Then go back and star the ones that are really important to you. And, if you think of your own dynamics or questions—add them in!

Geographical Environment

1. Would you prefer to work or live in a specific geographic area, locality, or a certain type of physical environment? If so, based on what? Availability of suitable work, a certain size city or town, demographics, feels like home to you, recreational opportunities, natural beauty, peace, excitement, another family member's needs, the weather suits your clothes?

2. Do you prefer an urban, suburban, or rural environment?

3. Are there certain cities, towns, regions, or countries that you need to, or want to, live in? Any that you do not?

Physical Environment and Activity

1. Indoors or outdoors—how much of each?

2. How much travel required—extended trips, occasional, rarely, or never away from home?

3. Your physical location—sit at a desk, visit several locations each day, in front of a group of people, traveling constantly, work on top of a phone pole?

4. Do you prefer an office-oriented environment, workshop, medical facility, classroom, etc.?

5. Private office or cubicle? A desk in a large office with lots of other people around you?

6. How large an office? Is the status of your office space important?

7. Are there factors, such as lighting, noise, pollutants that affect you or the quality of your work?

Organizational Environment and Culture

1. Employee or self-employed?

2. Profit, nonprofit, government, academia, other?

3. Service organization or producer of goods?

4. Mammoth organization, big, medium, small, tiny, or just you and the dog?

5. Organizational purpose, philosophy, style?

6. Every organization has a lifespan. Start-ups, developing companies, established businesses celebrating their 150th anniversary. Each stage of its life creates a different organizational environment with different advantages and disadvantages. Is this important to you? If so, what stage fits you?

Start-up Phase—Being in at the very beginning, maximum opportunity to influence the basic structure of the organization, fewest rules, long hours, pioneering spirit, biggest opportunity to carve out a big chunk of personal territory and/or significant ownership, most risky, prone to an early death.

Entrepreneurial Phase—The excitement and rewards of quick growth, risky, unstable, filled with the unexpected, environment tinged with adventure and uncertainty, creative problem-solving is highly valued and rewarded, pioneering spirit, opportunity to create the perfect niche for yourself, usually requires long hours, good chance for quick promotion.

Leveling-Off Phase—Safer, less need for battlefield problem-solving skills, but still room for creativity and new thinking, perfect for those seeking to build a well-oiled and stable system and for those who want stability and security as well as growth and creativity, may require long hours.

Stability Phase—Everything is worked out, organization run by a fixed set of policies and procedures, even keel, everything stays the same, safest nest for the security-minded, lower level of appreciation for creativity and individualism, usually has conservative values, likes the steady step-by-step approach, you feel like a cog in the wheel because that's exactly what you are.

Decline Phase—Like stability phase in character, except has more pathological tendencies than other phases. Not a healthy place to be for anyone except those who love to save sinking ships. Innovative people are often brought in to try to save the ship, but their ideas are not implemented because the organization is still run by stability-phase management people who would rather sink than change.

Opportunities for advancement based on performance or political maneuvering or seniority?

Social Environment

1. How will you relate with other people at work? Super social, all business all the time, friendly and professional . . . ?

2. Is the pace of your workday relaxed, moderate, or fast?

3. What combination of extroverted and introverted activities? What percentage of your workday will consist mainly of face-to-face conversations with a constant stream of people? Is your introverted time to be spent alone with the door closed or working by yourself with others around?

4. With whom will you relate or be in contact—fellow workers, customers, clients, adults, children?

5. What's the reason for meeting with them?

6. What do you get from being with them? What do they get?

7. What population do you work with or serve: young, old, professionals; people with problems or in need; people seeking to purchase something, to learn something, or solve a problem; people from other countries and cultures; people from a particular profession or from a particular background or socioeconomic group? If more than one kind of relationship, what percentage of each?

8. If there is a teamwork approach, what sort of a team? How big? How varied the members' jobs?

9. Degree of collaboration toward a common goal?

10. Degree of independence and interdependence?

11. What sort of people are your fellow employees? What special qualities or characteristics? Professionals, technical, support, blue collar, traditional, liberal, conservative, creative, supportive, cooperative, highly motivated, not dysfunctional, young, and so on?

12. How connected or isolated will your work environment be from the rest of your life?

Organizational Goals and Priorities

1. Who does your work benefit? The organization, the less fortunate? Specific groups? The environment?

2. How defined are your responsibilities and goals?

3. What kind of problems do you work on?

4. How much variety does your work provide? Do you do many things in many areas? Specialize and perform one or a few specific tasks?

5. Do you have a set schedule and routine or is there a high degree of variability?

Leadership and Decision-Making Environment

1. Are you supervised? How much? How often? What style?

2. Type of supervision structure: traditional top-down approach or something else?

3. How much structure to your supervision? Clear lines of authority necessary? Will the people you work with be the people with whom you spend your leisure time?

4. Do you have a managerial or leadership role?

5. What do you want to have responsibility and authority for?

6. Do you want to set all of your own goals or have them provided for you?

7. Do you want to direct, delegate, and supervise others?

8. What kind of decisions do you make? Is your work detail-oriented? In what ways? Big picture? In what ways?

Once you're done, you know the drill. Look back over this inquiry for Clues. Add whatever you find to your Clues list. Ask, "Is there anything I am willing to choose as a Career Component?" Add anything you choose to your Career Components list. Do any new careers/jobs come to mind? If so, add them to your Career Ideas list. Remember to keep working with your Clues, moving them toward selecting new definite components.

SECTION 4

PUTTING IT ALL TOGETHER

Congratulations on all the work you have done so far. Throughout Section 3, you explored, questioned, pondered, considered, and made decisions about important aspects of your future work. It's time to prepare to, and make, your final choices and decisions. In this short but powerful section, you will move through several steps:

Chapter 16: My Components and My Career Design

In this chapter, you will gather, organize, and power up your Components list and prepare to investigate the facts and details of your Career Ideas.

Chapter 17: Researching Career Ideas

In this chapter, you will research facts and information about your Career Ideas.

Chapter 18: Career Evaluation and Comparison

In this chapter, you will incorporate your Career Components into your research and spend time searching for new Career Ideas of interest. Then you will use a new tool, the Career Comparison Worksheet, to evaluate and compare your Career Ideas.

Chapter 19: My Career Choice

It's time to make a choice. If you haven't already done so, you'll do some final research and reflection and choose. There is also some guidance for what to do if you get stuck or can't decide.

Hang in there. For many people, this is the scary part. It is not always easy. Stick with it, do the work, and you will succeed in your extraordinary commitment. You will achieve your goal or identifying work or career that, for you, fits what you are good at and what is most important to you.

CHAPTER 16

✦

MY COMPONENTS
AND MY CAREER DESIGN

To be yourself in a world that is constantly trying to make you
something else is the greatest accomplishment.

—RALPH WALDO EMERSON

Good News

Assuming you have followed our suggestions and have been working your way through this book chapter by chapter and Inquiry by Inquiry, you have invested quite a bit of time and done a lot of work! Congratulate yourself on your commitment and effort. Think about where you started and where you are now. If you kept a copy of your very early Clues, Components, and Career Ideas lists (i.e., what you *knew* when you started) and compared it to those lists now, we have no doubt that you have had many insights. You have increased your self-awareness and have a new degree of certainty and clarity about what work is right for you. Grand!

More Good News

If you have worked your way through the Inquiries in this book, regardless of your *current* degree of certainty about your future career choices, you have already done most of the heavy lifting. That doesn't mean that there isn't more to do—there is—but working through the Inquiries and developing a Career Components list of important criteria is the key to the proverbial kingdom.

Still More Good News

Your Components list need not be *anywhere* near perfect for you to achieve your goal of making a great choice about your future work. Even if you feel disorganized and incomplete, if you have done the work, you are in a good place. We still have some critical steps to take, but even if you still feel quite uncertain about what work is a great fit for you, you can still achieve your goal of choosing a career. What you are about to do will help.

The actions you take in this chapter will help you clarify your Components.

The actions you take throughout this section will help you identify the career choices that are right for you!

Organizing the Chaos

Keep your eyes on the stars and your feet on the ground.

—Teddy Roosevelt

The more you've kept on top of reviewing and updating your list of Components, the less work you will have on this next step and in this next Inquiry. If you've been diligent and created Components as you went along, you probably have minimal chaos to manage. You'll just need to double-check. If you haven't been so diligent, have notes and scribbles on scraps of paper and Post-it notes, and have some of your work somewhere in Google Docs, you will have some additional work to do. The more Inquiries you skipped or didn't finish, the less organized your work, the more chaos you currently have, the more work you have to do now. But here is some super, fabulous, bonus good news for the messy, incomplete, and disorganized: right now you are going to handle it. You are going to complete your work, gather the mess in one place, and get it organized. And the greater your current lack of organization and completeness, the bigger the difference this next Inquiry will make for you. Win-win—right?!

These next Inquiries may take you a while to complete. While you shouldn't worry about doing them perfectly and don't need to microanalyze every possible point—give them some real thought. It will pay off.

INQUIRY 29

Review Your Work and Gather It on Your Clues, Components, and Career Ideas Lists

In this Inquiry, you are going to review and collect all the takeaways from all the chapters and exercises onto your three lists: Clues, Components, and Career Ideas.

Prior to this chapter and this inquiry, you have read fifteen chapters and have completed twenty-six Inquiries. Each Inquiry has addressed a topic or topics that has been shown to be important to many people seeking a career that fits them beautifully. Way back in chapter 3, we introduced three terms to you: Clues, Components, and Career Ideas. In chapter 4, you started a notebook and started lists of each. These lists are gathering places for your insights, your declared criteria, and your Career Ideas.

If helpful, review chapters 3 and 4 for a refresher on Clues, Components, and Career Idea lists. If there are any Inquiries you skipped or left incomplete, go back and complete them now. (This, of course, is optional, but recommended.)

Now it is time to look back over your notes and work on each of the Inquiries. (If you have already done this, you are ahead of the game. Work this step to the degree it is helpful.)

Review each of the chapters and Inquiries you completed. From each, what insights can you add to your Clues list? Add them now to your Clues list.

Reminder: Clues are experiences, insights, preferences, and opinions.

Examples: *"I love hedgehogs." "My favorite part of playing pickleball is the comradery." "My favorite college course was Philosophy 101."*

You don't need to self-edit your Clues. This is a gathering place for thoughts and ideas.

As you review each chapter and Inquiry, what is your takeaway? What stands out as significant to you? Is there anything that you are clear that great-fit work for you would include? Anything that great-fit work for you would avoid? See if you can create one or more Components from each of the subjects and Inquiries you have completed.

Reminder: Components are criteria, or aspects of work, that you have identified as being significant to you. They are individual elements that you declare as being important in your future work.

Examples: *"My work will allow me to instruct, teach, or train others." "My workplace will walk the talk and have policies and procedures assuring diversity and inclusiveness." "I will be valued and rewarded for my attention to detail and my unwillingness to ignore sloppy work."*

Any Career Ideas pop to mind while revisiting your work? Add them to your Career Ideas list.

As with Clues, Career Ideas are simply that: ideas. No need to overly edit yourself. If it pops to mind—add it to your list. We will be prioritizing and dealing with reality soon.

Now that you've gathered all of your insights, criteria, and career ideas onto these three lists, let's review your Clues list. Is there any insight or preference on your list that is gnawing away at you or that your attention keeps going back to? Look for potential Components.

Developing Components from Clues

Soon, we are going to focus in on your Components and Career Ideas lists and pay less attention to your Clues. Before we move on, let's review your Clues list and see if are any items or preferences that you would like to develop into Components.

Review your Clues list. Star or highlight those that stand out to you as being important or significant to you.

This is something you need to suss out yourself. If it seems important, or like it might be important for you, let's work with it.

For those Clues that you starred, translate them (if needed) into Components and add them to your Components list.

Here are a few examples of Clues developed into Components.

Now you've updated your Components list. You still might have a jumble of items. We're going to spend some time with it.

Clue	→	Component
"People tell me that I am great with other people and help them feel comfortable in any situation."	→	"My work will value and reward me for my ability to be great with others and help them feel comfortable."
"I enjoy explaining complex ideas to others in a simple way they can understand."	→	"My work will involve breaking down complex ideas and explaining them to others."
"I cannot stand the sight of blood and sick people creep me out."	→	"I will not work around sick or injured people." "I will not work in environments where I or others face physical harm or injury."
"I don't want to work to further line the pockets of rich people."	→	"I will not work for a company that only cares about profits for share-holders." "I will work for a nonprofit or not-only-for-profit organization."

Organizing and Powering Up Your Components List

Your Career Components list consists of individual elements and aspects of work that you have identified as being important to you. We want them to be as helpful for you as possible. Doing all the work it took you to build your list of Components was valuable in itself—we bet that you already have a vastly increased understanding and will make better career decisions based on what you are good at and what is most important to you. We're going to take that clarity two steps further to make the Components list as useful as possible. Then we're going to see if there are ways to improve it, or power it up.

Component Check-In

If you were (or are) unhappy at your job, or have never found your work satisfying or fulfilling, you may have come to this process with a few clear ideas about what you did not want or like. You may have quickly been able to create some Components that described the stupid job or boss that you were never going to deal with again ("I will not work for a micromanager"; "My work will not be something that any monkey can do"). But it may not have been quite so easy to create Components for other topics, like natural roles, values, or talents.

A good Components list consists of a list of items that are meaningful to you. A great Components list consists of a diverse, well-rounded list of items that cover most, if not all, of the important aspects of the working world.

This next Inquiry is here to help you check out that you have a number of different bases covered. It may also point out any areas with which some additional clarify may be helpful.

Career Component Check-In

Below you will find an outline of a number of different aspects that you could—and should!—consider when working out what career would suit you. Not all of the topics listed have had entire chapters devoted to them in this book, but, by now, you have had a lot of practice creating Clues and Components, so don't let that stop you.

Review your Components list and consider all the career exploration work you have done. For how many of the subtopics do you have, or can you create, a Component?

Reminder: There are no right answers. Do your best. Perfection is not required.

Aim for at least one per subtopic or three per section (A through G)

A. Logistics—Where, How Much, and When

1. Location, Geography (Where you want to live and work)

2. Income (specific numbers) (How much money?)

3. Schedule—flexibility, stability

4. On-site, Remote, Hybrid, Travel

5. Employed or Self-employed

B. My Background, Experience, Training, Skills, and Education That I Want to Leverage

1. Natural Talents and Abilities

2. Skills and Knowledge

3. Education and Experience

C. More About Me—My Nature, Personality, and What I Need to Thrive

1. Personality and Temperament

2. Natural Roles/Archetypes

3. Ways I work with, or interact with, others

4. Miscellaneous Quirks/Preferences

5. Risk Tolerances (personal/physical safety, income/job stability, etc.)

D. What I Do

1. Subject Matter, Interests

2. Field/Industry

3. Job Functions—what I spend my time doing

4. Leadership/Management/Independent

E. Why I Do It

1. Values

2. Motivation/Rewards/Accomplishment

3. Passions/Meaning/Purpose

F. Where I Will Do It

1. Organization's Legal Structure—(corporation, small company, not-for-profit, etc.)

2. Organizational Culture and Dynamics

G. Misc Components (Add your own.)

1. _____

2. _____

3. _____

4. _____

Powering Up Components

Remember: Your Components list is so much more than a list of insights. It is more than a set of criteria to define great-fit work. A great Components list is a fabulous tool you can use to:

A. Locate relevant data and information about careers of interest.

B. Evaluate career ideas and options.

C. Refer to when you write your résumés, cover letters, and online profiles.

Is your Components list a fabulous tool now? There is an easy way to check.

Here's how you check if your Component is great. If, when you enter it into an internet search field, or ask someone about it, you get relevant results and responses.

It is natural to use common expressions or vague descriptions when we create Components. "I want to be creative at my work" and "I want to earn a decent income" are two examples. We tend to phrase things this way because we're usually trying to capture complex ideas that could play out in several ways. We are unsure about what we mean or we want to leave our options open. Completely understandable.

The problem, in this situation particularly, is that it's not helpful to use broad and general descriptions. It's not helpful because it forces you to stay in the "I'll recognize it when I see it" camp and it requires you to guess and interpret a lot. You will not have a lot of success pinpointing great-fitting jobs in your field by searching on those that let you "be creative" and "earn decent income."

It is immeasurably more helpful to have powerful Components that are specific and measurable. Great Components are worded in such a way that you could ask someone, "Hey, would that job allow me to X, Y, Z . . . ?" and they would quickly understand what you mean and be able to answer you with specific facts and information (and not with additionally vague and interpretive opinions). They would also be worded in such a way that you could use them to seek out job opportunities, or career options, that meet your criteria (i.e., Components).

Note: You will also find your Components list, and the tools you'll use in this chapter, to be excellent tools for researching additional Career Ideas and continuing your job search.

Examples of How to Power Up Your Components

The best (well, probably the *easiest*) way for us to provide guidance on how to power up your Components is to give you a few examples. La voilà.

Good Component	→	Great Component
"I will earn a good income."	→	"I will earn at least $75,000/year."
"I will have good work-life balance."	→	"I do not work weekends." "I am not expected to answer work calls or emails after business hours."
"My work will not be boring and repetitive."	→	"I will not spend more than 10% of my time doing data entry." "I will not have to make cold calls." "I will have a variety of tasks each day and am able to constantly learn and develop new skills."

Good Component	→	Great Component
"I will find my work rewarding and meaningful."	→	"I will be able to see the difference I make for people by looking in their faces." "I understand how my work positively impacts the daily lives of those who use my product/service."
"I can be myself at work."	→	"My colleagues find my purple hair and Death Slayer fangirl T-shirts charming."

You can see from these few simple examples how the Components become more specific. Each "power-up" addresses a particular aspect of a position or organization that you could research or inquire about.

INQUIRY 32

Powering Up My Components

This Inquiry is for those who really want a great set of Career Components with which they can search for, inquire about, and evaluate Career Ideas, organizations, and specific jobs or roles. By reviewing each of your Components and powering up those that are vague, generic, or bland . . . you will not only have rock star clarity about what you are looking for, you will be able to better target potential opportunities and save a lot of time and effort.

The instruction for this Inquiry is simple:

Review each of your Components. Is there a way you can make them more specific or measurable? Power up your Components list.

Would a stranger be able to tell you whether or not a specific career or job would fit your Component?

Are you avoiding common or overused expressions (e.g., "work-life balance," "not boring," "good income")?

Tip: When in doubt—test it out! Not sure about one . . . share your Component(s) with someone else. Do they know exactly what you mean?

CHAPTER 17

✦

RESEARCHING CAREER IDEAS

We are now heading into the home stretch. You are about to take the next and last step before deciding which career path you will pursue. Hooray!

In chapter 16, you reviewed all the work you have done so far and focused on creating a well-rounded, powerful set of Components. In this chapter, we will set you up to conduct some dynamite research on each of your Career Ideas. We'll discuss places and ways to research your Career Ideas and suggest specific information to capture.

Exciting, right?! Let's get started.

A Day in the Life?

So you think you would like to be a lawyer, or a graphic designer, or a data scientist. Fabulous. But, as we mentioned in our discussion about job functions, those are umbrella titles under which there can be a lot of variation and range. What kind of law would you like to practice? Would you prefer to work for a large, private firm? Be the general counsel for a global nonprofit? Work to protect the interests of the nation by impacting government policy? Do you actually know what *a day in the life* of a graphic designer entails? Do they all use the same tools and processes? Is a college degree necessary for that or would a certification suffice? How about a data scientist—what kind of projects do they work on? What's the difference between a data scientist and a data analyst? What background, education, or training is required for them? What fields and industries hire data scientists? All of them?

Before you can make a conscious decision about your future and your career path, you need to thoroughly investigate the career options you are considering. You need facts and information. You need to do some research.

Research

Over the course of this journey, you have been working on building a list of Career Ideas that might fit you. It's time to turn to the real world. You need to investigate, check your thinking, and discover if reality matches your vision and beliefs.

In this stage of the process, you need to:

- Learn about fields and career areas you are considering—research current information from multiple resources.

- Consider if and how specific jobs and careers fit your specifications.

- Find people, especially industry leaders, to add to your network of support.

- Find out what you need to do to get into a new field.

- Identify and learn about potential employers.

Best Practices and General Guidance for Research

While there is no single best research tool, there are resources to use and paths to take that work better than others. Do everything you can think of to learn what you need to know. Find what works for you.

Here are some things to remember, though, as you go:

1. **The internet is a blessing and a curse.** The World Wide Web puts a virtually unlimited amount of information at your fingertips. In seconds, you can ask any question and have millions of results and responses. The problem is, you'll have to sift through that information to figure out what is true, and helpful. Don't try to find everything, and consider the quality of your sources.

2. **Don't lump research and a job search together.** While there is definitely overlap between *career idea research* and a *job search*, you need to separate these two activities in your mind. After all, they have different goals. You will probably switch back and forth between the two activities, but both will be more effective if you keep this in mind.

   Researching your career ideas is a fact-finding and information-seeking mission. The main goal is to *learn about* the positions and careers you are considering with an open mind. You should seek out information from multiple sources, scanning the full breadth of the career landscape and gathering pieces of the puzzle.

A job search looks a lot like research, but the main focus is different. When conducting a job search, you need to be *more evaluative* in your approach. You use your criteria (aka Components) to help you narrow down your search results to those potential job and career options that are the best matches to you.

3. **Do the things you don't want to do,** when nearly everyone does the opposite. Driven by comfort, we tend to avoid what might be a little scary or outside our everyday experience. Introverts may resist talking with people they don't know and asking tough questions; extroverts may not read enough about the subject of their interest. Bite the bullet, and notice the parts you should do more of (it is *not* what you have already been doing lots of, by the way). Get some support if you need it—send some emails and request fifteen-minute informational interviews from ten people—or sit down and take some quality time, wading through pages of web results and taking notes.

4. **Seek out multiple sources of information.** The more points of view you access, the more accurate a picture you will get. Different resources will share different information and perspectives. For any given field, career, or job title you investigate online, there will be a considerable amount of variation in their respective responsibilities and qualifications described. If you speak with real people, read their blogs, or watch their vlogs, you will be provided with a good dose of personal perspective, bias, and opinion. Identify multiple information sources. Focus on finding and learning from established and well-respected databases. Communicate with experts and people with deep experience. Don't get lost in the endless and mindless digital chatter of people with lots of opinions and little experience. Always consider the source.

Suppose, for instance, you are considering the field of physical therapy. You speak to two PTs who don't like their jobs, while a third tells you you'll never get accepted at a good school. If you stopped there, you'd kill off this field as a possibility entirely. But if you speak with ten physical therapists, and read some articles or internet entries, you might find that most talk about loving the work, and offer tips on getting into PT school. That can at least keep physical therapy in the running, and it doesn't doom what you might find to be the perfect new career for you.

5. **Resist trying to prove what you want to believe.** Give your hopes, dreams, and preexisting beliefs a rigorous examination, if not a rest. Watch for a tendency to seek evidence that stacks the deck in favor of what you want to believe. It may not match reality. This is not easy, but avoiding that trap will pay off. Law schools pour out an endless stream of graduates who would have made different choices if they had done more research and critical thinking before signing up. Be especially wary when you think you have found the answer. Check it out broadly and deeply. The best way to do this is to gather information from multiple resources.

Use Multiple Information Sources

Using multiple sources of information will help you gain a well-rounded perspective. This is helpful when you seek to make great decisions. Consider where you can turn to for information. Here are a few suggestions on where to look:

- **Your network.** Look to your friends, family, relatives, and others who might be able to connect you to more details about a position or field you are interested in. Talk to them. Put together a list of questions and ask them to share their personal experience and knowledge. It is not just a matter of talking to people you know. Get out there and create a wider and deeper pool of people who can inform you and otherwise be of assistance. Start reaching out to people now. Consistently nurturing and growing that network and relationships is a great career practice. It will pay of tenfold any time you are seeking a new job or position.

- Look for general descriptions of career fields and specific job titles. **Federal and state governments have free, detailed online career resources and databases,** and can be particularly helpful.

- Look in your city—there might even be a **career services office** near you—you can walk in the door and get direction and resources from a knowledgeable professional.

- **Colleges and universities** often have great online career resources. **Community colleges and trade schools** often have job search data and information. Can't find it online? Call the career services department at a college or university— tell them what type of information you are looking for. Ask them for any suggestions or resources.

- Go direct to the **websites of companies or organizations of interest to you.** Look at their Employment/Careers pages. Read the Job Postings. Read the Roles and Responsibilities and Qualifications section of the Job Postings.

- **Recruiters, Headhunters, and Hiring Managers.** Have a field or industry of interest? Reach out to a professional matchmaker or decision-maker. Ask them for a short (fifteen- to twenty-minute) informational interview. Ask them to share their experience and knowledge of the field.

As with all informational interviews—be prepared. Be specific. Have a set of questions to ask, respect their time, thank them when you are done.

- **Blogs, Vlogs, and YouTube channels.** Online, you can find people who are deeply knowledgeable about everything under the sun. Even left-handed bagpipe repair people probably have some sort of online group. And people on the internet are generally very friendly and willing to share what they know. Every group seems to have a range of participants from the newly curious to a few real old masters. The problem is always sorting out who are the masters and who just want to appear to be experts. Seek wisdom before opinion and learn to separate the two. Be discriminate and figure out who really knows their stuff.

- **Books** are another good source for in-depth research. To learn about a field, read a wide range of books that look from different perspectives: books written by people in the field, books about leaders in the field, books about the field by journalists, and textbooks teaching the subject matter you would need to learn.

- **The public library** is the resource not to overlook. Your library can be a useful source for a wide range of research tools unavailable online. Try to find the library in your area with the largest specialty collection of career information. There you will (hopefully) find an array of books on various occupations, the growth outlook for different careers, employer directories, and much more. Many libraries now also have extensive computer resources, links to other library databases and the internet, and will sometimes host career or job-seeker events or groups. Your best resource at the library is the information resources professional, otherwise known as the reference librarian.

- **Trade publications** are a good way to gain real insight into any field of interest. When you read commercial and association trade journals, you find out what is really happening in the industry, what insiders think, what concerns and worries they have, what problems you might like to help solve. There is no better way to transport yourself into the pulsing heart and soul of a field. You can also learn who is who and what topics are hot—valuable stuff if you start to look for specific roles, mentors, or get called in for an interview down the line.

- **Conferences, conventions, trade shows, seminars, and industry-specific clubs** are a great way to meet decision-makers, the people who might eventually hire you. You have an opportunity to meet people at all levels, from CEOs on down, speak with experts, and visit booths offering a wide range of related products. You can usually find a way into industry events, even if you might have to join an organization or apply some *Mission: Impossible* techniques to get into some. Participating in professional development seminars in a field of interest and joining industry-specific groups are other great methods for meeting people and learning at the same time.

- **Trade associations** are an excellent source of information on the careers within the industry they serve. They often have materials developed specifically for people interested in pursuing these careers. Their more senior employees usually have a stethoscope on the pulse of the industry. You might even be able to talk them into letting you use their libraries, which are often voluminous collections of materials in their specialty.

- **Your professional career coach,** if you have one, is your partner in research. Most likely, they won't actually go out and *do* the research for you, but will help you design an effective research strategy, suggest resources, point you in the right direction, and help you make sense of what you uncover.

- No matter how many people you speak with or how many books you read, there is no substitute for actually working in a field that is of interest. **Volunteering and internships** take you into the very heart of a field, so you can find out what it is like from the inside. One caution, though: volunteers and interns usually are given the lowliest of work to do. If you are thinking of becoming the captain of a Greenpeace ship, intercepting whalers on the high seas, licking envelopes in the local office may not give you the authentic experience you seek. Remember: use the opportunity to observe, listen, ask questions, and get a good sense of what people do.

- **Shadowing.** Shadowing is kind of a hybrid of an *informational interview* and an *internship*. This is not an option typically "advertised"—you may need to politely and proactively request to shadow someone in a specific role or position of interest to you. Hang out with a professional for an afternoon, observe what they do and how they do it. Get a sense of the flow and work environment they operate in. You will probably also gain an opportunity to ask questions and (bonus!) give them a chance to see how wonderful and employable you are.

Four Tips to Help Your Career
Research Get You to the Goal Line

1. **Do twenty times as much research as you feel like doing.** We sometimes have clients come back from doing research as a homework assignment, thinking they're done, when they have only scratched the surface. It is not enough to talk with one or two people or read a book or two—you are deciding what to do with your life! The career you choose will be how you spend your days, year after year. We recommend speaking with ten people, or reviewing ten digital or written resources, in each field of interest, at minimum. The more, the better. Read and ask until you don't get any new information from additional resources.

2. **Seek to discover new questions as well as answers.** The more you learn, the more new and important questions you will uncover. Don't be afraid to ask or pursue them.

3. **Capture the information.** Write it down. Copy and paste. Save the URL. Don't read over and forget—who knows, you may want to go back to a company's website and apply for that job later. Wouldn't it be better to have that web address handy?

4. **Think like a detective.** Be creative in how and where you pursue information. Read a news article about a ridiculously cool new piece of technology created by Super Company X? Go to their company website. What do they do? What kind of projects do they work on? Who works for them? Is there a list of employees? Job descriptions? Is there a Careers with Us page of job postings? Follow the clues until you see the whole puzzle.

Now that we've suggested some places to look for information and how to more broadly examine it, what should you make sure to pay attention to?

In the next Inquiry, we will suggest key questions for you to consider as you research individual career ideas.

INQUIRY 33

Career Idea Research, Part 1

Below is a set of questions you can consider as you begin your research. While we love writing by hand, this is a good point in the process to go digital and work on a computer. Not only is it easier to modify templates and documents to fit your growing research, you can also copy and paste descriptions and URLs and take screenshots. Always work in a way that fits your style, but . . . don't give yourself extra work.

We recommend that you create (or download) a template, or repeatable document, to help you organize and access your information on individual Career Ideas. You can find (free!) downloadable template options on Monica's website: https://incareermatters.com. Or create your own. On the next page, you will see an example of one way you could organize these universal questions.

Create or download a document to help you organize your research on individual Career Ideas. (See example, next page.)

Copy or duplicate one document for each new Career Idea.

Amend the template as helpful to you.

Make sure to add the name of the career or job title to your document. Also create or copy a brief general description of the job. (In figure 1, the space for this is in the center of the page.)

Begin your research on your Career Ideas. As you research each of your Career Ideas, consider the questions and characteristics outlined below.

You are seeking the best overall picture of what is typical for the specific Career Idea of Job Title (if there is anything typical).

Note if there is a lot of variation in daily tasks and responsibilities or in qualifications.

Are you noticing groups or subcategories that have similar characteristics or requirements?

Refer back to this Inquiry and its questions as you do your research.

Career Title: Mechanical Engineer			
Research Steps	Talents and Personality	Subject Matter and Meaning	Workplace Environment
1. Unknowns	Do I have the right talents to excel in this field?	Do I care enough about the problems that mechanical engineers solve?	Not sure of the range of companies that hire mechanical engineers
2. Questions	Who can I talk with to learn what talents are needed in this field?	What are the major problems they solve and niche areas they work in?	Which are the innovative companies, and where are they geographically?
	How do I know whether I have the right talents?	What industries hire mechanical engineers?	With what type of company do my talents and personality traits fit best?
	What kind of people go into this field, and am I like them?	Why am I attracted to this field? What am I trying to get out of it?	What kind of human and work culture setting would be best for me?
	What job functions do they typically perform?	Do I care about this subject matter enough?	What are the typical pay and benefits?
3. Resources and Research to Do	Talk to three college professors, and at least ten mechanical engineers. Read engineering journals and websites. Visit an engineering library on campus.	Find professional associations; get recommendations for books to read. Read books to learn about the niches and problems solved in this field. Ponder internally as to my true motivations; get clear why I would care to do this kind of work. What are my metagoals here?	Find out about about engineering companies and their work environments from talking with engineers.
4. Answers and Findings	Mechanical engineers are high in spatial reasoning and analytical reasoning talents. Most are strong introverts with logical, practical mindsets. I am exactly like this; I would be in my element in this field.	A large percentage of jobs in this field are in the aerospace, defense, home appliance, and automotive industries. I love cars and am very excited about helping to develop technology like alternative-fuel engines.	Work environments vary widely; it depends on whether they are innovating new products or mass-producing them. I am an innovator, so a small, dynamic firm that designs new products is where I fit best.

Basic Questions and Information to
Identify from Multiple Sources as You Research

Description: In a concise way, how can you describe this career/job?

Alternative Job Titles: As you research this career, look for alternative, related, or similar job titles. Collect them as you go along. (This will be very helpful later when you conduct job search activities.)

Roles and Responsibilities: What are the main duties and responsibilities for someone in this career? You will find variations in what is described or reported. Add to this list as you research. You might "*" or find a way to identify any characteristic that is either super common or is unique.

Traits and Aptitudes: In descriptions or job postings, or with your common sense, are there specific personality traits, reasoning abilities, natural talents, or aptitudes that are prominent and important for this work? For example, if you were interested in becoming a technical writer for NASA space equipment, having a strong analytical reasoning ability and a strong ability to solve 3D problems with objects would both be very important. For a less serious example, if you are super chatty and love to laugh and share your thoughts with everyone, a career as a silent retreat manager may not be the best fit for you.

Skills and Tech: Is an advanced ability to design with data visualization applications like Tableau important to this job or in this field? Are there coding languages you must know? Do you need to be able to run a seven-minute mile or carry fifty pounds of dead weight up a flight of stairs? Are there key skills or tech that seem important in this career?

Subject Matter and Knowledge: What are the broad or specific areas of knowledge and subject matter important to this career/job? (Biology, chemistry, mediation and arbitration, natural resources, international financial instruments, human migration, the history of the Roman empire?)

Qualifications: As you research, job descriptions will provide you with typical qualifications, while real people may share the "unofficial" what it takes to get hired. As you receive that information from both those sources, note it down. Are there universals? Do you have to pass a state licensing exam, for example? Is there a wide variety of qualifications? Look for patterns.

Salary and Logistics: What is the salary range? What is typical? Is it common to go to an office? Work remotely? Hybrid? How many hours a week? Do you need to live in a particular city, state, or environment? Would this job require travel? How much? What about the type of hours you work—is it typical to be on call? Are evenings and weekends going to be prime work time for you? Note down the whens and wheres and how muches of things.

Workplace Culture and Environment: Is the work or workplace highly regulated and security-conscious? Is it innately hierarchical and structured like the military or state governments? Does it lean toward embracing very progressive values with a lot of diversity and inclusion training? Can you bring your dog to work? Will you be expected to work eighty hours a week and to be money-ambitious? Look for patterns or tendencies for certain cultural dynamics.

Misc. and Quirks (not shown here): Why do you keep seeing references to "hazard pay"? Knowing that your work schedule follows the average temperature or time of sunrise might be something of note. Feel uncomfortable around sick people? Most nursing roles might be a poor fit for you.

Make sure you have a page or document to capture and record the best sites you visited.

If you find a website that describes all the subdisciplines of psychology really well, and provides examples of each . . . make sure you can easily get back to that website.

Monica is a big fan of the multi-tabbed spreadsheet. Look to her website (incareermatters.com) for templates to make your research easier.

+

CHAPTER 18

CAREER EVALUATION AND COMPARISON

Here, with a possibly harsh lack of fanfare, we are going to merge your well-earned list of Career Components into your research efforts and evaluate how well each of your Career Ideas fits you and your career design.

Researching with Your Career Components

In Inquiry 33, you were provided with a set of fundamental topics and questions to consider as you investigate. Did you intuitively start incorporating your Components, and the criteria they illuminate, into your search criteria? If you haven't already done so—it's time to start.

Your Components are more than a wish list—they are a set of criteria. In plain language, they capture what is most important to you and what you want in a career. They are full of key words and terms that you can use to search, not only for information about your existing Career Ideas, but also to identify new job and career options—some you haven't yet thought of! It's time to incorporate your Components into your career research.

INQUIRY 34

Career Idea Research, Part 2

Prep

1. Pull up your Career Components list.

2. Start a second document titled something like "Key Words & Search Terms."

- A key word is a word or phrase of significance. You probably use them all the time when you look for things online. Key words are terms that your browser will try to match to specific information and sites on the web. "Computer, IT, remote work, mission-based, collaboration, detail-oriented, and history" are all key words. "If, and, and but" are not.

3. Read over your Components list and look for "key words." Add them to this new document. Make sure to leave space to add additional key words as you continue your research. Look over your Career Ideas and Clues lists also. Add any meaningful terms.

4. Create a new document, or come up with a plan, to capture your research on relevant careers, organizations, and resources. You could add relevant info and links to individual research pages (see Inquiry 31) or create a new document titled something like "URLs & Resources."

Mix, Search, and Capture

5. Enter your first combination of key words into an internet browser. We recommend mixing them up to include terms relevant to a variety of the topics you explored (e.g., subject matter, job function, values, work environment, etc.).

   - For example, one combo of terms could be "marketing, environment, policy, stewardship, team, interagency, future."

6. Review the results of your search on multiple pages (roughly five to ten). Click into any site that captures your attention. You are looking for more than job postings and specific job descriptions—you are looking for like-mindedness. The results you investigate may be for an organization, like The Nature Conservancy, or they may be for a government report by the EPA. They may be to a news article about a public-private partnership to save a wetland, or they may be a job posting.

7. As you go, capture the URLs, and any key terms or data, for any new career ideas, organizations, projects, companies, or possible networking partners you find.

8. Also update your Key Words, Career Idea Research pages, Clues, Components, Career Ideas, and URL and Resources documents.

Rinse and Repeat

9. Repeat the process above (#5–7) many times using different groups of words.

- Switch up the word order.

- Add in a couple of location terms (e.g., New York, Seattle, Toronto) or terms like "job, business, company, position" and see what happens.

- Keep a lookout for synonyms and additional terms to add to your Key Words list. If the terms you are using aren't getting you results of interest to you—change the terms you are using and try again.

How do you know you are done? Only you can answer this question. Some people spend ten, twenty, one hundred hours searching in this way. If you stop seeing new and relevant results—and you've built a strong list of key words and mixed and matched them for hours and hours—you might be done.

Move back and forth between actions outlined in Inquiries 32 and 33 in a way that makes sense for you. And remember—your ultimate goal is to make a choice about what work or career to pursue. You should start paying attention to narrowing down your Career Ideas list to only those with some real potential!

Career Comparison Tool

Wherever you are in your in-depth research efforts, it is time to introduce you to a new tool: the Career Comparison Worksheet. This worksheet will be your primary tool as you evaluate and narrow down your career options. Find a colorful template on Monica's website, www.incareermatters.com, or create one of your own (there's an example later in this chapter).

Which Careers Fit Best?
The Career Comparison Worksheet

The goal of this Inquiry is to check out how well your various careers fit your specifications (aka you and your Career Design). A note: It may take time!

Career Comparison Worksheet						
Career Design Components	Brain Surgeon	Underwater Welder	Career #3	Career #4	Career #5	Career #6
Mark columns to show where components match up with a career						
3D spatial	5	3				
Make $400K	5					
Use my hands	5	3				
No weekend work	0	4				
Score	15	10				

Across the top row of your worksheet, list the career ideas or job titles that you want to formally evaluate. The exercise you're about to do takes thought and effort. We recommend choosing careers that you think might be a great fit to you and your Career Design Components.

Down the left-most column of your worksheet, list your Career Design Components.

The order of your Components is up to you. Some people put the most important, "nonnegotiable" Components at the top. Some people group them by category (similar to those outlined in the Components Check-In Inquiry).

Evaluate

Pick a career option, go down the column of Components, and rate that career by how well it fits each Component. You may or may not need to do additional research on the career as you do this.

There are different ways you could "rate" the Components. You could use a scale of 1 to 5 or some type of pass/fail rating. Do what makes sense to you.

The more thorough your earlier research on this career idea, the quicker this Inquiry may go for you.

Some of your Components may not be easy to rate for one reason or another. Components addressing "workplace environment and culture" tend to be tricky to rate. How do you evaluate a career idea for "My colleagues are warmhearted and laugh a lot" or "I have a big office with lots of windows and plants" without walking in the door of a specific organization or company? You may want to create a little code to distinguish those Components that are "organization specific" or use your imagination and guess. Do your best to be as accurate as you can.

If you notice that you have too many "It depends" responses, you may want to narrow down your Career Idea to be more specific. Maybe you can create subcategories. If you split a broad idea into a few subcategories, it will not only be more helpful, it will make your life much easier. For example, if you have "writer" as a Career Idea, that is so generic, you would be hard-pressed to define or evaluate much. "Technical writer for a software company," or "speech writer," or "long-form journalist" will be much easier to research and evaluate.

Continue working thorough your Career Ideas. Do more research as needed. Add or power up your Components as they come to you.

When you've done your best to evaluate your selection of Career Ideas, add up the final score. Notice which if any come out as "winners."

Start a B List and Keep Going

After doing your research and evaluating your options on the Career Comparison Worksheet, are there any Career Ideas that you have realized are not strong candidates for your final choice?

Create a B list of Career Ideas and move any weak candidates from your main worksheet to the B list.

You don't want to destroy the info and your evaluation, but you do want to remove it from your prime document. This will leave space for you to . . .

Add new Career Ideas to your worksheet and repeat steps 4 through 6 until you have identified a select few (one to three) top contenders! Keep in mind, though, that these numbers are to help you objectively compare your options in a quantified way—it does not mean that the career with the most points is "the right one." The point is to explore, compare, and evaluate. Use this as a tool to make an informed choice.

And the winner is . . .

CHAPTER 19

✦

MY CAREER CHOICE

If you have already made a choice—Congratulations! You can jump straight to Section 5 for guidance on creating personal marketing materials and pursuing your choice.

If you have *not* made a final choice, you should have narrowed your choices to two to four finalists. This chapter provides you with some final guidance to help you across that finish line.

Final In-Depth Research

To conclude that a career satisfies all or most of your Career Design Components and is a good fit, you have to turn over a lot of rocks. You have to have your unanswered questions—answered. You need to have an informed sense of what each career really entails, flushing out details and getting a glimpse of the flow of a typical workday. The point of all this is twofold: find out enough about a career to predict how well it will fit, and move beyond any romantic fantasies toward the real deal.

Now is the time to get your remaining questions answered and make your final choice.

INQUIRY 36

Answering the Lingering Questions

If you have diligently worked through the Inquiries and put your heart into your research and are unable to identify a great-fitting career choice, you probably have some lingering, unanswered questions. There may be some concern or fact lurking in the back of your brain. It's time to bring it into the light and get clarity.

List your unknowns. Take a pause. Stop gathering new information and look at your Career Comparison Worksheet. What is missing? What haven't you addressed in your research or in your Components? What information is inadequate or missing? Identify the major unknowns you have. Write them down. You may have incomplete knowledge, missing information, distorted generalizations, and flawed understandings about the careers you are considering.

For example, one client we worked with did a brilliant job on her Career Design and in her research. When it came down to making a choice, though, she was unenthused. When asked, "What's missing?" she thought about it for a minute and declared, "Excitement!" None of her choices had the element of the unknown and uncovering mysteries and patterns that she sought. She then had to go back, think about what "exciting" looked like for her, and do some more investigation. (She eventually chose epidemiology, with a focus on minimizing hospital infection spreads.)

Yeahbuts? Do you have an unaddressed concern or fear that is in the way? Write down your Yeahbuts. Many of them can be resolved or overcome with some specific information.

For example, if you have a Yeahbut that says, "To be a veterinarian, I need to get accepted into a program and find a way to pay for it. What if I can't get in? What if I can't afford it?" Both are very reasonable concerns that could absolutely be in the way of choosing to become a veterinarian. Both are also resolvable. You could do additional research and find specific information on the qualifications and application process for veterinarian school. You could find out the cost of the program and speak to someone about the availability of grants, scholarships, financial aid, or student work programs.

Look inside. There are answers to questions that cannot be found outside of you. Sometimes the best answers are internal, such as "Am I willing to live near a big city?" Look inside and see if there is a choice or preference needed that only you can create.

Make up an answer. Sometimes you won't find the answer internally or externally. There are no facts or norms to find in the world. There is no right answer. You've looked for your "inner truth" during three hours of mediation and still can't muster an "insight." In cases like these, you may find great freedom in simply making up an answer. You can choose for no reason other than you say so. Perhaps the career you most want to do is less predictably attainable than others are. You want to be an actor, but you know "success" is incredibly hard to predict. Success, and the ability to earn a stable income, is not as easy to achieve as an actor as it would be as a tax accountant or government employee. Sometimes, you just have to make the leap into the unknown, and make a bold declaration, like the guys who signed the Declaration of Independence, or President Kennedy declaring that "man will walk on the moon." It may be a matter of making an existential choice—just making the choice you know is right for you.

Go realistic. Give sufficient attention to the availability of the work you are considering, the likely future growth of opportunities in the field, and how much of a risk you are willing to take.

Keep at it until you have answered all your important questions.

And, Finally, Make the Choice

For some, the final decision will not be too challenging. The choice may be obvious.

For others, you may face choosing between more than one career that fits your specifications. If that is the case, are they similar enough in a major way that you should look for a way to pursue them as a career path? Or do you really need to choose just *one*?

There are a few special situations when it may be appropriate to have your final choice include more than one specific career:

- More than one very similar job would be equally appealing, and you are willing to split your job search between them.

- You are a college student or otherwise in a situation where you feel that you have narrowed your choice sufficiently, for the present, and want to get some more experience or maturity under your belt before you make the final decision.

- You have decided to have more than one career and divide your time between them.

While many people today have more than one career trajectory, it is not always advisable to pursue more than one. Pursuing a meaningful and rewarding career usually takes a 100 percent effort to get off the ground. However, some people run several part-time businesses and make it work. Reluctance to make one final choice may just be an attack of Yeahbuts. So, you could simply take a deep breath and go for it!

Remember: only you can choose.

You just need to do it. It is your final created commitment. "I will be a . . ."

When the choice is made, you may not feel excited or relieved. If your choice extends you out into new territory, you may feel apprehensive or suffer an even more massive attack of Yeahbuts than usual—a version of the phenomenon known to all salespeople as "buyer's remorse." This is perfectly normal, and, in fact, it may happen regularly. If it does, don't let it sway your resolve. If you read the biographies of people who have accomplished extraordinary feats, you realize that doubts are inevitable. Once Nick asked his explorer friend, John Goddard, if he suffered from attacks of doubt in the midst of expeditions into new territory. Mr. Goddard said sometimes the doubts were constant, especially at times of great difficulty and duress. He said that he treated them like mosquitoes. You can do the same. Know that you will have to put up with many mosquitoes and that they will draw some blood. But don't let them keep you from your destination.

INQUIRY 37

It's Time

What's it going to be? Which career or career path have you identified as being a great fit to you and what is most important to you?

   Write a statement to yourself, declaring your career choice. Include a few main reasons why this choice is a great choice for you.**

** If you are still struggling to make a choice, see the special section in the back of this book, "What If I Can't Decide?" You might also benefit from some professional coaching services—working with someone who knows their stuff and is an expert in helping you choose.

You Did It!

Congratulations. If you are reading this paragraph, you have either designed a great career or chosen work that is a big improvement over the past. We know it took something extraordinary to work through the entire Career Design Project. We know you kept going when the going got tough, when there was no light at the end of the tunnel, even when the Yeahbuts were doing their best to keep you down. You persisted through all of it to arrive here.

   Take a pause and acknowledge yourself for your hard work.

   When you are ready, you will find advice on how to communicate effectively and pursue specific job and career opportunities that light you up!

SECTION 5

COMMUNICATING YOURSELF AND YOUR TALENTS TO OTHERS AND STAYING IN ACTION

A successful pursuit of your brilliant future is all about communicating yourself and your choices with others. This final section of *The Pathfinder* provides you with classic and timeless wisdom on how to market yourself and actively pursue work and career opportunities of interest to you.

Chapter 20: How to Write a Masterpiece of a Résumé

Chapter 21: Effective Job Search

Putting your best foot forward at least keeps it out of your mouth.

—MORRIS MANDEL

✦

How to Write a Masterpiece
of a Résumé

Be brave enough to show the world who you really are.

—NVE

A great résumé does not necessarily follow the rules. It does not have to be one page or follow some special format. In fact, it should be like you: unique. Every résumé is a one-of-a-kind communication, reflective of your situation and your needs.

This résumé guide is most appropriate for people looking for a job in the United States. In the U.S., the rules of job hunting are much more relaxed than they are in much of Europe and Asia. Rules and norms also shift for certain industries, including the government, law, academia, and highly technical engineering and science fields. Do your research to make sure that you are following the best practices for your specific target industry. Then use the principles in this chapter to maximize your presentation and its effectiveness.

With some extra effort, you can create a résumé that makes you really stand out as a superior candidate for a job you are seeking. You can present yourself in a way that stirs the interest of prospective employers and gets you invited to an interview.

Let's focus on the most basic principles of writing a highly effective résumé.

• • •

Intention and purpose. Why do you have a résumé in the first place? What is it supposed to do for you?

Here's an imaginary scenario: You find and apply for a job that seems absolutely perfect for you. You send your résumé with a cover letter to the prospective employer—and so do plenty of other people. A few days later, the employer is staring at a pile of several hundred résumés. *Several hundred?* you ask. *Isn't that an inflated number?* Not really. A job offer often can attract between one hundred and one thousand résumés these days. So, you are facing a great deal of competition. Okay. Back to the employer and the stack. This person isn't any more excited about going through this pile of dry, boring documents than you would be. But they have to do it, so they dig in. After a few minutes, they are getting sleepy. They are not really focusing any more. Then they run across your résumé. As soon as they start reading it, they perk up. The more they read, the more interested, awake, and turned on they become. Most résumés in the pile have only gotten a quick glance. But yours gets read, from beginning to end. Then it gets put on top of the tiny pile of résumés that made the first cut. These are the people who will be asked in to interview.

This is what we're hoping to accomplish. Here's how we can.

The Purpose of a Résumé

The résumé is a tool with one specific purpose: to win an interview. It's an advertisement, telling an employer what you have done, and making a promise that, if they hire you, they will gain specific, needed benefits. It presents you in the best possible light. It convinces the employer that you have what it takes to be successful in this new position or career—that they would be missing out if they didn't give you a call.

Aren't there other ways it can be helpful? Of course! A résumé can be useful to:

- Pass the employer's screening process (requisite educational level, number of years experience, etc.) and give basic facts that might favorably influence the employer (companies worked for, political affiliations, racial minority, etc.).

- Establish you as a professional person with high standards and excellent writing skills, based on the fact that the résumé is so well done.

- Help in other phases of the job-hunting process: to give to friends and contacts who may in turn pass them on to potential employers, to give to your job-hunting contacts and professional references, to provide background information.

What a Résumé Isn't

Most people write a résumé because everyone knows that you have to have one to get a job. They write their résumé grudgingly, to fulfill this obligation. Writing the résumé is only slightly above filling out income tax forms in the hierarchy of worldly delights. If you realize that a great résumé can be your ticket to getting exactly the job you want, you may be able to muster some genuine enthusiasm for creating a real masterpiece, rather than the feeble products most people turn out.

It is a mistake to think of your résumé as a record of your past, a personal statement, or some sort of expression of self. Sure, most of the content of any résumé is focused on your job history—but that information can be shaped and displayed in a way that responds to a specific question or need. Write from the intention to create interest, to persuade the employer to call you. If you do, your final product will be very different than if you write to inform or catalog.

Specialized Industries or Cultures

If you are applying to a niche industry, for a government or academic position, or to a company or organization in another country or culture, you have alternative or additional etiquette to consider. If you are applying to a company or organization with special or unique norms or procedures, you need to conduct some additional research.

For example, if you're applying to a Swiss company, before submitting your résumé, you could search "proper résumé format for applying to jobs at Swiss companies." Did you know that the Swiss (and several other European cultures) use the term *CV* (Curriculum Vitae), and not *résumé*? They also prefer your CV to emphasize your work history, to be formatted in reverse-chronological order, and to be written in the language in which the advertisement or posting was written. See how five minutes of research could quickly and profoundly impact how effectively your application would be received?

Application norms and protocols differ substantially between the private and public sectors in the U.S. Before applying to a position with the U.S. federal government, you should investigate "résumé protocols for applying to U.S. federal government jobs." With government applications, there are specific rules to follow. With some additional attention, you will also find a number of valuable suggestions. Tips such as "use verbs and adjectives that match key words used in the job posting," "highlight and loudly list your accomplishments," and "focus on the mission of the agency" can make all the difference as to whether or not you make it through the first stage. While these are good practices for most résumés and applications, following this guidance makes a particular difference with the government's highly structured and standardized application processes.*

The same extra attention should be paid when interested in working within distinct or specialized cultures or industries. Particularly, if you are not highly literate in the professional practices of a niche community, you should consider engaging a specialist. Look for a résumé writer, or job search or career coach, who has specific knowledge and experience in the culture or industry you are pursuing. Your

---

* https://www.dol.gov/general/jobs/tips-for-writing-a-federal-resume

additional investment will make an immense difference. You always want to present yourself in the most appropriate, expected, and familiar way. The more specialized the industry or culture, or the less familiar you are with it, the more attention you should pay to presenting yourself fittingly.

Consider the value of engaging an insider. Many of the career coaches trained by Rockport Institute are members of the Orthodox Jewish community. They have unique knowledge and insight on how to properly and effectively navigate the religious, social, and cultural norms within this community's professional world. How hard would it be for a professional outside of this community to match the culturally savvy résumé and career advice that these coaches could provide?

What If I'm Not Sure of My Job Target?

The Pathfinder's main purpose is to help you identify jobs, positions, careers that are a great fit to you. If you are not sure of what you are looking for—go back and do some work in the first 350 pages of this book.

Okay, that was a bit dramatic. Maybe you aren't 100 percent sure or have a couple of options in mind, or don't know exactly the right job titles. You can still work on your résumé, but it requires additional work.

If you are headed for an uncertain job target, still curate and design your résumé to directly respond to each job you are applying for. Do some research and figure out exactly what they want in a candidate and use that framework to put forth what will be most useful. Use the key words that will work with them. Look up similar listings and use key words that will work. There will be more about this later in the chapter.

How to Knock the Socks Off the Prospective Employer

Research has shown that only one interview is granted for every fifty to one hundred résumés received by the average employer—and that those résumés are being quickly scanned, rather than evaluated. The time you have to persuade a prospective employer to read more into you is about **seven seconds**.

This means that the top half of the first page of your résumé will either make you or break you. By the time they have read the first few lines, you have either caught their interest, or your résumé has failed. To write an effective résumé, you have to learn how to write powerful, but subtle, advertising copy. Not only that, but you must sell a product in which you have a large personal investment: you.

You do not need to hard sell or make any claims that are not absolutely true. You do need to get over your modesty and unwillingness to toot your own horn. People more often buy the best-advertised product than they buy the best product. That is good news if you are willing to learn to create an excellent résumé. With a little extra effort, you will find that you will usually get a better response from prospective employers than people with better credentials.

Focus on the Employer's Needs, Not Yours

Putting it a different way: imagine that *you* are the person who will be doing the hiring. It may be a recruiter, someone in HR, or the person who will be responsible for the bottom-line productivity of the project or group you hope to be a part of (or a combination). These folks care deeply about hiring the right person to fulfill the needs of the job. Your résumé should appeal directly to them. Ask yourself: What would make someone the perfect candidate? What accomplishments or special abilities would this person have? What would set a truly exceptional candidate apart from a merely good one? What does the employer really want?

If you are seeking a job in a field you know well, you probably already know what would make someone a superior candidate. If you are not sure, you can gather hints from the job listings you are answering, from asking other people who work in the same company or the same field. You could even call or email the prospective employer and ask them what they want. Don't make wild guesses unless you have to. It is very important to do this step well, and that every successive step in producing a finished document should be part of your overall intention to convey to the prospective employer that you are a truly exceptional candidate.

Start Putting It Together

Start brainstorming about why you are the person who can best fill this role. Write down everything you have ever done that demonstrates that you fit perfectly with what is wanted and needed by the prospective employer. The whole idea is to loosen up your thinking enough so that you will be able to see some new connections between what you have done and what the employer is looking for. You need not confine yourself to work-related accomplishments—use your entire life as the palette to paint with. Cover all possible ways of thinking about and communicating what you do well. What are the talents you bring to the marketplace? What do you have to offer the prospective employer?

If you are making a career change or are a young person and new to the job market, you are going to have to be especially creative in getting across what makes you stand out. This brainstorming will be the raw material from which you craft your résumé. One important part of the planning process is to decide which résumé format fits your needs best. Don't automatically assume that a traditional format will work best for you. More about that later.

Build It Out

A great résumé has two sections.

In the first section, make simple and bold statements about your abilities, your qualities, and your achievements. Write powerfully, but honestly. Make the reader immediately perk up and realize that you are a unique individual with something special to offer. In the second section, you will provide the supporting details, the evidence, that backs up your initial bold assertions.

The first section is usually short and to the point. Leave the reader wanting more. Leave them with a hint of mystery. That way, they have even more reason to reach for the phone.

You should start by naming your intended job. This may be in a separate "Objective" section, or may be folded into the second section, the "Summary." If you are making a change to a new field, or are a young person not fully established in a career, start with a separate "Objective" section.

The Objective

Good advertising is directed toward a very specific target audience. When a car company is trying to sell their inexpensive compact to an older audience, they show Grandpa and Grandma stuffing the car with happy, shiny grandchildren and talk about how safe and economical the car is. When they advertise the exact same car to the youth market, they show it going around corners on two wheels, with plenty of drums and power chords thundering in the background. You want to focus your résumé just as specifically.

This requires that you be absolutely clear about your career direction—or, at least, appear to be clear. The way to demonstrate your clarity of direction or apparent clarity is to have the first major topic of your résumé be your **objective,** or a statement that you're the one.

Let's look at a real-world example: Suppose the owner of a small software company is seeking an experienced software salesperson. A week later they have received five hundred résumés. The applicants have a bewildering variety of backgrounds. The employer has no way of knowing whether any of them are really interested in selling software. They remember all the jobs they applied for that they didn't really want. They know that many of the résumés they received are from people who are just using a shotgun approach, casting their seed to the winds. Then they come across a résumé in the pile that starts with the following:

A software sales position in an organization where an extraordinary record of generating new accounts, exceeding sales targets, and enthusiastic customer relations would be needed.

This wakes them up. They are immediately interested. This first sentence conveys some very important and powerful messages: "I want exactly the job you are offering. I am a superior candidate because I have the qualities that are most important to you. I want to make a contribution to your company." This works well because the employer is smart enough to know that someone who wants to do exactly what you are offering will be much more likely to succeed than someone who doesn't. (And will probably be a lot more pleasant to work with.) What's more, the candidate is communicating from the point of view of making a contribution to the employer, not a self-centered or self-serving point of view. Even when people are savvy enough to have an objective, they often make the mistake of saying something like "a position where I can hone my skill as a scissors sharpener" or something similar. The employer is interested in hiring you for what you can do for them, not for fulfilling your private goals and agenda.

Here's how to write your objective. First of all, decide on a specific job title to direct your objective toward. Go back to your list of answers to the question "How can I demonstrate that I am the perfect candidate?" What are the two or three qualities, abilities, or achievements that would make a candidate stand out as truly exceptional for that specific job? The person in the above example recognized that the prospective employer, being a small, growing software company, would be very interested in candidates with an ability to generate new accounts. So, they made that the very first point they got across in their résumé. Be sure the objective is to the point. Do not use fluffy phrases that are obvious or do not mean anything, such as: "allowing the ability to enhance potential and utilize experience in new challenges." An objective may be broad and still somewhat undefined in some cases, such as: "a mid-level management position in the hospitality or entertainment industry." Remember, your résumé will only get a few seconds attention, at best! You have to generate interest right away, in the first sentence they lay their eyes on. Having an objective statement that really sizzles is highly effective. And it's simple to do. One format is:

Objective: *An X position in an organization where Y and Z would be needed.*

X is the name of the position you seek. Y and Z are the most compelling qualities, abilities, or achievements that will really make you stand out above the crowd of applicants. The research you have previously done, to find out what is most important to the employer, will provide the information to fill in Y and Z.

If you are not really sure what job you are after, you should adapt your résumé to each type of job you apply for. There is nothing wrong with having several different résumés, each with a different objective, each specifically crafted for a different type of position. You may even want to change some parts of your résumé for each job you apply for. Have an objective that is perfectly matched with the job you are applying for. Remember, you are writing advertising copy, not your life story.

A Few Examples of Separate Objective Sections

- Senior staff position with a bank that offers the opportunity to utilize my expertise in commercial real estate lending and strategic management.

- An entry-level position in the hospitality industry where a background in advertising and public relations would be needed.

- A position teaching English as a second language where a special ability to motivate and communicate effectively with students would be needed.

Now that you have your objective, it's time to move on to your summary.

The Summary of Qualifications

The "summary" or "summary of qualifications" consists of several concise statements that focus the reader's attention on the most important qualities, achievements, and abilities you have to offer. It is your one and only chance to attract and hold their attention, to get across what is most important, and to entice the employer to keep reading. This is the spiciest part of the résumé. It may be the only section fully read by the employer, so it should be very strong and convincing, and feature professional characteristics that may be helpful in winning the interview. It should look something like this:

A short phrase describing your profession
Followed by a statement of broad or specialized expertise
Followed by two or three additional statements related to any of the following:

    Breadth or depth of skills
    Unique mix of skills
    Range of environments in which you have experience
    A special or well-documented accomplishment

A history of awards, promotions, or superior performance commendations
One or more professional or appropriate personal characteristics
A sentence describing professional objective or interest

Below are some examples. Notice that they show how to incorporate your objective in the "Summary" section. If you are making a career change, your "Summary" section should show how what you have done in the past prepares you to do what you seek to do in the future. If you are a young person new to the job market, your "summary" will be based more on ability than experience.

A Few Examples of "Summary" Sections

- Highly motivated, creative, and versatile real estate executive with seven years of experience in property acquisition, development, and construction, as well as the management of large apartment complexes. Especially skilled at building effective, productive, working relationships with clients and staff. Excellent management, negotiation, and public relations skills. Seeking a challenging management position in the real estate field that offers extensive contact with the public.

- Over ten years' experience as an organizational catalyst/training design consultant with a track record of producing extraordinary results for more than twenty national and community-based organizations. A commitment to human development and community service. Energetic self-starter with excellent analytical, organizational, and creative skills.

- Financial management executive with nearly ten years of experience in banking and international trade, finance, investments, and economic policy. Innovative in structuring credit enhancement for corporate and municipal financing. Skilled negotiator with strong management, sales, and marketing background. Areas of expertise include [a bulleted list would follow this paragraph].

- Health-care professional experienced in management, program development, and policymaking in the United States as well as in several developing countries. Expertise in emergency medical services. A talent for analyzing problems, developing and simplifying procedures, and finding innovative solutions. Proven ability to motivate and work effectively with persons from other cultures and all walks of life. Skilled in working within a foreign environment with limited resources.

- Commander—chief executive officer of the U.S. Navy, Atlantic Fleet. Expertise in all areas of management, with a proven record of unprecedented accomplishment. History of the highest naval awards and rapid promotion. Proven senior-level experience in executive decision-making, policy direction, strategic business planning, congressional relations, financial and personnel management, research and development, and aerospace engineering. Extensive knowledge of government military requirements in systems and equipment. Committed to the highest levels of professional and personal excellence.

- Performing artist with a rich baritone voice and unusual range, specializing in classical, spiritual, and gospel music. Featured soloist for two nationally televised events. Accomplished pianist. Extensive performance experience includes television, concert tours, and club acts. Available for commercial recording and live performances.

Skills and Accomplishments

In this final part of the evidence section of your résumé, you go into more detail. You are still writing to engage the reader, not to inform them. Basically, you do exactly what you did in the previous section, except that you go into more detail. In the summary, you focused on your most special highlights. Now you tell the rest of the best of your story. Let them know what results you produced, what happened as a result of your efforts, what you are especially gifted or experienced at doing.

You are still writing to communicate the following: if you buy this product, you will get these direct benefits. If it doesn't contribute to that message, don't bother to say it. Remember, not too much detail. Preserve a bit of mystery. Don't tell them everything.

Sometimes the "Skills and Accomplishments" sections is a separate section. In a chronological résumé, it becomes the first few phrases of the descriptions of the various jobs you have held. We will cover that in a few minutes, when we discuss the different types of résumés. When it is a separate section, it can have several possible titles, depending on your situation:

ACHIEVEMENTS
ACCOMPLISHMENTS AND SKILLS
ACCOMPLISHMENTS
SUMMARY OF ACHIEVEMENTS (OR ACCOMPLISHMENTS)
ACCOMPLISHMENTS AND EXPERIENCE
PROFESSIONAL HIGHLIGHTS

There are a number of different ways to structure this section. In all of these styles, put your accomplishments and skills in order of importance for the desired career goal. If you have many skills, the last skill paragraph might be called "Additional Skills."

Here are a few ways you could structure your skills and accomplishments section:

1. A listing of skills or accomplishments or a combination of both, with bullets

Example:

SELECTED SKILLS AND ACCOMPLISHMENTS

- Raised $19,000 in twenty-one days in canvassing and advocacy on environmental, health, and consumer issues.

- Conducted legal research for four assistant U.S. attorneys, for the U.S. Attorney's Office.

- Coordinated board of directors and community advisory board of community mental health center. Later commended as "the best thing that ever happened to that job."

2. A listing of major skill headings with accomplishments under each. The accomplishments can be a bulleted list or in paragraph form. The material under the headings should include mention of accomplishments that prove each skill.

Example:

SELECTED ACCOMPLISHMENTS

National Training Project / Conference Management.
Director of "Outreach on Housing," a national public education/training project funded by USAID, foundations, and all the major church denominations—Designed, managed, and promoted three-day training conferences in cities throughout the U.S.—Planned and managed 32 nationwide training seminars and a five-day annual conference for university vice presidents and business executives.

Program Design: Universities
Invited by Miscatonic University president H. P. Lovecraft to develop new directions and programs for the university's Office of Summer Educational Programs, first director of Miscatonic's "Pre-College Program," first editor of "Midnight at Miscatonic."

3. A list of bulleted accomplishments or skill paragraphs under each job (in a chronological résumé).

Example:

Director of Sales and Marketing 2019–2023
DELAWARE TRADE INTERNATIONAL, INC. Wilmington, DE

Promoted from Sales Representative within one year of joining company to Director of Sales and Marketing. Responsible for international sales of raw materials, as well as printing and graphic arts equipment. Oversaw five sales managers. In charge of direct sales and marketing in seventeen countries throughout Europe and the Middle East.

- Recruited, trained, and managed sales staff. Developed marketing strategy, prepared sales projections, and established quotas. Selected and contracted with overseas subagents to achieve international market penetration.

- Negotiated and finalized long-term contractual agreements with suppliers on behalf of clients. Oversaw all aspects of transactions, including letters of credit, international financing, preparation of import/export documentation, and shipping/freight forwarding.

- Planned and administered sales and marketing budget, and maintained sole profit/loss responsibility. Within first year, doubled company's revenues, and produced $7–9 million in annual sales during the next eight years.

Outsmarting AI and ATS Scanners

Today, for better or for worse, many sophisticated organizations use an applicant tracking system (ATS) to process your résumé. Your résumé may be discarded because it has the wrong information or does not contain the best key words. ATS software is designed to help the employer improve the hiring process and lighten the load. They streamline the recruiting process by evaluating candidates, automate the hiring process, and make better decisions based on data.

Be wary of answering the questions asked. Use the words and terms the application system used in your responses. Failure to do so may cause your résumé and application to be passed over. Specific key words include or discard your résumé. Some of the most sophisticated ATS systems are able to create a profile of an ideal candidate, identify skills and talents, and even predict success factors to maximize the higher. Some of them will search online candidate résumés in addition to sorting through applied candidates. They can simplify an organization's struggle to identify and recruit high-end talent, create dynamic job descriptions, pre-interview applicants, and offer skill assessments using AI to create skills profiles.

In writing your summary section, one important task is to try to figure out what key words will get you through the dragon's doorway. You can do this in a number of ways. For example, one organization may search for candidates that graduated from certain top universities. If you an took online course from that school, be sure to mention it. Sometimes it's worthwhile to take the course just to get the name of the elite university on your résumé. Then, once the résumé is through the scanner, a human being will read it, who will most likely care less about your educational affiliation than they will your superior qualities and experience. This is the place to be both crafty and honest to help you get through the software scan. Your summary section is your key to the lock.

When you submit an application online, the ATS scans your résumé and extracts information like skills, job titles, and educational background. To increase your chances of passing an ATS scan, learn how it works from the point of view of an employer. Read some of the sales pitches from ATS companies to learn how they go about what they do. The more you know, the better.

This is why your summary section is the most important part of your résumé. It's the place to put all the keywords to slide you through the ATS process so that your résumé reaches the desk of the decider.

Even though people argue about the best file type for ATS, all up-to-date scanners can read PDF, Word, and Google files. It is best to send a PDF file because the employer may not use the software you used, which may create issues with formatting.

The Supporting Details and Evidence Section

By evidence, we mean all the mandatory information you must include on your résumé: chronological work history with dates, education, affiliations, list of software mastered, etc. All this stuff is best placed in the second half of the résumé. Put the hot stuff in the beginning, and all this less exciting information afterward. It gives the employer the details about where you worked, how long, your education, etc. This is the standard stuff that any résumé book can help you with, so we will not cover it here in detail. We divided the résumé into a "hot" assertions section, and a staid "evidence" section for the sake of communicating that a great résumé is not information, but advertising. A great résumé has no evidence section. It is all one big assertions section. In other words, every single word is crafted to have the desired effect, to get them to pick up the phone and call you. It is all one big ad disguised as a history of your working life. The decisions you make on what information to emphasize and what to de-emphasize should be based on considering every word of your résumé to be an important part of the assertions section. The evidence includes some or all of the following sections:

Experience

List jobs in reverse chronological order—meaning your current or most recent role at the top—and don't go into detail on the jobs early in your career. (Another trick is to summarize a number of the earliest jobs in one line or very short paragraph, or list only the bare facts with no position description.) Decide which is, overall, more impressive: your job titles or the names of the firms you worked for. Then consistently begin with the more impressive of the two, perhaps using boldface type.

You may want to describe the firm in a phrase in parentheses if this will impress the reader. Put dates in italics at the end of the job, to de-emphasize them: don't include months, unless the job was held less than a year. Include military service, internships, and major volunteer roles if desired, because the section is labeled "Experience." It does not mean that you were paid.

Other headings: "Professional History," "Professional Experience"; not "Employment" or "Work History," both which seem more lower-level.

Education

List education in reverse chronological order, degrees or licenses first, followed by certificates and advanced training. Set degrees apart so they are easily seen. Put in boldface whatever will be most impressive. Don't include any details about college except major and awards, unless you are in still in college or just recently graduated. Include grade point average only if over 3.4. List selected coursework if this will help convince the reader of your qualifications for the targeted job.

Do include advanced training, but be selective with the information, summarizing the information and including only what will be impressive for the reader.

No degree received yet? If you are working on an uncompleted degree, include the degree and in parentheses the expected date of completion (expected xxxx).

If you didn't finish college, start with a phrase describing the field studied, then the school, then the dates (the fact that there was no degree may be missed).

Other headings might be "Education and Training," "Education and Licenses," "Legal Education/Undergraduate Education" (for attorneys).

Awards

This section is a must if you have received awards. If you have received commendations or praise from some very senior source, you could call this section "Awards and Commendations." In that case, go ahead and quote the source. If the only awards received were in school, put these under the "Education" section. Mention what the award was for if you can (or just "for outstanding accomplishment" or "outstanding performance").

Professional Affiliations

Include only those that are current and will be relevant and impressive—leadership roles, too, if appropriate. This is a good section to include to get across your status as a member of a minority targeted for special consideration by employers, or if there is an association membership to show it and this would be helpful in hiring and otherwise unclear on the résumé.

This section can be combined with "Civic/Community Leadership" as "Professional and Community Memberships."

Community Leadership

This is good to include if the leadership roles or accomplishments are related to the job target and can show skills acquired, for example: a loan officer hoping to become a financial investment counselor who was the financial manager of a community organization charged with investing its funds. Any board of directors memberships or "chairmanship" would be good to include. Be careful with political affiliations, as they could be a plus or minus with an employer or company.

Publications

Include only if published. Summarize if there are many.

Personal Interests

Advantages: Can indicate a skill or area or knowledge that is related to the goal, such as photography for someone in public relations, carpentry and woodworking for someone in construction management. Can show well-roundedness, good physical health, or knowledge of a subject related to the goal. Can create common ground or spark conversation in an interview.

Disadvantages: Are usually irrelevant to the job goal and résumé purpose, and may be meaningless or an interview turnoff ("TV and reading," "Fundraising for the Hells Angels").

You probably should not include a personal interests section. Your reason for including it is most likely that you want to tell them about you. But, as you know, this is an ad. If this section would powerfully move the employer to understand why you would be the best candidate, include it; otherwise, forget about it.

References

You may put "References available upon request" at the end of your résumé if you wish. This is a standard close (centered at bottom in italics), but is not necessary—it is usually assumed. Do not include actual names of references. A references list can be done as a separate sheet and brought to the interview to be given to the employer if requested.

A Few Guidelines for Presentation

As mentioned above, the résumé's first impression is most important. It should be exceptionally visually appealing, to be inviting to the reader. Remember to think of the résumé as an advertisement.

Simple clean structure. Very easy to read. Symmetrical. Balanced. Uncrowded. As much white space between sections of writing as possible, sections of writing which are no longer than six lines, and shorter if possible. Absolutely no errors. Have a couple of detail-oriented people go over your résumé and look for small errors.

Highlight your strengths. Make careful and strategic choices as to how to organize, order, and convey your skills and background. Consider: whether to include the information at all, placement in overall structure of the résumé, location on the page itself or within a section, ordering of information, more impressive ways of phrasing the information, use of design elements (such as boldface to highlight, italics to minimize, ample surrounding space to draw the eye to certain things).

Use of power words. For every skill, accomplishment, or job described, use the most active and impressive verb you can think of (which is also accurate). Begin the sentence with this verb, except when you must vary the sentence structure to avoid repetitious writing.

A List of Power Verbs

accelerated
accomplished
achieved
acquired
added
addressed
administered
advised
allocated
analyzed
answered
appeared
applied
appointed
appraised
approved
arranged
assessed
assigned
assisted
assumed
assured
audited
awarded
bought
briefed
broadened
brought
budgeted
built
cataloged
caused
changed
chaired
clarified
classified
closed
collected
combined

commented
communicated
compared
compiled
completed
computed
conceived
concluded
conducted
conceptualized
considered
consolidated
constructed
consulted
continued
contracted
controlled
converted
coordinated
corrected
counseled
counted
created
critiqued
cut
dealt
decided
defined
delegated
delivered
demonstrated
described
designed
determined
developed
devised
diagnosed
directed
discussed

distributed
documented
doubled
drafted
earned
edited
effected
eliminated
endorsed
enlarged
enlisted
ensured
entered
established
estimated
evaluated
examined
executed
expanded
expedited
experienced
experimented
explained
explored
expressed
extended
filed
filled
financed
focused
forecasted
formulated
found
founded
gathered
generated
graded
granted
guided

halved

handled

helped

identified

implemented

improved

incorporated

increased

indexed

initiated

influenced

innovated

inspected

installed

instituted

instructed

insured

interpreted

interviewed

introduced

invented

invested

investigated

involved

issued

joined

kept

launched

learned

leased

lectured

led

licensed

listed

logged

made

maintained

managed

matched

measured

mediated

met

modified

monitored

motivated

moved

named

negotiated

observed

opened

operated

ordered

organized

oversaw

participated

perceived

performed

persuaded

planned

prepared

presented

processed

procured

programmed

prohibited

projected

promoted

proposed

provided

published

purchased

pursued

qualified

ranked

rated

received

recommended

reconciled

recruited

redesigned

reduced

regulated

related

reorganized

replaced

replied

reported

represented

researched

resolved

responded

revamped

reviewed

revised

saved

scheduled

selected

served

serviced

set

set up

simplified

sold

solved

sorted

sought

sparked

specified

spoke

staffed

started

streamlined

strengthened

stressed

stretched

structured

studied

submitted

substituted

succeeded

suggested

summarized

superseded

supervised
surveyed
systematized
tackled
targeted
taught
terminated
tested
toured
traced
tracked
traded

trained
transferred
transformed
translated
transported
traveled
treated
trimmed
tripled
turned
uncovered
unified

unraveled
updated
used
utilized
verified
visited
waged
widened
won
worked
wrote

Some Other Power Words

ability
capable
capability
capacity
competence
competent
complete
completely
consistent
contributions
demonstrated
developing
educated
effective
effectiveness
efficient
enlarging
equipped
excellent
exceptional

expanding
experienced
global
increasing
knowledgeable
major
mature
maturity
nationwide
outstanding
performance
positive
potential
productive
proficient
profitable
proven
qualified
record
repeatedly

resourceful
responsible
results
significant
significantly
sound
specialist
substantial
substantially
successful
stable
thorough
thoroughly
versatile
vigorous
well-educated
well-rounded
worldwide

Indicate that you are results-oriented. Wherever possible, prove that you have the desired qualifications through a clear strong statement of accomplishments, rather than a statement of potentials, talents, or responsibilities. Indicate results of work done, and quantify these accomplishments, whenever appropriate. For example: "Initiated and directed complete automation of the XXX Department, resulting in time-cost savings of over 25 percent." Additionally, preface skill and experience statements with the adjectives "proven" and "demonstrated" to create this results orientation.

Be consistent, but not repetitive. Don't repeat a verb or adjective twice in the same writing "block" or paragraph. Use commas liberally, to clarify meaning and make reading easier. Remain consistent in writing decisions; for example, use of abbreviations and capitalizations.

Production. It should look typeset. Use a standard conservative font in 11 or 12 point. Don't have your résumé look like you squeezed too much on the page.

Length. Everyone freely gives advice on résumé length. They don't need to be one page. That makes no sense for some people. It should highlight relevant experience and be relevant to the industry and position to which you are applying. It should be long enough to lead the prospective employer to pick up the phone and call you—but no longer than that. Do what works. Sometimes it is appropriate to have a three-pager. Look to others in your profession to see if there is an established agreement about résumé length in your field. Don't bore them with too many details. Let them call you and ask you!

Professions with specific résumé formats. If you are in a profession that demands a specific résumé format, like law, or academia, follow that format exactly.

Verb, person, and tense. Résumés can be written using either the first- or third-person verb tense. Use whichever you choose consistently.

Verb tenses are varied and based on accurate reporting. If the accomplishment is completed it should be past tense. If the task is still underway, it should be present tense. If the skill is something that has been used and will continue to be used, use present tense ("conduct presentations on member recruitment to professional and trade associations"). A way of "smoothing out" transitions is to use the past continuous ("have conducted over forty presentations . . .").

No lengthy blocks of writing. A good rule is to have no more than six lines of writing in any one writing "block" or paragraph (summary, skill section, accomplishment statement, job description, etc.). If any more than this is necessary, start a new section or a new paragraph.

Ordering of experience and education sections. Experience sections should come first, before education, in most every case. This is because you have more qualifications developed from your experience than from your education. The exceptions would be (1) if you have just received or are completing a degree in a new professional field, if this new degree study proves stronger qualifications than does your work experience; (2) lawyers, who have the peculiar professional tradition of listing their law degrees first; (3) an undergraduate student; or (4) someone who has just completed a particularly impressive degree from a particularly impressive school, even if they are staying in the same field; for example, a MBA from Harvard.

Telephone numbers. Be sure the telephone number on the résumé will, without exception, be answered by a person or an answering message Monday through Friday, 8 a.m. to 5 p.m. You do not want to lose the prize interview merely because there was no answer to your phone and the caller gave up.

A Few More Tips

Put most important information on the first line of a writing "block" or paragraph—the first line is read most.

Use bold caps for the name on page one. Put your name at the top of page two, on a two-page résumé. Put section headings, skill headings, titles, or companies (if impressive), degrees, and school name (if impressive), in boldface.

Spell out numbers under and including ten; use numerical form for numbers over and including 11 (as a general rule). Spell out abbreviations unless they are unquestioningly obvious.

What Not to Put on a Résumé

The word "Résumé" at the top of the résumé
Fluffy rambling "objective" statements
Salary information
Full addresses and zip codes of former employers
Reasons for leaving jobs
A "Personal" section, or personal statistics
Names of supervisors
References

Accuracy, Honesty, Stretching the Truth

Make sure that you can back up what you say. Keep the claims you make within the range of your own integrity. There is nothing wrong with pumping things up in your résumé so you communicate who you are and what you can do at your very best. In fact, you are being foolish if you seek to convey a careful, balanced portrayal of yourself. You want to knock their socks off! Remember, this is an ad with a purpose of landing an interview, not a history of your past.

CHAPTER 21

+

EFFECTIVE JOB SEARCH

Today's Job Search Reality

Have you ever heard it said that the most stressful things people go through are divorce, the death of a close loved one, and moving? Applying for jobs should definitely be on the list. We've heard from many of our clients that the whole idea of seeking a new job fills them with horror. We understand. We are here to help. And . . . the reality is that, unless you get super lucky, your job search experience is unlikely to feel quick and painless. You will likely have to deal with rejection. You may have to spend hundreds of hours and several months engaged in activities that are outside your comfort zone, but don't panic. The more focused and effective the job search method you use, the sooner you will have the job you want.

Job Search Effectiveness

Personal Marketing. The one most basic principle of job searching is that every step in the process is a form of personal marketing. The person who gets the job is often the one who does the best job of marketing themselves. To compete successfully, you have to understand why one person gets selected over another and design your campaign so that you will be that person. Each phase of the job search provides an opportunity for you to come up with a creative strategy to boost the effectiveness of your campaign.

A lot of action. Presenting yourself in the best possible light requires a great résumé, a consistent plan, and a lot of action. You are going to give yourself the best possible shot at it by being clear what you want and why you are a great candidate, having a well-written, tailored résumé and online profile, identifying the best target companies and opportunities, and then . . . applying to many of them.

You would be shocked by how much of a job search is a numbers game. If you speak with two hundred people who might turn out to be your next boss, you will have ten times the chance of landing a job than if you talk with twenty. If you spend thirty hours a week engaged in an effective search, you will have ten times the chance of landing a job than if you do it three hours a week. Double the transactions, double your chances. It's that simple.

Network with Decision-Makers and Centers of Influence. High-quality connections depend on creating and managing relationships with people who can hire you, will hire you, or can recommend you as an exceptional candidate. The more decision-makers and influencers you connect with—the more efficient your job search will be.

Your Job Search Is a Project

Just as you did with your Career Design, treat your job search as a project. Create a specific goal, make a plan, and then wake up each morning and follow your plan. Implementing a creative action plan is what gets you to your goal, not doing what is in your everyday bag of tricks.

Step 1: Write a description of exactly what you are looking for.

Do you have a clear picture of the jobs or roles you are looking for? If not, go back a few steps and do more work on your Career Design Project. Keep your Career Components in front of you.

Step 2: Define and list your target market.

"Target market" in advertising terms refers to people a company aims to turn into customers. In your job search, your target is the collection of specific organizations that might hire you to do what you want, where you want to do it. You choose the organizations that make it to your target list. If you don't have criteria for companies and organizations to approach, review chapter 15 on Workplace Environment.

Once you have identified organizations that might hire you to do what you want, find out everything about them. What is it like to work there? How well do they do what they do? What's their history and likely future, their financials, their strengths and weaknesses? What are their main concerns? What kind of people do they prefer to hire? Do they seek the best candidate or take a conservative hire-the-one-with-the-best-résumé approach? Who are the decision-makers? What are they like? How could you get to them? Who do you know who might have access to them? Do you have the qualifications they require? What's their hiring philosophy? How well do you fit it?

This takes a lot of detective work. The main value of the internet in job searching is this kind of research. Networking is, by far, the best way to find out what you need to know.

Prioritize your target organizations once you have developed your target list and done some research. You want to put the bulk of your effort into the most likely places you might work.

Step 3: Write an effective, targeted résumé.

See chapter 20 for some wisdom on how to approach, and what to prioritize, on your résumé.

Step 4: Plan and work your job search project.

Plan your search campaign and the steps you will take. Make up a daily and weekly plan of action. What will you accomplish each day? Be specific: instead of "ask friends . . . ," note exactly who you will talk to about what. And your plan must include talking to people, not emailing them. How much time will you spend? How will you keep track?

Step 5: Get in action. Concentrate on the most effective activities.

Most job seekers spend too little time each week on their job search. Once again, this is a numbers game. You get twice the results from twice the effort. When someone tells us they have been searching for a job for more than a year, we ask how much time they have spent on their search in the last week, and they usually admit to spending very few hours. The few that have put in sufficient time have usually spent that time on low-payback activities.

> *I'm a great believer in luck, and I find that the harder I work,*
> *the more of it I have.*
>
> —THOMAS JEFFERSON

Step 6: Keep at it until you reach your goal.

It's okay to mess up, slack off, or cry. Just regroup and get back on the proverbial horse. You don't fail unless you quit.

Last words of wisdom. There are plenty of other things you need to do: plan your job search campaign, research organizations, learn more about decision-makers, write letters, and keep track of your search project. Focus on coming face-to-face with as many decision-makers as possible. Each step in the job search prepares you, in one way or another, for the one thing vital to this process: talking directly with people who can offer you the job. The more, the better.

Remember, even when hiring managers have strict parameters to meet, and protocol to hire, they want to hire someone they like, someone they think will fit in, and someone with the enthusiasm and work ethic to get the job done right. If you can make yourself a real person—a face, a name, a personality—do it! By adding boldness and personality to your résumé, cover letters and emails, messages, and online profiles—you give yourself a fighting chance. If you can—get face time with influencers and decision-makers. Have your face on your online profiles. Use your name. Use their name. If you take this approach to your job search, you need to find ways to give decision-makers a chance to know you, to discover your sterling qualities.

Success is the ability to go from one failure to another with no loss of enthusiasm.

—SIR WINSTON CHURCHILL

Final Words of Encouragement, Inspiration, and Congratulations

Remember, the final step is to celebrate. Go have yourself an amazing party. You deserve it!

SPECIAL SECTION I:
THE TYPE AND TALENT INDICATOR

Note: This chapter depends on your having completed chapters 7, 9, and 10.

The following is a list of charts suggesting careers that may fit combinations of your personality type on Maestro/Tribal and spatial/non-spatial scales. Then it takes it a step further and divides those lists into careers that fit spatial, tangible, and non-spatial people.

The best way to use these lists is to check out the list of careers that fit your type and talents. Notice what the careers have in common. Notice which ones are attractive to you and ask yourself why. Notice which ones are not attractive to you and what it is about them that makes them so. The intent is to help you find good clues.

Very important note: Do not take any of this too literally. This is a generative exercise, meant to prompt larger thought, enthusiasm, and investigation. It is not a definitive diagnosis. More than one type and talent profile fits any career. You may fit careers that are suggested for other types. Study the whole set, and follow what speaks to you.

Maestro ENFP		
Non-spatial	**Tangible**	**Spatial**
actor: theater	adventure education: program designer, instructor	alternative medicine practitioner
coach: personal growth, career change, life planning	alternative therapist: biofeedback, virtual-reality therapy	evolutionary biologist, sociobiologist
consultant: communications, education, HR	cognitive scientist: personality, psychobiology	film director: independent production
drama coach	documentary filmmaker	fine artist
law: entertainment, media	Outward Bound guide	holistic medicine: naturopath
motivational speaker, self-help seminar leader	photojournalist	life sciences professor
organizational development consultant	professor: humanities, film, arts	neuropsychologist
psychologist: relationship, spiritual, career	psychologist: sports psychology	performing arts: dance instructor
social entrepreneur	theater director	physician: family, psychiatry, preventive
social scientist: emphasis on teaching	therapist: neurolinguistic programming (NLP)	primatologist
		therapeutic humorist
		yoga and meditation instructor

Tribal ENFP		
Non-spatial	Tangible	Spatial
activist: education reform, health-care reform, peace	buyer: educational products, arts, books, music	art therapist
admissions counselor: college	film producer: feature films	athletic coach
agent for actors, artists, writers	internal consultant: HR, organization development	dance/movement therapist
clergy in low-dogma faiths	music therapist	design arts (team leader): set design, new urbanism
counselor: career center staff, outplacement firm	nonprofit director: public health, international development	film director: Hollywood production
diplomat: senior level	nurse: counseling, psychiatric	neurotherapist
fundraiser	passenger service representative	nurse: midwifery, psychiatric
journalist: human interest	political campaign manager	physician assistant: family practice, preventive
lobbyist: social causes	recreation leader	teacher: spatial arts, computer graphics, dance
marketing/communications director	recreation therapist	team leader: life sciences, technology projects
marketing research	religious activities director	trainer: technology fields, sciences, engineering
meeting facilitator	teacher: high school social studies, history, English	
nonprofit director: social issues, arts/culture advocacy	trainer: applied social sciences, counseling, education	
ombudsman: corporations, universities, government agencies		
public relations director		
school psychologist		
social marketer		
training and development: program designer, trainer		

Maestro INFP		
Non-spatial	**Tangible**	**Spatial**
actor	cognitive scientist: personality, psychobiology	alternative medicine practitioner: naturopath, bodywork
attorney: social change, international human rights	documentary filmmaker	archaeologist
coach: career, life, personal growth	evolutionary biologist	architectural historian
consultant: education, organizational behavior	fine artist: impressionist, abstract	choreographer: dance, performing arts
counselor: relationship, spiritual, career change	forensic psychologist	dancer: jazz, improvisational
creative writer: poet, novelist, playwright	historian: history of science	engineer: human-computer interaction, ergonomics
cultural anthropologist, ethnographer	life scientist: wildlife biology, sociobiology	fine artist: sculpture
curriculum designer	photojournalist	industrial designer
drama coach	psychologist	music video filmmaker
economist: family, public, labor, health, education	science journalist	performer: Cirque du Soleil, acting
historian: social, art	software designer: educational application	physical anthropologist
humanities scholar	software developer: graphical user interface	physician: psychiatrist, family, holistic
independent scholar: social sciences, humanities	survey methodologist	primatologist
law professor: psychology of human emotions		screenwriter: independent feature
linguist		set designer
mythologist		somatic psychologist
nonfiction writer: self-help, personal growth		symphony conductor
professor: humanities, social sciences		yoga and meditation instructor
psychology: evolutionary, educational, organizational		
researcher: social sciences, humanities		
social entrepreneur		
social scientist: sociology, social policy, regional studies		
songwriter/musician		

Tribal INFP		
Non-spatial	**Tangible**	**Spatial**
activist	commercial arts: greeting card designer, advertising	architect: green design, monuments, memorials
advertising: copywriter, web content writer	foreign service officer: U.S. State Department	artist: 3D animation, spatial arts
campaign strategist	human-computer interface designer	athletic coach (mental and physical game)
clergy in low-dogma faiths	human-factors engineer	design artist: feng shui, interior design, historic parks
fiction writer: historical novels, memoirs, romance	IT: database designer, graphical user interface	screenwriter: educational, sitcom, TV, Hollywood
human resources: training specialist, career coaching	military officer: human intelligence, psychology ops	set design: theater, film, costume
journalist: editor, staff writer, freelance	nurse: psych, counseling	urban planning: new urbanism designer
librarian: specialized in social science, arts, humanities		video game designer
mediator		website designer: graphic design and information architecture
nonprofit researcher: societal issues		
speechwriter: politics		
training and development: program designer, trainer		

Maestro ENFJ		
Non-spatial	**Tangible**	**Spatial**
career coach	art historian: emphasis on teaching	alternative medicine practitioner
communications consultant: meeting facilitator	art therapist	athletic coach: college level
communications director	documentary filmmaker	film director: independent production
consultant: HR, training program design specialist	music therapist: neurobiological disorders	naturopath
drama coach	professor: life science, medicine	neurotherapist
humanities professor	sports psychologist	physician: family, holistic, preventive
law: mental health, race relations, disability rights		professor, instructor: architecture and design
life coach: personal development, relationships		yoga instructor
psychologist		
public speaker: social causes		
sex therapist		
social sciences professor		
social work counselor: addiction disorders		
trainer: leadership development, team building		

Tribal ENFJ		
Non-spatial	**Tangible**	**Spatial**
administrator: health care, adult education	camp director	athletic coach: high school level
admissions counselor: college	information architect: project manager	design arts manager
advertising account executive	nurse manager	film director: Hollywood production
agent for actors, artists, writers	outplacement counselor	military officer: broadcasting director
association executive	producer: films, TV programs, television promotions	physician assistant
clergy	speech pathologist	urban planning: project manager
counselor: career, public health, student adviser	supervisor, manager, team leader	
dean, university president	teacher: visual arts, graphic arts	
diplomat: senior level	website producer	
fundraiser		
human resources director		
marketing director		
mediator		
newscaster: human interest		
nonprofit director: social causes, arts promotion		
political consultant: campaign strategist		
politician: state senator, U.S. senator		
public relations		
recruiter		
sales manager		
teacher: high school English, history, music		

Maestro INFJ		
Non-spatial	**Tangible**	**Spatial**
coach: career, life, personal growth	art appraiser	acupuncturist
consultant: education, human resources	art historian	alternative medicine practitioner: naturopath
counselor: relationship, spiritual, career	composer: film scores	archaeologist
drama coach	information science specialist	architectural historian
entrepreneur: education- and human-development-related	IT: database designer	artist: sculptor
humanities scholar: history, literature, musicology	playwright	challenge course designer: outdoor adventure
law professor	training and development: program designer, presenter	computer game designer
lawyer: art, civil, employment, comparative family law	website design: information architect	engineer: human-computer interface, ergonomics
nonprofit: director of writing and research		geographer: economic, political, cultural, historical
organizational behavior and development specialist		holistic therapist: mind/body connection
politician: U.S. senator		organic farmer: environmental educator
psychologist/therapist: narrative therapy, neurolinguistic programming		screenwriter: feature-length screenplay
researcher: political think tank		symphony conductor
social scientist		
social work: researcher, program development		
songwriter/musician		
writer: biographer		

Tribal INFJ		
Non-spatial	**Tangible**	**Spatial**
activist	commercial artist: graphic arts, advertising	architect: sustainable development, green
advertising: copywriter, website content writer	film editor	design arts: designer of sets, monuments, historic parks
clergy in low-dogma faiths	human-computer interface designer	exhibit designer: museum, living history exhibits
director: education or social service nonprofit	human factors engineer	industrial design artist
editor: book, magazine, newspaper journalist	information architect	physician assistant: psychiatric, preventive
grant writer	jury consultant	screenwriter: TV, sitcom
human resources: career planning and leadership trainer	marketing research analyst	software developer: graphical user interface
meeting facilitator, mediator	nurse: psych, counseling, midwife	urban planning: landscape architect
paralegal: researcher, law librarian	physician: psychiatrist, family, preventive	
public policy analyst	reference librarian: college library	
public relations/communications: writer, researcher	script reader: film	
researcher/writer: advocacy, nonprofit, policy think tank		
résumé writer		
social marketer		
speechwriter		
strategic planner		
TV sitcom writer		

Maestro ENTP		
Non-spatial	**Tangible**	**Spatial**
academic professor: law, social sciences, public policy	academic professor: mathematics, computer science	academic professor: engineering, physical and life sciences
consultant: change management, social change projects	consultant: MIS, telecommunications, business systems	architecture: sustainable development consultant
foreign service officer: U.S. State Department	documentary filmmaker	consultant: engineering, medicine, science applications
humanities scholar	entrepreneur: new technologies, scientific research	ecologist
investment broker	epidemiologist	evolutionary scientist
investment fund manager: emerging markets	executive coach	inventor
lawyer: constitutional, intellectual property	math tutor: coach high schoolers how to pass SATs	life and physical scientist: chief researcher
political pundit, columnist	social entrepreneur	neuropsychologist, neuroscience, neurology
political scientist		physician: medical scientist, preventive medicine
social critic		software and engineering design: technical team leader
social policy researcher: think tank, nonprofit		space exploration: NASA scientist
social scientist: emphasis on teaching		.
venture capitalist		

Tribal ENTP		
Non-spatial	**Tangible**	**Spatial**
agent: literary, film	advertising, creative director	architect: marketing role, educator
campaign strategist	business systems analyst	construction manager
journalist: investigative reporter	CEO, high-tech companies	design engineer: research and development (all fields)
lobbyist	corporate executive: special-projects developer	industrial designer: new-product innovation
manager: leading-edge company	design arts: project manager	instructor/professor: medicine, science, engineering
marketer	film producer	physician assistant: neurology, cardiology
political analyst	intelligence agent: U.S. Homeland Security, CIA, FBI	project manager: physical sciences, engineering
politician: U.S. senator, U.S. congressman, U.S. president	intelligence analyst: CIA, FBI, DIA, NSA, DEA	real estate developer: green buildings
public relations publicist	military officer: counterintelligence, interrogator	science/math teacher: high school AP courses
strategic planner		

Maestro INTP		
Non-spatial	**Tangible**	**Spatial**
comedian: comedy writer, performer	artificial intelligence research	archaeologist
cultural anthropologist	bioinformatics	biologist: all subspecialties
economist: international, development, game theory	computer programmer	biomedical engineering: virtual-reality engineer
historian: prehistory, ancient, world	documentary filmmaker	chemist: all subspecialties
independent scholar: social sciences, humanities	economist: environmental and natural resource	computer scientist
judge: federal courts and Supreme Court	epidemiologist	design engineer: research and development (all fields)
law: constitutional, intellectual property	evolutionary scientist: sociobiology	ecologist: global warming research
linguistic scientist	fiction writer: sci-fi, horror, screenwriter	film: special effects and animation artist
mathematician: theoretical, operations research	fine artist	forensic artist
musician: jazz/classical guitarist, violinist, pianist	law: international environmental law	forensic paleontologist
musicologist	political cartoonist	forensic scientist: biochemist, geneticist
nonfiction writer: sciences, politics, technology	psychologist: psychometrics, cognitive science	geneticist
philosopher	researcher: computer science, new technology	inventor
political pundit, columnist	social entrepreneur: new technologies	lawyer: patent
political scientist		life and physical scientist: emphasis on research
psychiatrist		nanotechnology scientist
researcher: social sciences		neuroscientist, neuropsychologist
social critic		optical engineer: lasers, holography
social policy researcher: think tank, nonprofit		physician: medical scientist, academic research
social science professor		physicist: all subspecialties
sociologist		researcher: life science, physical science
statistician		robotics research
		software architect, designer, developer
		surgeon: plastics, neurology, cardiology

Tribal INTP		
Non-spatial	**Tangible**	**Spatial**
editor: social sciences, public health, public policy	advertising artist	architect: green technologies, new urbanism
financial analyst	environmental planner	industrial designer
grant writer	intelligence agent: U.S. Homeland Security, CIA, FBI	interior design, interior planner
investment analyst: mutual fund, stock/ bond analyst	intelligence analyst: CIA, FBI, DIA, NSA, DEA	physician assistant: surgery, oncology, neurology
journalist: media criticism, politics, science, health	military officer: counterintelligence, interrogator	urban designer
law: researcher, district attorney, military lawyer (JAG)	technical writer	video game animator
marketing researcher	urban planner	yacht and marine designer
public policy: researcher, analyst		
strategic planner		

Maestro ENTJ		
Non-spatial	**Tangible**	**Spatial**
college professor: economics, law, political science	college professor: IT, MIS, computer science	architect: consultant
credit investigator	consultant: management, business systems, IT, MIS	college professor: engineering, physical sciences
economic consultant	engineering executive	computer security specialist
Federal Reserve: economic analyst, board member	entrepreneur	engineering consultant
financial planner	epidemiologist	medicine: environmental, virology, immunology
judge: federal courts and Supreme Court	executive coach	sales rep: pharmaceutical, medical equipment
law: ethics, health policy, trial		
lobbyist		
military officer: lawyer, judge		
mortgage banker		
SEC analyst		
stockbroker		
strategic planner		

Tribal ENTJ		
Non-spatial	**Tangible**	**Spatial**
administrator: college dean, university president	business manager: high-tech, engineering	architect: project manager
corporate leadership: CEO, board of directors	business systems analyst	athletic coach
journalist: reporter	chief information officer (CIO)	computer systems analyst
manager: sales, marketing	federal agency director: FEMA, EPA, FDA, FCC	construction manager
mutual fund manager	general manager, senior level	design engineer: technical team leader
mutual fund trader	intelligence agent: U.S. Homeland Security, CIA, FBI	manufacturing executive
nonprofit: director, program designer	intelligence analyst: CIA, FBI, DIA, NSA, DEA	patent agent, attorney
politician: U.S. president, U.S. senator	law: public defender, district attorney	project manager: engineering, software, IT
project team leader	sales: high-tech	shop foreman: auto-repair service
public policy analyst		U.S. foreign service: medical officer
sales: banking, securities		U.S. surgeon general

Maestro INTJ		
Non-spatial	**Tangible**	**Spatial**
curriculum designer	artificial intelligence scientist	acoustic engineer: concert hall, recording studio designer
economist: financial, business, history of economics	bioinformatics expert	biologist: all subspecialties
forensic accounting expert	computer programmer: software development consultant	biomedical engineer
historian	consultant: business, information technology	chemist: all subspecialties
journalist: technology, political columnist	forensic psychiatry	computer forensics specialist
judge: federal courts and Supreme Court	information technology: network and database design	computer hardware engineer
law professor	lawyer: housing, criminal, health-care, public health	computer security specialist
law: constitutional, immigration, international finance	mathematician: applied problem-solving	design engineer: all fields
musicologist	psychologist: research, psychometrics, cognitive science	economist: urban and rural, agricultural, development
political science professor	science writer	environmental engineer
psychiatrist		forensic scientist: biochemist, geneticist
social policy researcher: think tank, nonprofit		genetic engineer
sociologist		inventor
statistician		lawyer: patent, antitrust, technology, land use, cyberlaw
		pharmacologist
		physician: neurology, cardiology, facial reconstruction
		physicist: all subspecialties
		robotics engineer
		software architect, designer, developer

Tribal INTJ		
Non-spatial	**Tangible**	**Spatial**
CEO, high-tech	computer programmer: banking, financial applications	architect
financial analyst	electronics engineer, technician	computer programmer: engineering, manufacturing applications
grant writer	environmental planner	computer systems analyst
investment analyst: mutual fund, stock/bond analyst	intelligence analyst: CIA, FBI, DIA, NSA	industrial designer
journalist: editor, staff writer	lawyer: public defender	landscape architect
loan officer: banking, mortgage, small business	military enlisted: electronic technician	patent agent, examiner
marketing researcher	urban planner	physician assistant: cardiovascular surgery
military officer: lawyer, judge		structural engineer
public policy analyst		transportation planner
SEC analyst		urban designer
strategic planner		

Maestro ESFP		
Non-spatial	**Tangible**	**Spatial**
actor	animal trainer, pet psychologist	art appraiser
comedian	athlete	athlete: gymnast
entrepreneur: specialty products and services	botanist	chiropractor
language professor	Outward Bound instructor	cinematographer
music teacher	public health scientist	dance instructor, choreographer
pharmaceutical sales representative	recreational therapist	dermatologist
singer, performer	restaurant manager, host, hostess	makeup artist
social worker: young adults, teens at risk	sport psychologist	midwife
	wellness and fitness nutrition expert	naturopathic doctor
	wine steward, sommelier	sports medicine practitioner
		wildlife biologist

Tribal ESFP		
Non-spatial	**Tangible**	**Spatial**
advertising account executive	B&B owner, manager	athletic coach
communications director: associations, nonprofits	entrepreneur: restaurant, hospitality, retail	cheerleader
diplomat	health promotion manager	chef
foundation manager	health spa manager	firefighter
fundraiser	merchandiser, product buyer	George W. Bush: 43rd U.S. president
marketing director	personal shopper, image consultant	gym teacher
mediator	personal trainer	hairstylist
military officer: public affairs officer, broadcast manager	police officer	kindergarten teacher
newscaster	politician: city council, mayor	nurse: emergency, sexual assault forensics
press secretary	salesperson: fashion, housewares	paramedic
producer/promoter: film, TV	sales rep: manufacturers, distributors, service providers	physical therapist
public relations, public affairs specialist	teacher: elementary school, science, physical education	U.S. foreign service: health practitioner
salesperson	travel: agent, tour guide, TV program host	
talk show host: travel, food, entertainment	website producer	

Maestro ISFP		
Non-spatial	**Tangible**	**Spatial**
actor	animator: film, video games, cartoons	animal rescue officer
animal trainer, pet psychologist	art therapist	art and antiques appraiser
entertainer	bodybuilder	art conservator
meditation and relaxation teacher	botanist	artisan, craftsman
musician, performer, singer	cartoonist	athlete
music teacher	cheese maker	baker, cake maker
occupational/vocational counselor	color specialist	chef
social work: teens at risk, inmate rehab	dietitian	cinematographer
songwriter	fashion model	dancer, ballerina, figure skater, gymnast
special education tutor	fitness trainer	fine artist: portrait, mural, landscape, sculpture
training and development specialist	graphic artist, multimedia specialist	forester
travel writer	nutritionist: clinical specialist	gardener, plant nursery, landscaper
	painter: ornaments, fine wood, home interiors	luthier: instrument maker/repairer
	pastry chef	makeup artist
	perfumer	massage therapist: sport, Rolfing
	photographer: fashion, nature, advertising, travel	military: plastic surgeon, dietitian, counselor
	poet	naturopathic doctor, holistic medicine
	public health scientist	performer: Cirque du Soleil gymnast, acrobat
	wildlife biologist: nature photographer, conservationist	performing arts medicine: musician injuries
	wine and cheese shop owner	physician: plastic surgeon, audiologist, emergency, sports MD
	wine steward, sommelier	potter, glassblower, stained glass maker
	yoga instructor	restoration specialist: historical homes and buildings
		stonemason, woodworker
		veterinarian

Tribal ISFP		
Non-spatial	**Tangible**	**Spatial**
communications expert: PR, public affairs, public outreach	advertising artist: photography, 2D art	advertising artist: 3D graphics
customer service representative	bartender, waiter/waitress	aerobics instructor
editor	childcare provider: day care center	bodywork: massage, Rolfing, etc.
employment counselor	children's book writer, artist	drafting technician: computer-aided design
guidance counselor	entrepreneur: retail, personal services, B&B owner	dressmaker: wedding, special occasions
interpreter	fashion buyer, sales	firefighter
language teacher	interior decorator	hairstylist
matchmaker: dating service	personal assistant	interior designer
mediator	police officer	jewelry designer
recruiter, staffing adviser	product buyer	landscape architect
student adviser, admissions counselor	secret shopper	nurse: emergency, psych, first-assist
teacher: preschool, K–12, ESL	U.S. foreign service: health practitioner	set designer, costume designer, film location scout

Maestro ESFJ		
Non-spatial	**Tangible**	**Spatial**
genetic counselor	antiques dealer	animal rescue officer
hospice counselor	caterer	chiropractor
job counselor: unemployment office	food service specialist	medical technologist: allied health
language professor	health educator	personal trainer
religious educator	nutritionist	physician: gynecologist, obstetrician, pediatrician
social work counselor: mental health, drug rehab	recreation therapist	physician: palliative care, pain management, geriatrics
special education teacher	sales rep: manufacturers, distributors, service providers	physician's assistant
trainer: customer service, sales	shopkeeper: specialty items	space planner: retail, grocery, commercial
weight management counselor	special event designer	sports physician
		veterinarian (primary care)

Tribal ESFJ		
Non-spatial	**Tangible**	**Spatial**
account executive: sales, marketing	assisted-living attendant	athletic coach
administrator: social services, public health	bartender, host/hostess, waiter/ waitress	dental hygienist
advertising sales: hospitality, human resources, health	funeral home director	engineering manager
concierge	grocery store manager	food service manager
customer care liaison	hospitality manager: hotel, restaurant, innkeeper, health spa	general contractor
diplomat	interior decorator	hairstylist
health-care administrator	nurse manager	health club manager
human resources manager	office manager	hospitality manager: restaurant, hotel, B&B, resort
marketing manager	personal shopper	household/holiday crafts maker
military: public affairs officer, personnel manager, recruiter	politician: city mayor, municipal government council	nurse: gerontology, midwife, pediatric
news reporter, broadcaster	real estate agent	occupational therapist
personal secretary	retail management	physical therapist: recreational, pediatric
receptionist	sales engineer	police officer
recruiter	teacher: preschool, kindergarten, elementary, ESL	property manager
retail sales	travel agent, planner	window display designer: retail
sales party host: cookware, cosmetics, jewelry	wedding planner	
school principal		

Maestro ISFJ		
Non-spatial	**Tangible**	**Spatial**
counselor: drug rehab, hospice, geriatric, crisis hotline	animal trainer	acupuncturist
language professor	art and antiques appraiser	animal rescue officer
law: family, divorce, human resources, tort, and accident	art therapist	artisan, craftsman
librarian: information science specialist	baker	art restoration specialist
mediator	botanist	chef
meditation teacher	calligrapher	curator, conservator
religious educator, scholar	cheese maker	dentist: orthodontics, endodontics
special education tutor	color specialist	food scientist
training and development specialist	entrepreneur: retail, personal services, B&B owner	forester
	gardener	furniture maker
	nutritionist: clinical specialist	industrial designer
	organic farmer	instrument maker
	perfumer	medical technologist: allied health technician
	sport psychologist	midwife
	technical sales support	military officer: plastic surgeon, dietitian
	trainer: hardware/software technologies	nurse: research
	wine and cheese shop owner	optometrist
		pastry chef
		physician: family practice, pediatrician, internist

Tribal ISFJ		
Non-spatial	**Tangible**	**Spatial**
administrative assistant, secretary	childcare provider: day care center	anesthesiologist
customer service representative	children's book writer	dental hygienist
editor	clinical dietitian: home health, rehab facility	fashion designer
educational administrator	dietetic technician	firefighter
guidance counselor	health service worker	graphic artist, multimedia specialist
human resources administrator, generalist	innkeeper	hairdresser, cosmetologist
insurance agent	interior decorator	interior designer
interpreter, translator	IT network administrator	jewelry designer
librarian, archivist	librarian: multimedia management	landscape architect
magazine editor	manager: restaurant, retail, personal services	massage therapist
matchmaker: dating service	PC technician: help desk	nurse: generalist, rehab, hospice, occupational
medical transcriptionist	personal chef	occupational therapist
paralegal	pet groomer	paramedic
personal assistant	police officer	physical therapist, exercise physiologist, kinesiologist
priest/minister/rabbi/monk/nun	product buyer	respiratory therapist
receptionist	retail store clerk, cashier	speech pathologist
social worker administrator: adoption, foster care	teacher: preschool, K–12, ESL	veterinary assistant
student adviser, admissions counselor		website designer
		zookeeper

Maestro ESTP		
Non-spatial	**Tangible**	**Spatial**
business consultant	athletic coach	astronaut
corporate lawyer	auctioneer	athlete
entrepreneur: specialized products and services	ecotourism guide	driver: tank, truck, construction, and heavy equipment
financial planner	fitness instructor	earth sciences: geology, volcanology, seismology
negotiator	lawyer: military, sports	explorer
stockbroker	outdoor-challenge course guide	home inspector
tax consultant	pharmacist	IT: PC and network troubleshooter, problem solver
	photographer: adventure, wartime correspondent	physician: internist, oncologist, physiatrist
	retail store owner: specialty products	pilot: military training
		racer: auto, boat, motorcycle
		real estate developer
		resource extraction engineer: mining, petroleum
		Special Forces: Navy SEAL, Green Beret, special ops
		stunt actor
		surgeon: emergency medicine, battlefield ER
		veterinarian

Tribal ESTP		
Non-spatial	**Tangible**	**Spatial**
actuarial manager	agriculture: farm manager	air traffic control manager
auditing manager, supervisor	bicycle tour guide	construction manager
broadcast news reporter	drug enforcement agent (DEA)	firefighter: urban, forest
lawyer: corporate	engineering manager: all specialties, field and test	food service manager
marketing presenter	executive: hands-on, operations, manufacturing	forestry: land manager
retail business manager	field agent: CIA, FBI	mechanic supervisor
sales manager	insurance adjuster: natural disaster claims	military officer: artillery, missile systems, tank
tax manager	law enforcement: detective, CSI, police officer	paramedic: ambulance driver, EMT, helicopter pilot
white-collar crime investigator	project manager: business, technical	physical therapist: sports medicine
	real estate agent: commercial	search and rescue worker: FEMA, National Guard
	recreational therapist	trades: carpenter, plumber, HVAC technician
	Secret Service agent	
	teacher: math, physics, chemistry	
	technical sales: engineering, medical, heavy equipment	
	travel tour manager	

Maestro ISTP		
Non-spatial	**Tangible**	**Spatial**
accountant: forensic, auditing, forecasting, tax	agriculture: organic farmer, beekeeper, farm manager	adventure education: outdoor challenge-course designer
actuary	animal scientist	astronaut
business consultant	diplomatic security: special agent	athlete: golf, baseball, basketball
entrepreneur: practical products and services	ecotourism guide	chef
financial planner	horticulture: botanist, winemaker, gardener	construction: surveyor, landscaper
lawyer: mergers and acquisitions, securities regulation	IT: PC and network troubleshooter, problem solver	dentist: emergency surgeon, forensic dentistry
statistician	operations research scientist	driver: tank, truck, construction, and heavy equipment
stock analyst	Outward Bound guide	earth sciences: geology, volcanology, seismology, geomorphology
tax consultant	personal services: barber, personal chef	forestry: forester, arborist, ecologist, land manager
technical writer	pharmacist	gemologist
venture capital analyst	photographer: news, wartime correspondent	home inspector
	soil scientist	hunter, fisherman
		lifeguard
		martial arts instructor
		mechanic: general, race car, motorcycle, aircraft
		military: fighter pilot, infantry officer, machine gunner
		mining engineer, mineralogist
		mountain medicine: altitude illness, hypothermia, frostbite
		nurse: ICU, emergency room
		optometrist
		petroleum engineer: offshore drilling, geochemistry
		physician: ophthalmologist, orthopedic surgeon, forensic pathologist
		pilot: military, news, stunt, recreational

Maestro ISTP		
		racer: auto, boat, motorcycle
		scuba diver: industrial underwater welder
		Special Forces: Navy SEAL, Green Beret, special ops
		sport physician
		stunt actor
		surgeon: ER, military flight or field surgeon
		surveyor/mapper

Tribal ISTP		
Non-spatial	**Tangible**	**Spatial**
chief financial officer (CFO)	athletic coach	dental assistant
chief information officer (CIO)	bicycle tour guide	engineer: all specialties, field and test, Army Corps
chief operations officer (COO)	drug enforcement agent (DEA)	firefighter: urban, forest
corporate executive (all levels)	executive: hands-on, operations, construction	paramedic: ambulance driver, EMT, helicopter pilot
executive secretary	insurance adjuster	search and rescue worker: FEMA, National Guard
financial analyst	intelligence field agent: CIA, FBI	teacher: high school physics, geometry, shop
lawyer: corporate, contracts, copyright	law enforcement: detective, CSI, police officer	trades: carpenter, electrician, plumber, mason
	production operations analyst	
	project manager: business, technical	
	recreational attendant	
	Secret Service agent	
	teacher: math, biology, chemistry	
	technician: allied health, lab, IT, telecom, TV/radio	
	video camera technician	
	white-collar-crime investigator	

Maestro ESTJ		
Non-spatial	**Tangible**	**Spatial**
auditor	computer programmer: technical team leader	chef
business consultant: accounting, auditing	dietitian	computer security analyst
business systems analyst	FBI field agent	computer systems analyst
certified public accountant (CPA)	funeral director	conservationist
entrepreneur: practical products	industrial engineer	earth science: geologist, hydrologist
financial planner	IT consultant	engineering consultant (all specialties)
insurance agent, broker, or underwriter	pharmaceutical sales representative	field technician: HVAC, telecom, cable TV
IRS agent	technical sales: engineering, medical, heavy equipment	medical equipment representative
judge: municipal court		physical therapist: speech pathologist, occupational
lawyer: corporate, tax, real estate, estate planning		physician: oncology, urology, orthopedic
stockbroker		quality inspector: USDA, FDA, EPA, indoor air, safety-space planner

Tribal ESTJ		
Non-spatial	**Tangible**	**Spatial**
actuarial manager administrator: health, school, government	business operations manager: all industries	construction manager
audit supervisor	engineering manager	dental hygienist
bank manager	event planner	engineer: team-centered
cashier	food service manager	fireman, paramedic, EMT
chief executive officer (CEO)	homeland security analyst	general contractor
chief information officer (CIO)	immigration officer	manufacturing: foreman, supervisor
chief operations officer (COO)	insurance adjuster	military manager: communications, supplies
corporate executive (all levels)	office manager	nurse: RN, case manager, rehab manager
project manager: all industries	purchasing agent	patent agent
executive assistant	police chief	physician's assistant: orthopedics
loan officer	real estate agent	production operations manager
mutual fund trader	real estate management	shop foreperson: auto repair
sales manager	retail store manager	
school principal	sales rep: manufacturers, distributors, service providers	
stockbroker	teacher of practical material: math, gym, shop, technical	
tax manager	travel tour manager	

Maestro ISTJ		
Non-spatial	**Tangible**	**Spatial**
actuary: health, life, annuities, property, pensions insurance	computer programmer	adventure guide
auditor	conservationist	airline pilot
business consultant	defense intelligence analyst	applied mathematician
business systems analyst	dietitian	chemist: inorganic
certified public accountant (CPA)	electrical engineer	computer security analyst
compliance analyst	entrepreneur: practical products	dentist: general, periodontics
financial planner	historian: military, Civil War	earth science: geologist, hydrologist
forensic accountant	industrial engineer	engineering consultant: civil, mechanical, reliability
lawyer: business, tax, real estate, estate planning, mergers	IT: database and network administration, PC technician	entomologist
mutual fund accountant	operations research scientist	environmental engineering
statistician	pharmacist: compliance specialist: pharmaceuticals, biotech, chemistry	farmer, hunter, fisherman
stock analyst	quality assurance specialist: engineering, biotech	field technician: HVAC, telecomm, cable TV
tax analyst	technical writer: computer, software-related	forest ranger
technical writer: business-related		green architecture specialist
		heavy-equipment operator
		historic restoration specialist
		lawyer: patent, property, land use
		machinery operator
		metallurgist
		meteorologist
		physical therapist: speech pathologist, occupational
		physician: surgeon, pathologist, podiatrist, radiologist
		technical writer: engineering related
		woodworking specialist: furniture maker

Tribal ISTJ		
Non-spatial	**Tangible**	**Spatial**
accountant: general	chef: short-order cook, line chef	athletic coach
administrator: public health, school, health care, government	clinical research librarian	AutoCAD technician
bank teller	event and travel planner	combat engineer: U.S. Army
business manager: Fortune 500	FBI analyst	computer systems analyst
chief financial officer (CFO)	homeland security analyst	construction manager
chief information officer (CIO)	immigration officer	engineer: all specialties, field and test
chief operations officer (COO)	insurance adjuster	engineering manager
corporate executive (all levels)	manager: retail store, operations, projects	firefighter, paramedic, EMT
executive assistant	property management	materials engineer
financial analyst	purchasing manager, inventory control, supply chain	mechanic: aircraft, auto, diesel, heavy equipment
government employee	quality inspector: USDA, FDA, EPA, indoor air, safety	military: resource management analyst, aircraft navigator
IRS agent lawyer: corporate, business law, bankruptcy	real estate manager	nurse: OR, radiology, generalist
librarian	reference librarian: business research	patent examiner
office manager	security engineering officer: U.S. State Department	police officer: civil servant, military police
paralegal	security guard	production operations manager
school principal	summer camp director	roadway engineer
	teacher: math, gym, shop	teacher: shop, vocational
		technician: lab, science, engineering, health, TV/radio
		trades: carpenter, electrician, mason, plumber
		wastewater/drainage engineer

SPECIAL SECTION II:
WHAT IF I CAN'T DECIDE?

The darkest hour has only sixty minutes.

—MORRIS MANDEL

Sometimes it all clicks together perfectly. You generate Career Components that point toward one or more fitting careers. Then it is just a matter of research and whittling down the possibilities to make the best choice.

Sometimes, it's harder to hear the click.

Few careers fit every specification. Don't get discouraged if you can't find the perfect match. In reality, almost no career would be "perfect" anyway. That is okay. You are aiming for a great fit—not a perfect fit. And, remember, you are being extraordinary in your commitment to consciously choosing a career that you love. The taller an order your Career Components add up to, the bigger the challenge to find what you want. Let's see what may be going on.

Here are some common thoughts you might have if certain steps in the process are not coming as easily, and how we can move with, around, and through them.

Things are feeling too complicated.

They might be. Simplify. Pare down your Components to only those that are *essential*. Can you reword them in a simple (but specific) way? Do some more searches with only these simplified, reworded Components. Choose a few of the most important design components, the ones you would never give up, and then see if anything matches. Pare down, use plain language, and reapproach. The essentials might steer you right to the gold.

I'm having trouble finding matches to my Components.

Have you searched thoroughly enough? Shake things up, clear your browser history, go incognito. Mix and match and reapproach. Find three new resources. Are you using words in a way that other people could understand what you are looking for? Share your list of Components with a few others and ask them what they think would fit your specifications. If they ask you what you mean by something, share more with them until they understand. Look for an alternative way to communicate your Components—then use them in your research.

One of our clients who wanted to explore less obvious options narrowed down his specifications to a short, focused, powerfully worded list and stapled posters downtown offering a reward for the winning career idea. He found a career that fit everything, one nobody had thought of before. Compromise does not necessarily equal sacrifice. If you've followed our Career Design Method fully, you have taken the high road and sought perfection or close to it. This method has a huge advantage over the way most people make a choice. They usually take the middle road, with compromises unconsciously built into the design. You have been wonderfully unreasonable, reaching for the stars in your Career Design. By seeking the ideal, you have more room to adjust and still wind up successful and satisfied. Try altering your Design Components a little. Identify the snag—the Component or Components that push your design into the "nothing fits" territory. See if you can drop or alter this specification. Loosen up a little. Add a little more flexibility into your design or tweak some other Components. For example, one client's sticking point was security. This was a critical Component for him, but the way he had defined security meant he would have to work for a large, soulless, bureaucratic company. By expanding his definition of security, far more attractive possibilities instantly opened up.

What I want doesn't exist.

It might not. If all the careers you've found are too narrow in scope, and you want to use a broad range of talents, don't worry: you're not going crazy or asking too much. Most jobs do not provide a lot of breadth. Even complex, high-level jobs often force the worker into a narrow range of functions. These days many people want more than a cookie-cutter job, and they're willing to custom-design one. If you can't find a career that has everything you're committed to, perhaps you'll have to make one up. You would be amazed how many people have convinced a decision-maker to hire them for a job that didn't previously exist.

There are a few organizations in which employees define the parameters of their projects and daily functions. Since this approach produces the happiest employees, in time it is likely that more organizations will adopt a more flexible approach. But you are dealing with reality today. If you want to make full use of a broad palette of talents, traits, and functions, and have the most say in how and what you do, the obvious solution is the self-designed job. This may translate into convincing someone to let you do what you want in their organization, starting a business, or working on your own.

I'm not qualified to do what I want to do.

You might not be. You may need to take interim steps to reach that perfect job, like additional training or education. You may need to reach the goal indirectly, by working in a bridge job that takes you partway there. Find out the career path for others in the role or position you are interested in. What did they do before? What degree or training do they have? Get the facts about the likely amount of time, training, and expense that you would incur to become qualified. Then . . . decide if you are willing to do it!

What if I can't decide?

If you have trouble deciding on your future career, it's not a character flaw. Most people, including those revered for great leadership, wrestle with decisions that have far-reaching consequences. There are also consequences, however, for sitting on the fence. There's an old saying in the military that a decision is better than no decision. You want to be in action and heading in a chosen direction. Consider making a choice and knowing that you can be adaptable and flexible along your career path. If you discover you missed some information or made a bad choice—you can correct course.

Let's dig into this, though, because it really isn't as uncommon as you'd think. Typically, indecision stems from various fears. The way to combat them is to match it to a reality.

Fear: I might make a mistake and pick the wrong career.

Reality: It is certainly possible to make the wrong decision about anything: where to live, with whom to spend your life, and what to do with that life. There are few guarantees. One of them is that we all will make many mistakes. The way to minimize those mistakes is to be prepared. Insufficient preparation is by far the main reason people wind up in careers that do not fit. They selected their work with too little thought, using methods unlikely to produce the intended result. You can, most likely, make a choice you won't regret if you apply the tools in this book. If you break the process down into smaller pieces, find good clues, fully investigate those clues, ask and answer the important questions, build strong definite components, do the research, and talk with many people engaged in the same work you intend to do, you have a high probability of success. Career choice is not like an algebra problem. There is no guarantee. You may just have to take the leap.

Fear: I'm not sure I will get it right on my own.

Reality: Earlier in the book, we suggested going through a Career Design coaching program that includes in-depth testing of innate natural talents. We did not write that to sell services, but because we strongly believe that Career Design is a complex process for which most of us have no training. Using professional coaching is by far the most effective way to design your future career. If you find it difficult to reach certainty and total specificity about your future work, check out the Career Design coaching programs at incareermatters.com. Or, use another organization that does similar programs. If one-on-one coaching is not for you, form a small group of fellow adventurers with similar goals to work with you through this project. In any event, if possible, don't go it alone.

Fear: My Components are not good enough.

Reality: It is possible to have a long list of Components that do not point to anything definite. You may have decided you are going to live in Chicago, wear casual clothes to work in a leading edge but noncompetitive environment that values individual contribution more than seniority and has a good health-care plan. It uses your planning talent with your outgoing personality. But, hmmm, what fits those specifications? A list like that can go on and create more confusion the longer it gets.

That doesn't mean, though, that they cannot be useful. Try to reframe.

Here is a useful test of the quality of your components: If you read your list to an audience, are they able to make a few specific suggestions? Try this out on some friends. If they come up with ideas that are all over the map or can't think of anything specific, you've got to develop more gold and silver definite Career Design Components to help narrow down the possibilities.

Here's the kind of specificity you're looking for: financial industry in a consultative capacity. When combined, those Components turn to gold, since they point to a very limited number of jobs. They are specific enough to generate a few strong possibilities. What about analytical problem-solving or working with three-dimensional objects? If you were to try either of those two out on an audience, people would offer specific suggestions you could research and pare down to an even more specific few to seriously consider. Some other gold/gold combinations: teaching/training adults, administrator in academic or nonprofit, marketing concepts/ideas.

Not to decide is to decide.

—Harvey Cox

Fear: I feel like I don't have enough time to make the right decision.

Reality: When people say, "I want to think about it for a while" or "I need to process this further," they are sometimes fooling themselves. And you may be making an unconscious decision to not decide. Not deciding is a valid choice, but it would be useful to raise it to a conscious level where you can be a powerful player in your own life, responsible for the consequences of your decisions.

Fear: If I don't keep my options open, I'll miss out on something great.

Reality: Some temperament types prefer to wait and see, let the situation develop, keep all possibilities open, or adapt as the situation changes. They naturally resist deciding. If your four-letter personality type has a *p on the end, you may fit into this group, and deciding is not as natural for you as it is for people with big, strong decision-making muscles. If your nature is to let it all flow, choose a career where that characteristic fits the work. But, to do that, to have a career that fits you perfectly, you have to push yourself to choose.*

If you feel you are cutting off other wonderfully attractive options when you make a decision, it's true. But you make decisions all day long without a great deal of angst. You could be doing a million other things, but you are reading this book. Not one waking moment goes by that you could not spend doing something else. You constantly make decisions about what you are going to do that exclude everything else. You are not going to change. You need to make a decision to move forward and have workability. Grab someone in your life who is supportive of you and is very decisive. Ask them to help you make a decision. They will probably bring a rational and simplistic clarity to your issue.

Fear: I have so many things I want to do, and I might lose the time to do them.

Reality: Most of the people you admire do one thing well. They sing or create businesses or make discoveries or whatever. Only a very few people succeed in multiple arenas. Most of them completely mastered one game and then expanded into a new area. Then again, there is nothing wrong with having multiple careers at the same time. But it can be a bit like dating ten people at once; you have to keep track. If many things sound interesting, pick one to do next. Commit to going for it for the next three to five years. Know you can reassess and re-choose again. The fact of the matter is that we cannot do it all now. We are human beings with limited time, limited energy, and a limited lifespan. Doing something you love, doing it brilliantly, and getting paid well for it is a lot better than avoiding choosing one direction.

Fear: I don't actually know enough about what jobs exist out there in the real world.

Reality: You are never going to know about 1/1,000 of the real career options that exist. New careers are invented every day. There are niches and corners and boutique businesses and start-ups. You are never going to know about the vast majority of them. And . . . this is okay. Pick one, stay in action, learn as you go, shift, modify, or change course as you gain new experiences, knowledge, and perspective.

Fear: I am not ready to decide.

Reality: Sometimes there are valid reasons to hold off on making the final choice. There are times when you need to know more than it is possible to know at the time. If you are a younger person, you may need more experience or maturity to provide a framework to weave a choice. You need to take some courses or take on some internships to explore options, or spend a year backpacking around the world to gain breadth and perspective. If you are a person of any age who just had a major tragedy that demands much of your attention and energy, holding off may be a good call. As one of the world's most ancient books, *I Ching*, says, "Strength in the face of danger does not plunge ahead but bides its time, whereas weakness in the face of danger grows agitated and has not the patience to wait."

Fear: What I want seems unobtainable.

Maybe it is. If you want to be president of the United States and you were born in Norway, you need to find a new dream. If you are not very strong or agile and are five foot two, you are not going to play pro basketball. Most of the time, however, thinking the dream is impossible is just a Yeahbut. What seems impossible is usually just difficult.

The Bottom Line

Are you willing to do what it takes to get from here to there? We occasionally have clients who can define what they want, but falter when it looks difficult to turn the dream into reality. Sometimes they haven't been sufficiently realistic about how far they are willing to stretch into new territory. It is one thing to take a peek outside the box, but quite another to actually jump out. One way to deal with this apparent impasse is to assess the benefits and costs of leaving the old box far behind. For example, continuing on your present path may risk a life of stress, boredom, or lack of fulfillment. A change involves different risks, such as uncertainty. Both options are risky. The easy road of staying where you are may bring continual, long-term, chronic stress along with the subsequent risks to your health, longevity, and relationships. On the other hand, the seemingly more difficult road of making a difficult choice may result in massive short-term stress, which, if you have chosen well, will disappear. Which risk do you choose?

SPECIAL SECTION III: TECH, THE FUTURE, AND YOUR CAREER CHOICES

Nothing New

Throughout the history of human civilization, new ideas and technologies have developed that have radically transformed culture and our lives. Most of these changes have resulted in many positive, and some negative, impacts.

From harnessing the use of fire, humans could cook their meat and have access to more calories and nutrition. Much later, they could use this control to work metal and build skyscrapers. This same control also enabled individuals to, by accident or purpose, start forest fires and lay waste to thousands of acres of precious forest and forest life.

The Industrial Revolution, and its use of machines, greatly reduced the amount of human labor required to produce goods and services. Societies were able, again, to produce items of value in a time frame, and at a cost, that was previously impossible. This same advancement created massive shifts in the amount, and type, of labor required. It also resulted in a shift to an increasing disparity of income between workers and owners.

More recently, the internet radically transformed the type, speed, availability, and comprehensiveness of information and knowledge that humans had access to. No longer did we need to travel to a library to find a book or two, written previously, on a subject. In seconds, we had access to a functionally infinite amount of information. And, largely, for free. The impact of this development, and that which has allowed almost anyone to immediately, and without censure, place content and opinions on the web, cannot be overstated. It created a boon of creativity and self-expression, with people able to share and collaborate with greater ease and with new media. Open-source platforms allow scientists to share knowledge with one another; family members can talk face-to-face with one another across the globe. It is a gift beyond measure. These same platforms and technologies have also given rise to increased polarization in politics and the widespread plague that is false information and propaganda. In the U.S. alone, the news outlets and media are no longer trusted. There is a glut of information available and a dearth of ways to verify it. It seems many people have stopped trying to, or even being concerned with the validity or truth of the media they consume. Our society is in crisis.

The global health pandemic of 2020 instigated not only economic and financial strain and loss of life. It also impacted how business is conducted and what is expected of workers. As people were unable to gather communally, including at work, technology stepped in, creating new norms. Videoconferencing became normal and new policies and procedures were put in place to allow remote working. In a very short period of time, worker expectations shifted to include a desire or demand for remote work. Remote work and other communication and collaboration technologies have made being on-site less and less necessary for many businesses and professions. No longer do people need to be local to work for a company or business. Many positions and functions can be filled by workers living or located almost anywhere! The extent of competition for any one job just skyrocketed. Online applications and automated systems further exacerbate the issue. No longer do you type and hand-deliver your résumé and cover letter for a job in your vicinity, and compete against one, five, or twenty fellow applicants. You may now be competing with hundreds or thousands of faceless applicants living in different time zones.

The examples above only touch on the extent to which technology changes the working world, and explain why you need to stay on your toes.

The New Kid on the Block

The democratization of generative AI a way of creating all types of content (e.g., images, text, audio, conversations, videos, stories, customer service responses, new Beatles songs), harnessing the mass of data available online and using genius coding and machine learning techniques, is the new kid on the block. The new superhero, magical, mysterious, all-powerful(?) kid on the block. Or is it a supervillain? A number of people have big concerns about this tech. Could it lead to the destruction of civilization? Could the machines "learn" that humans were destructive and maleficent and decide they need to go? Has Pandora's box already released the Terminator and HAL 9000?! It's possible. It's not probable.

In the interim, it is worthwhile to consider the impact of today's technology, particularly artificial intelligence, on the world of work and career choice.

Artificial intelligence, with its promise and peril, is poised to continue reconfiguring the way we work and the way we conceive of jobs and careers. Our ongoing incorporation of AI and machine learning will keep reshaping our career choices. Some will diminish or be negatively affected, others will require extensive retraining, and new careers will emerge and grow.

AI excels at data processing, pattern recognition, and executing repetitive, predictable tasks. It reviews mammoth amounts of data, recognizes patterns and probabilities, and recombines them in novel ways. This is how it "creates." There are things that it does not do the way humans can—some forms of creativity, complex problem-solving, empathy, and understanding nuance and context. How this will change and develop is yet to come.

For years, clever programming and artificial intelligence has demonstrated transformative effects across industries and disciplines, from health care and finance to education and entertainment. It is worth your while to consider how today's technology is steering the world of careers and the job market.

Career Paths Likely to Diminish

The influence of AI has the potential to diminish or drastically alter certain career paths. Jobs characterized by routine, predictability, and repetitive tasks are particularly at risk, regardless of their pay or industry. Such jobs are susceptible to automation because AI systems can learn to perform these tasks more efficiently, accurately, and consistently than humans, without fatigue or the need for breaks. Millions of workers have already been displaced. Ironically, the tech industry has suffered some of the biggest losses. What used to be highly skilled coders are now replaceable. Writers are also suffering. Film and television creative writers are in crisis and striking to protect their rights in Hollywood as new AI tech can produce the newest episode of a sitcom in moments. They are hoping to use the legal system to keep AI from replacing them. There have already been too many changes to count. The turn of the wheel of the future will surely be full of surprises, but here are a few areas most likely to be majorly affected.

- **Manufacturing and Warehousing:** Automation has been reshaping these sectors for decades. Now, with advancements in AI, tasks such as assembly line production, quality inspection, machine operation, inventory management, and packing, previously handled by humans, are increasingly being delegated to machines. Being able to communicate with, troubleshoot, and fix software and machines will become more important.

- **Semi-Skilled Jobs:** Traditional positions and roles of all kinds, which require minimal training, knowledge, or creativity to complete, will face a loss in the number of job opportunities. Most likely, the nature of what "a semi-skilled job" includes will probably shift to AI-friendly tasks and responsibilities.

- **Transportation, Delivery Services, and Logistics:** Autonomous vehicles and drones present significant challenges to truck drivers, delivery personnel, and taxi operators. AI-driven optimization algorithms are also streamlining logistics, reducing the need for lower-skilled human operators. Tech-savvy, specialized, and unique operators will be more in-demand.

- **Office Workers:** As AI takes over many routine tasks, as well as many of the jobs for staff and executives, a great reshuffling may take place. Remaining flexible, attending to changes in technology, and shifting roles changed by the new tech will be key for those with traditionally clerical or administrative support roles.

- **Retail, Telemarketing, and Customer Service:** AI is now sophisticated enough to handle basic customer service roles. Automated telemarketing and chatbot customer service representatives can manage simple inquiries and complaints, working 24/7 without the need for human intervention. A pizza restaurant with no human workers can function as well, or better, than what we have now. Each pizza can be a masterpiece.

- **Illustrators and Some Artists:** Why pay someone hundreds of dollars for an illustration or painting when AI can create a wide range of possibilities for free? There will substantial job loss for artists who aren't generating their own material in a unique way. Being able to incorporate new technologies and generative-AI techniques into one's processes may be helpful and become mainstream.

To reiterate, while AI can automate certain tasks within a job, it does not necessarily mean the entire job will disappear. Most likely, some roles will require significant transformation or re-skilling, while most will simply evolve to incorporate AI tools and technologies.

Careers Requiring Extensive Retraining

The advent of AI is driving changes in roles and functions, demanding extensive retraining in several careers. These include:

- **Health Care:** While AI can enhance health-care delivery through precision medicine and quicker diagnoses, physicians and nurses will need to understand and adapt to these technologies. For example, radiologists may need to learn how to integrate AI tools that can detect anomalies in imaging scans. The human touch will always be crucial.

- **White-Collar Office Workers:** A great reshuffling occurs as AI becomes our more perfect assistant, personal guide and coach, chief of staff, technical expert, strategy and tactics expert, marketing guru, and much more. The people who will continue to thrive in corporate work will need to do some major retraining, and shifting within the corporate world. Leadership will still remain a human domain.

- **Teaching and Education:** With the rise of AI-enabled personalized learning platforms, educators must learn how to effectively incorporate these technologies into their teaching methods.

- **Marketing and Sales:** AI can automate certain marketing tasks and provide powerful insights about customers, but sales and marketing professionals must understand these tools to leverage them successfully.

- **Education:** As EdTech develops, educators will need to adapt to new tools and methods of teaching, such as AI-based adaptive learning systems. Teachers and trainers may require retraining to integrate these technologies effectively into their practice. Every student should have a computer on their school desk so they can learn at their own pace. AI may make this mandatory.

- **Finance:** AI algorithms are revolutionizing financial services from trading to risk assessment. Professionals in this sector will need to learn how to leverage these tools to deliver better outcomes for their clients.

- **Law:** AI can help scan through and analyze large amounts of legal documents in less time. Legal professionals will need to adapt to and understand these systems to stay relevant. Lawyers will probably still be better at arguing than AI.

In all of these professions, the fundamental role of the human worker is unlikely to disappear. Instead, individuals in these fields will need to learn to collaborate with AI, using the technology to enhance their productivity and decision-making capabilities.

Emerging Careers and Growth Opportunities

The advent of AI and machine learning has the potential to open up a variety of new career paths. Here are some that will likely grow in the era of AI.

- **Robotics Engineers and Technicians:** As robots become more commonplace, particularly in manufacturing and health care, there will be an increased demand for professionals who can design, maintain, and repair these machines.

- **Cybersecurity Specialists:** As we rely more heavily on digital systems and AI, protecting these systems from cyber threats becomes crucial. Cybersecurity specialists will be in high demand to protect sensitive information.

- **Health-Care Technologists:** From AI-powered diagnostic tools to robotic surgery, technology is transforming health care. Health-care technologists who can develop, use, and maintain these tools will be critical.

- **Personalized Education Providers:** AI has the potential to personalize education to individual students' needs. Educators and technologists who can leverage AI to create personalized learning experiences will be in demand.

- **Data Privacy Experts:** With more data being collected than ever before, privacy concerns are rising. Data privacy experts will be needed to ensure compliance with regulations and best practices for data privacy.

- **Renewable Energy Managers:** As the world moves toward cleaner energy sources, professionals who can manage the generation and distribution of renewable energy—potentially using AI and machine learning for optimization—will be vital.

- **Smart City Planners:** Cities around the world are becoming "smart," using AI and IoT devices to improve efficiency and quality of life. Urban planners with knowledge of these technologies will be in demand.

- **Virtual Reality (VR) and Augmented Reality (AR) Specialists:** VR and AR are emerging technologies with potential applications in gaming, training, and remote work. Specialists in these areas will be needed.

- **Digital Marketing Analysts:** As marketing becomes increasingly digital and data-driven, professionals who can analyze marketing data and derive insights will be valuable.

- **Telemedicine Professionals:** With AI and improved internet connectivity, remote health care or telemedicine is booming. This creates jobs not only for doctors but also for remote medical assistants, health informaticists, and telemedicine facilitators.

- **Bioinformatics Specialists:** The field of bioinformatics—the application of computational methods to the analysis of biological data—is growing rapidly. AI and machine learning are crucial tools in this field.

- **Military and Police Specialists:** As warfare changes to one AI fighting with another, human experts will manage and command these interactions. AI will provide extraordinary benefits to conventional warfare. Police will have new, wide-ranging tools to identify evildoers and locate them.

- **Agricultural Technology Specialists:** AI has significant potential to improve farming efficiency through predictive analytics and automation. Professionals who can develop and apply these technologies in an agricultural context will be needed.

- **Human-Machine Teaming Managers:** These individuals will coordinate how people and AI-powered systems work together effectively, helping businesses leverage the strengths of both.

- **Inventors:** Just as we humans have created all the previous breakthroughs, we are uniquely capable of extraordinary design and invention.

- **3D-Printing Engineers:** As 3D-printing technology advances, demand for professionals skilled in designing and creating 3D-printed products—potentially using AI-driven design processes—will grow.

- **Space Exploration Specialists:** With private companies aiming to explore and even colonize other planets, and AI playing a key role in analyzing space data and running spacecraft, specialists in space exploration technology will be increasingly needed.

- **Mental Health and Wellness Professionals:** As society grapples with the changes brought by AI, mental health support will be increasingly important.

- **Green Jobs:** AI can help address environmental challenges, but humans will be needed to manage these technologies and carry out environmental work.

- **AI Ethics Consultants:** As AI systems grow more complex and pervasive, ethical dilemmas will become more common. AI ethics consultants will be responsible for navigating these issues, ensuring AI systems are developed and used responsibly.

Careers Less Likely to Be Affected

Some professions are less likely to be significantly impacted. These roles typically require a human touch, emotional intelligence, creativity, complex decision-making, or a deep understanding of human behavior and context. "Unaffected" is not the same as "untouched." AI may still augment and change how these jobs are done, but the core of the work will still require human input.

- **Health-Care Professionals:** While AI can help with diagnosis, drug development, patient monitoring, and other tasks, the empathy, interpersonal skills, and hands-on care provided by doctors, nurses, therapists, and other health-care professionals cannot be fully replicated by AI.

- **Creative Professionals:** AI can assist in creative processes, but the unique and original creativity found in some roles for writers, artists, musicians, and designers will remain a largely human endeavor. Others that can be duplicated by AI will likely be replaced. Humans will still value the creations of fine artists.

- **Educators:** Although AI can provide personalized learning experiences, the role of teachers in motivating students, managing classrooms, and providing social and emotional education will likely remain critical.

- **Mental Health Professionals:** Psychiatrists, psychologists, and other mental health professionals require a deep understanding of human emotions, behaviors, and experiences. While AI can provide tools for therapy, the empathetic human connection is vital.

- **Senior Management:** CEOs, CTOs, and other high-level management roles involve making complex decisions based on a wide array of factors, some of which may be intangible or emotional. AI can assist with data analysis, but the ultimate decision-making will remain a human responsibility.

- **Social Workers:** These professionals provide support for people going through difficult times. Their job requires emotional intelligence and understanding of complex social issues, which are currently beyond the capabilities of AI.

- **Clergy:** Jobs that require a deep understanding of faith, spirituality, and providing religious guidance are unlikely to be replaced by AI.

- **Legal Professionals:** While AI can assist with tasks like legal research or contract analysis, the roles of lawyers, judges, and other legal professionals that require complex decision-making, negotiation skills, and courtroom presence will likely remain human-centered.

- **Researchers and Scientists:** These roles require creativity, critical thinking, and complex problem-solving skills that AI can assist with but not fully replace.

- **Human-Centered Fields:** Most of us depend on the input, advice, or guidance of other people.

Even in these fields, AI can still be a tool to aid in tasks and make work more efficient. For example, AI can take over routine paperwork in health care, assist in student evaluation in education, or help with initial design drafts in creative fields. However, the core responsibilities in these fields still require a human touch. The future of work is likely to be a collaboration between AI and humans, rather than AI fully taking over.

Preparing for the Future: AI and Career Development

To prepare for a future where AI is increasingly dominant, you could consider these strategies:

- **Further Education:** Depending on your career trajectory, you may need further education.

- **Adaptability:** The ability to quickly adapt to new technologies and methods is crucial. Embrace change and learning new tools and techniques.

- **Embrace Lifelong Learning:** The AI field is continually evolving, with new developments emerging regularly. Continuous learning is crucial. Be open to new learning opportunities. Embrace online courses, workshops, webinars, and certifications to stay abreast of developments in your field.

- **Develop Digital Literacy and Data Fluency:** These skills will be crucial in the AI-driven workplace. Understanding how to interpret and work with data and use digital tools will be beneficial in almost any career.

- **Focus on Human Skills:** AI is far from replicating uniquely human skills such as emotional intelligence, critical thinking, creativity, and complex problem-solving. Cultivating these skills can help future-proof your career.

- **Gain AI Literacy:** Even if you're not planning to become a data scientist, understanding the basics of AI, machine learning, and data science can be beneficial.

Many businesses are integrating AI into their operations, and having a foundational understanding can give you a competitive advantage.

- **Career Flexibility:** Given the fast pace of change, be open to switching careers or industries if necessary. Building transferable skills and maintaining a broad network can help make these transitions smoother.

- **Interdisciplinary Approach:** Combining knowledge from different fields can provide a competitive edge. For instance, a lawyer who understands AI could work on legal issues related to AI.

Human Skills: Emphasizing What Makes Us Unique

AI has a hard time replicating human skills, such as creativity, empathy, leadership, and some complex problem-solving. To stay competitive in the future job market, hone and leverage these skills.

- **Develop Emotional Intelligence:** Emotional intelligence—the ability to understand and manage our own emotions and those of others—is a crucial human skill.

- **Cultivate Creativity:** Creativity is not limited to artistic pursuits. It's about finding innovative solutions to problems, generating new ideas, and bringing unique perspectives. Cultivate creativity by exposing yourself to new experiences, ideas, and ways of thinking.

- **Focus on Complex Problem-Solving:** The ability to solve complex problems that require human insight will be invaluable. Develop this skill by seeking out challenges and projects that require you to devise sophisticated, innovative solutions.

- **Grow Your Leadership Skills:** Even if you're not in a leadership position, developing leadership skills such as effective communication, strategic thinking, and the ability to inspire and motivate others can enhance your career.

ACKNOWLEDGMENTS

We would like to acknowledge each and every client that has entrusted us with their uncertainties, their hopes, and their futures. All our work and effort has been in service of you having happy and successful lives. Your shared experiences and breakthroughs have contributed to us, and the writing of this book, more than you can imagine.

We would also like to acknowledge several of our former colleagues and associates—the core crew—who always went above and beyond and gave of themselves generously. All our respect and gratitude to Anthony Spadafore, Jules Myers, Nancy Chek, Rick Duff, Sheila Cahill, and Susan Kohm.

Our sincerest gratitude goes to the many talented individuals whose hard work and expertise made this book possible. We are indebted to Mac Lore for his exceptional artistry and stunning illustrations, which bring the pages to life. Our agent, Nick Mullendore, provided invaluable guidance and support throughout the entire process. We are grateful to Julianna Haubner, our initial editor, for her belief in our project and her insightful feedback. A special thanks to Amy Guay, who graciously stepped in as our editor and expertly guided us to completion. We deeply appreciate Rachael DeShano's dedication as our senior production editor. Her excellent communication and collaborative spirit made the editing journey smooth and enjoyable. We are grateful to our attentive and insightful copyeditor, Rob Sternitzky, for ensuring the text is polished and precise. We are also grateful to our fearless proofreaders, Lisa Geller and Lloyd Davis, for their meticulous attention to detail. Finally, our sincere thanks to Joan Shapiro for her expertise in creating a comprehensive and user-friendly index. The contributions of each of you are deeply appreciated. This book would not be the same without your invaluable input.

Nick would also like to acknowledge his wife, Mitra Mortazavi Lore, whose boundless love and support make everything possible. His mom, for love and genes; Sam Lightnin' Hopkins, first adult friend; Werner and Randy MacNamara; Bucky Fuller, who got him into this. John Goddard, great adventurer and loving soul; The Beatles, who showed him how mastery, magic, joy, commitment, and irreverence can play together in perfect harmony. Dylan, Robert Johnson, Rembrandt, Vermeer, W. Edwards Deming, Sid Gautama, and Yeshua the carpenter (two career changers).

Monica would also like to acknowledge her family. To her father, Steve, who plays full out and gives 110 percent to everything he cares about. To her sister, Amy, who is wise, witty, and beautiful, and the best teacher on the planet. To Sandi, who brings gentleness and kindness to the world. To Jenn, who makes sure that everyone is invited to the party, and, somehow, makes it all look easy. And lastly, but not leastly, to Lyla, her Mommy Dearest, who is loving, and silly, and bravest person she knows. I love you two times.

INDEX

Note: Page references in *italics* refer to figures.

About the Authors

NICHOLAS LORE is the originator of the field of career coaching and founder of Rockport Institute, an organization that has guided thousands of professionals, executives, high-tech people, artists, support staff, and government officials through career change, and helped numerous young people design their work. He has been commended for excellence by two U.S. presidents. He lives in Rockville, Maryland.

MONICA S. ROSE is the founder of Career Matters, a boutique company offering personalized career coaching and consulting services to clients worldwide. Drawing on her diverse background in psychology, research, business, statistics, and recruiting, Monica brings a mix of art and science to all she does. In addition to her extensive experience with individual clients, she has developed large-scale programs for private companies and a public school system. When not writing, creating new career programs, or working with clients, Monica can be found tromping around wetlands, woods, and prairies. Camera in hand, she'll be happily exploring and identifying birds. This is her first book.

For information and communications about the book, reach out to Monica at: ThePathfinder3.com, *info@ThePathfinder3.com*

For info on career coaching and aptitude testing programs and services, reach out to Monica at: InCareerMatters.com, *monica@incareermatters.com*

Career Guru Nicholas Lore can be reached at: *nicholaslore@gmail.com*

Artist and illustrator Mac Lore can be reached at: *maclore333@yahoo.com*